SUTURE

Fig. 1. Hieronymus Bosch, *Ship of Fools* (1490–1500)

First published in 2021 by punctum books, Earth, Milky Way.
https://punctumbooks.com

ISBN-13: 978-1-68571-014-9 (print)
ISBN-13: 978-1-68571-015-6 (ePDF)

DOI: 10.53288/0357.1.00

LCCN: 2021949833
Library of Congress Cataloging Data is available from the Library of Congress

Book design: Vincent W.J. van Gerven Oei
Cover image: Deeds Davis, "Guardians and Mediums."

spontaneous acts of scholarly combustion

HIC SVNT MONSTRA

KJ Cerankowski

Suture

Trauma and
Trans Becoming

Contents

Acknowledgments

First, a thank you to those who saw value in this work in its nascent stages, who gave some of these stories an audience or financial support:

A version of "I Don't Know If This Is About Trans Stuff, or What" first appeared in *The Account: A Journal of Prose, Poetry, and Thought,* Fall 2017, https://theaccountmagazine.com/article/cerankowski-17. I am grateful to editors Tyler Mills and Megan Milks for shaping that essay and giving it its first breath.

Portions of "What Testosterone Can Do" first appeared as "Praying for Pieces: A Practice in Building the Trans Body," CrossCurrents 68, no. 4 (2018): 515–24, DOI: 10.1111/cros.12339. Thank you to editor Stephanie Mitchem for shepherding that piece into existence. That research and writing was generously supported by *CrossCurrents* at Auburn Seminary/Coolidge Fellowship. Special thanks to Charles Henderson and Christian Scharen for making that research colloquium possible. And to a few special colleagues there who provided feedback on this work and made that summer in New York unforgettable: Elyse Ambrose, Wriply Bennet, Katie Horowitz, Eric Plemons, Elliot Ratzman, Cypress Reign, and Max Strassfeld, thank you for the laughs, the reflections, and the inspiration.

The production of this book was also generously supported in part by a Research Status Fellowship and a Grant-In-Aid from Oberlin College.

The writing of this book began while I was working as a lecturer in the Feminist, Gender, and Sexuality Studies program at Stanford University. I am forever grateful for the wonderful colleagues, friends, and students who made my work there so pleasurable and rewarding. With special love and gratitude to my office co-conspirator, Patti Hanlon-Baker, and to my mentors Paula Moya, Heather Love, Celine Parreñas Shimizu, Stephen Sohn, and Laura Frost.

Work on this book really picked up steam after I moved to Oberlin College. To my colleagues there who provide me laughter and support each and every day, to my students who remind me why I do what I do and who make each day in the classroom and in the office one of reward and purpose: thank you. With special gratitude to my Comparative American Studies colleagues who welcomed me with open arms and gave me an intellectual home of kin and friendship: Shelley Lee, Gina Perez, and most especially Wendy Kozol who read drafts, endured countless phone calls, and tirelessly dished out invaluable advice. To my Gender, Sexuality, and Feminist Studies (and beyond) colleagues who invited me to share an early draft of my chapter on the "time of pain," to all who attended that talk or read drafts of it and helped me think about that chapter in new ways, especially: Ann Cooper Albright, Charmaine Chua, Jack Jin Gary Lee, Greggor Mattson, Patrick O'Connor, and Rebecca Whelan.

It is difficult, when writing about abuse and trauma, to consider whether or not I owe some acknowledgment to those who have done me harm. In a sense, without them, this book would not exist. The lessons learned and growth achieved may have happened in different directions or not at all, or, I would not be the person I am today, as the adage goes. Of course, I would gladly trade much of the pain and suffering for a different path, to not have learned these lessons in the ways I did. But a part of me still feels a sort of debt to the people and circumstances that have pushed me to my limits and expanded my so-called growth-edges. Though I do not name them here, I want to acknowledge that in relation to those with whom this life has been difficult, there has been joy, love, and pleasure, too. Sometimes just hurt, yes. But sometimes hurt *and* goodness, sadness *and* delight.

And sometimes, pure joy and ease of love. Importantly, I want to acknowledge all the people in my life who held me up while I was flailing and falling, who did the carework, who supported this writing in their own big and small (sometimes unknown to them) ways, and who I truly feel so fortunate to have crossed paths with and to have journeyed with in this lifetime. With special thanks to: Kazim Ali, Grace An, Amanda Anderson, Emilia Bachrach, Swethaa Ballakrishnen, Lyndsey Beutin, Lisa Bhungalia, Cal Biruk, Yana Calou, Kyler Cerankowski, CJ Chasin, Dani Chau, Maxe Crandall, Regyna Curtis, Meiver De La Cruz, Anne Del Bane, Stephanie Eberle, Jay Fiskio, David Fryer, Alice Gambrell, Bill Gordon, Jessie Haas, Dana Hamdan, Erika Hoffmann, Rebekah Jean, Ryan Kane, Niki Khanna, Eunjung Kim, Wendy Kozol, Angie LaGrotteria, Lucas Lawrence, Clara Lewis, Danielle Lottridge, Talia Madrigale, Meghan Martiniere, Chris Marx, Elizabeth Mathis, Debra Mazer, Kathryn Metz, Cyle Metzger, Megan Milks, Tamika Nunley, Ianna Hawkins Owen, Leanne O'Rear, Eloine Plaut, Ethan Plaut, Nancy Qarmout, Milo Razza, heidi andrea restrepo rhodes, Mariela Restrepo Rhodes, Chelsea Rhodes and family, David Rollo, Aubrie Russo, Karen Sehein, Rob Sehein, Lora Silver, Danielle Skeehan, Toby Smith, Alyson Spurgas, Ruth Starkman, Corinne Teed, Stephanie Wike, Danielle Terrazas Williams, Regina Wright, Brian Thompson, Hale Thompson, Lola Thompson, and my Stonewall fam. Whether it was creating joint writing sessions, sharing resources, making home, being a friend, a rock, an emotional center, or all of the above, thank you thank you thank you. For giving me the language and the courage to write what needed to be written and for healing my spirit in ways for which I can never adequately convey my gratitude: Wendy Ormiston and Linda Garcia-Cruz. For getting me through heartbreaks and hard times, can't get out of bed times: Michael Scott and the crew at Dunder Mifflin; Meredith Grey and the whole team at Grey Sloan Memorial Hospital, forever and always.

This book would also not be what it is without the expert feedback and suggestions of insightful and careful readers. Any errors, of course, remain completely my own. To the publishers at punctum, Eileen A. Fradenburg Joy and Vincent W.J. van Gerven Oei, thank you for seeing the value in this book. To Vincent, in particular, many thanks for patiently fielding my million queries and for sharing a fiery enthusiasm for bringing this book home to punctum's magical, queer world. Thank you, Lily Brewer, editor extraordinaire, for reading with a keen, thoughtful eye and for polishing this manuscript into its best version of itself. For reviewing the entire manuscript with remarkable care and for unparalleled generosity, thank you Julietta Singh. For reading and witnessing early drafts and works in progress, for invaluably offering input that improved these pages and/or for cheering the work onward, thank you: Ian Barnard, Cynthia Barounis, Cal Biruk, Lauren Caprio, Edie Fake, Braveheart Gillani, Kristina Gupta, Scott Kraynak, Wendy Kozol, Hil Malatino, Ianna Hawkins Owen, Ela Przybylo, Milo Razza, Stephen Sohn, Corinne Teed, and the generous audiences at several National Women's Studies Association meetings, the DARE Ten Year Anniversary Symposium at Stanford, and the DC Queer Studies Symposium. Thank you, Deeds Davis for creating art the world needs, and for honoring this book's cover with your passion and shine. For reading (almost) every word, for celebrating this book every step of the way, for the brainstorms and suggestions, the intellectual exchanges, the reassurances through fear and doubt, and infinite sweetness: heidi andrea restrepo rhodes, you have shaped this book in ways you may not even see or know.

This book was written under the ancestral guardianship of many ghosts, particularly my grandfathers, tender men who taught me how to be and to dream of becoming, with gentleness and love. And lastly, I write with love and gratitude for my mother, who always worked hard and tried her best in spite of it all.

I know what I am doing here: I am telling of the instants that drip and are thick with blood.

— Clarice Lispector, *Água Viva*

sutures, palpable, here
it gapes wide open, here
it grew back together — who
covered it up?

— Paul Celan, "Stretto"

Preface, or, Seeking the Love Story

> I've injected a powerful elixir, the workings of which hurtle me
> into a web of energies and impulses I couldn't have anticipated.
> The doors are blasted open.
>
> — Max Wolf Valerio, *Testosterone Files*[1]

Storytelling is a kind of suturing. But I am also writing from within the cuts. Some cuts are more severe than others. Some are thick slicing gashes. Some are mere pricks of the needle. The cut can be deceiving. Sometimes the smaller wounds bleed much more than we expect them to. And those wounds that gape wide open may sometimes hurt a lot less than that minute needle prick. How we narrate the pains of the cuts, large and small, is how we live in them and with them, suffering even as we heal. Writing this book has been a reminder that wounds can always be reopened. New cuts can always be made. The stories I share here are undoubtedly one-sided and incomplete. They are fragmented and broken, imperfectly pieced together, creating a whole that is full of holes.

These pages are haunted by the gaps and silences of all that could not be written because it was too painful to share or too painful (impossible, even) to recall. I am still figuring out how

---

1   Max Wolf Valerio, *Testosterone Files: My Hormonal and Social Transformation from Female to Male* (Emeryville: Seal Press, 2006), 16.

to tell the stories, to gather up the shards, to knit the different strands together, to reopen the wound, to attempt to reseal it, or to leave it to gape. Some of the sutures are stitched tight, holding edges together as the flesh grows over, covering up what lies beneath. I am learning the art of tracing the scars and telling the stories of the dimples of flesh that mark the places where sutures and wounds once were. Scars mark the presence of something past. But not all stitches hold. Sometimes they tear and burst open — a dehiscence, a splitting, a spillage. The blood drips, thick and metallic, a roar in the ears, a tangy shock to the tongue, a ringing synesthetic din.

Writing in times of crisis makes a crisis of writing. In his account of his journey through illness in *Diving Makes the Water Deep,* Zach Savich writes, "every honest book is a crisis. I don't say about a crisis. I say a crisis."[2] If I am being honest here, I must also think of what it means to let this book *be* the crisis rather than *about* the crisis or crises, rather, a plurality of traumas and pains felt collectively and individually. How might this book *be* my trauma rather than *about* trauma? I think it is perhaps a little of both. An attempt to fasten together the scraps of one traumatic break after another, this book cannot help but be written in fragments, in a collage of pieces sewn or sutured together, made to fit haphazardly sometimes and never seamlessly. It is not only *about* trauma, but it *is* trauma, informed by trauma, and composed through and with the thinking that has come from decades of trauma's endurance.

It cannot be ignored that much of the theory that informs my thinking grew out of the catastrophic horrors and persecution of peoples that created a cache of trauma in collective memory and spurred an entire archive of thinking on inherited and collective pain right up through the ongoing persecution and state-sanctioned violence against people of color in the United States of America. The social-psychic wound remains open and festering. Sigmund Freud's psychoanalysis cannot be separated

2   Zach Savich, *Diving Makes the Water Deep* (Chicago: Rescue Press, 2016), 177.

from his Jewishness. Eric Kligerman writes of the "here" that gapes in Paul Celan's poem as being abyssal, noting that "with the opening and closing of this seam, we hear as well the open wound of Freud's depiction of melancholia."[3] So many selves lost in the mourning. So much of the *about* or *for* forgotten and lost to us in the surviving and living on. As Cathy Caruth suggests, trauma is experienced perhaps more through the act of survival than through the often consciously ungraspable, traumatic event itself.[4] We survive in the open wound of melancholia, that perpetual mourning. What do we cry about? For whom do we ache? There is only pain, gaping pain, a melancholic hum. Jacques Derrida, too, encourages us to read Celan's poetry "to the quick, to the point of bleeding, to the point of wounding," thus threading our reading to the wound and the scar.[5] A palpable suture. Which is to say, we must read and write in the presence of pain, as if we are being wounded with each word, as if the words are as much trauma itself as they are about trauma. Franz Kafka once wrote in a letter to Oskar Pollak that we ought to only read books that "wound and stab us," "that affect us like a disaster," "that grieve us deeply," that make us feel as though we are "banished into forests, far from everyone," that function as "the axe for the frozen sea inside us."[6] This book is an axe, grief, disaster, a banished walk through the haunted wood, a wound that gapes where sutures tug at the edges. It is its own cover up.

* * *

---

3   Eric Kligerman, *Sites of the Uncanny: Paul Celan, Specularity and the Visual Arts* (New York: Walter de Gruyter, 2007), 285.

4   Cathy Caruth, "Violence and Time: Traumatic Survivals," *Assemblage* 20 (1993): 24–25.

5   Jacques Derrida, *Sovereignties in Question: The Poetics of Paul Celan,* eds. Thomas Dutoit and Outi Pasanen (New York: Fordham University Press, 2005), 54.

6   Franz Kafka, *Letters to Friends, Family, and Editors,* trans. Richard Winston and Clara Winston (New York: Schocken Books, 1977), 15–16.

Taking inspiration from Savich as well as from Cris Mazza's approach to writing her memoir in "real-time," this book was written as events unfolded, as relationships began and ended, as pain came and went, as healing and harm moved in all different directions; in crisis, through crisis, as crisis. In the process of writing this book, I fell in love and out of love and in love again. I lost people in my life, but I also gained new friends, lovers, and family. As I was completing the writing of this book, I became suddenly ill. I had further complications, potentially connected to my testosterone use, that brought a new tenor to my meditations on what testosterone does and can do to a body like mine. This book is not meant to be one *about* transition or *about* testosterone. Rather, it investigates the powers of this strange elixir to not only shape and reshape the body, but also to blast the doors open, to instigate a confrontation with all the parts of one's being, becoming, and undoing. Which is to say, my time with testosterone has also been my time with pain, illness, and trauma.

As I have been writing in the wake of this new health crisis, I have not only been forced into new confrontations with the side effects of testosterone use, but I have also been faced with new questions of intersubjectivity, interdependence, and relationality. I have been reminded of how lonely the experience of illness can be, how we work to keep our pain from others and how those we entrust with it can often fail us. But I was also reminded of the salve of love and care that can buoy us in times of need, of the ways some of our dear ones cradle us in our pain and nurse us through. The living through and with the ongoingness of this new illness and the pain it brings has taken up life in these essays in ways I could not have anticipated when I began writing. Those recent events have shattered me into pieces that shimmer through this writing, in the quietness of new pain and struggle, in the gaps where the sutures break, where the wound refuses to close, still so fresh and raw.

Because this book was written in the mode of "real-time" writing, time is constantly out of joint. The time of this book — much like the time of trauma, the time of memory, the time of queerness, and the time of endless becoming — is non-linear. The present-tense of this writing exists over the span of at least five years, but the narrative is sometimes hurtled into a past of twenty or thirty years ago, made present by the visceral immediacy of memory rising in my body. Many of my friends joke about my steel-trap memory, counting on me to call up the specific details of an event, setting the scene to the last detail of the color of the paint on the walls and repeating dialogue nearly verbatim. But despite the many people impressed by my impeccable memory, I have had some people consistently accuse me of remembering falsely and making up my own version of events.

I know I, in fact, do not possess a perfect memory. I know sometimes I do misremember, and I do forget the details, both large and small. But with some people, I never seem to remember *anything* correctly. In writing about a sexual assault that occurred in her teenage years, Jeannie Vanasco addresses this question of the trustworthiness of memory, especially when confronting a past abuser. In particular, she notes how creative nonfiction authors are necessarily unreliable as a result of the inherent unreliability of memory. She follows this assertion with a famous quotation from Michel de Montaigne, "what do I know? I know what happened?"[7] Memory is undoubtedly faulty, and it rarely makes for sound evidence in and of itself. At the same time, memory is one kind of ghost we live with. What we remember and how we remember it becomes true for us, even if all the facts don't line up. What do we know? We know what happened. What do I know? I know what happened. Or at least I think I do.

Given memory's inherent unreliability and given the shadows of doubt that have been cast over my own memory by certain people and by myself, I must also acknowledge that these stories are written through memories of a past undoubtedly misremembered or made sense of after some latency, resurfac-

---

7   Jeannie Vanasco, *Things We Didn't Talk About When I Was a Girl: A Memoir* (Portland: Tin House Books, 2019), 95.

ing often in the presence of current triggers that skew, jar, or cut into the memory. I have continuously faced the dilemma that grows between wanting to trust my own memories and being uncertain if I am remembering everything or even anything correctly. And what, really, does it mean to remember correctly? Is it not enough to simply know what happened to me and for me as I remember it? This book reflects my ongoing and perhaps endless search for a way to tell the stories in the face of memory's unreliability. Thomas Page McBee writes, "the world is vicious and beautiful and, to some extent, unexplainable. But that doesn't stop us from wanting a story, all the same."[8] Despite the plaguing questions of memory's reliability, truthiness, or truthfulness, I remain committed to the search for the story of the beautiful in all the viciousness that might be culled from the pieces we recollect and string together.

The search for the story in the face of uncertain memory is about producing a counternarrative or countermemory to the demands of objective facticity over affective and subjective knowing in the blur of time. Michel Foucault describes countermemory as a "transformation of history into a totally different form of time."[9] Countermemory allows us to recover what traditional history has forgotten, to find a way to tell the stories that have been erased, and to shape them into the present ongoingness of our lives, an upending of the notion of a historical past that has passed and remains past. To create a countermemory, we must chase the ghosts down rather than chase them away. In *Ghostly Matters,* Avery Gordon imagines countermemory as a way of "making a contact that changes you and refashions the social relations in which you are located. It is about putting life back in where only a vague memory or a bare trace was visible to

---

8   Thomas Page McBee, *Man Alive: A True Story of Violence, Forgiveness, and Becoming a Man* (San Francisco: City Light Books, 2014), 147.

9   Michel Foucault, *Language, Counter-Memory, Practice: Selected Essays and Interviews,* ed. Donald F. Bouchard, trans. Donald F. Bouchard and Sherry Simon (Ithaca: Cornell University Press, 1977), 160.

those who bothered to look."[10] In following the ghosts, Gordon suggests we can write ghost stories that not only do reparative work but also "strive to understand the conditions under which a memory was produced in the first place, toward a counter-memory, for the future."[11] This book cannot wait for the future. I am writing toward a countermemory for today, for living with the ghosts in this perpetual now. I am searching for ghosts in the spaces where I have not previously bothered to look or where I have been too afraid to look. I am writing to (re)remember. I am writing toward repair, to make contact again and again with the ghosts that have changed me and continue to change me, to refashion their place in my life and in the collective imagination, to figure out how to live in the constancy of their haunting, and to understand and rework the memories of trauma, pain, and suffering into the bearable grit of living.

Importantly, these stories are more about the pain of memory rather than the memory itself. That is, they are about memory's mark; about the weight of bearing our pasts in our presents and futures; about recovery; about the impossibility I feel in becoming; about the marks and scars left by the past and every new transition; and about the ways we find ourselves in the words, narratives, and experiences of others. In the foreword to Yanyi's poetry collection, *The Year of Blue Water,* Carl Phillips describes the ways in which Yanyi's poems, as meditations on writing, teach us this valuable lesson: "a life of writing — actively writing for oneself as well as reading the writing of others — is a life of intentional love and generosity."[12] To want the story and to choose to tell the story are also ways to love and to offer something to the world. In this writing, I am doing my best to live intentionally with love and generosity, to give and receive love through the stories that make us. To live in love is to live with the ways the world both hurts and heals us, to remember that we

---

10 Avery Gordon, *Ghostly Matters: Haunting and the Sociological Imagination* (Minneapolis: University of Minnesota Press, 2008), 22.

11 Ibid., 22.

12 Yanyi, *The Year of Blue Water* (New Haven: Yale University Press, 2019), xii.

cannot and must not contain ourselves as we spill into the world and onto and into each other.

This spillage is about intersubjectivity — how we touch as we are being touched, how we leave marks on one another, how we leak onto and into one another, how we are always moving through each other, how we haunt one another, and how no story is ever just ours even as we have our own stories to tell. In many ways, these stories are ghost stories. The people I write about in these essays are my version of the people who have left their marks on me. Individually and collectively, I sometimes refer to them by initials that may or may not reflect their actual initials. The people who haunt these stories may resemble real people or agglomerations of real people. They may not actually be the people they resemble at all. Such resemblances may or may not be purely coincidental. They may be entirely figments of my faulty memory. Some of the people in these stories have left this world but remain so present in my life. Some of them have left my life yet remain present in this world. There are many ways to haunt and be haunted.

Of all my past partners, *R* and *L* haunt these pages the most, and, perhaps not so coincidentally, they are the only ones who "ghosted" me. A phrase we throw around so casually in our colloquial language, it never before struck me how appropriate the term, *ghosting*: in the aftermath, there's a lingering, a residue. They each haunt me in different ways. I am not sure there will ever come a time where a thought of one or the other does not rouse me from my sleep or keep me awake into the small hours of the morning, as I toss and turn in pain, anger, or grief, picking open all the old wounds. Ghosting can feel like such a cruelty, a refusal to close the wound of a relationship's end and to instead turn away as the lacerated heart pulses and spurts, leaving the broken to stitch together their own story of closure or resolution. For the one doing the ghosting, I suppose it is their way of healing their own wounds by turning away from the one who has also undoubtedly caused them pain. As I write this, I am glaringly aware of my own hypocrisy: some might say I ghosted my father, suddenly cutting off contact and refusing to take his calls.

I never gave him an explanation. I didn't know how to tell him how much he has hurt me and continues to hurt me. I am not sure if ghosting is my way of running from the pain or if it is an act of self-preservation, a way of setting a boundary, or a way of suturing my own wounds. It is probably a little of everything. Accordingly, I must make space for the ways in which ghosting can sometimes be the only option a person has to protect the self and to turn away from the pain or abuse of the other, even if that ghosting is also confusing or painful to the one left in its wake.

I have made a ghost of my father. In ghosting him, I suspect that I too haunt his life in some ways. I cannot help but wonder sometimes if I have become a ghost to my own ghosts, which is to ask if their memories of me haunt them, which is to ask more simply if they ever think of me. I am reminded of a time R shared with me a list she once wrote of "Things One Can Not Control." One of the items on the list always stood out to me: "whether the person who you are in love with thinks about you all of the time, some of the time, or never." In my most torturous moments, I have wondered how R or L could be in love with someone (me) one moment and, in the next moment, so readily excise someone (me) from their lives. I think about my father and the cut I made between us. But I was never in love with him. Rather, I wanted to love him as much as I wanted him to love me. I cannot help but wonder if R or L ever truly loved me and, if so, what that meant for them. Such fretting, I suppose, is my own way of coming to terms with all we cannot control when we make each other into ghosts. But mostly, I am preoccupied with the ways in which these ghosts follow me. Sometimes the anger swells out of seemingly nowhere, bubbling up from wherever it is I have kept it buried and pushed down. Sometimes I simply ache with loss, regret, or longing for what I wish could have been. Of course, I also play over and over the things I wish I would have said, should have said, or could have had the opportunity to say. I recognize my own attachment to some myth of closure, as if one more conversation would make a difference somehow, as if one more exchange of words might chase away their ghosts.

In calling up, recalling, and writing my grief and anger through this patchwork of lyric essay, poetry, and criticism, I think of what Sam Beam, who records music under the moniker Iron & Wine, sings of the work of song: "some call it talking blues, / some call it bitter truth, / some call it getting even in a song."[13] To sing my blues and to share my truths, no matter how bitter, I must confront the question of whether there is some sense in which I hope to "get even" as I drag these ghosts into the public sphere. What might it mean to get even with someone, to settle (or stir up?) their ghosts by writing the pain, the grief, and the abuses into the public eye? I resist the notion of airing one's dirty laundry as some sort of betrayal to the sanctity of self, others, or the relationships between the self and others. I have to tell these stories to heal. I have to tell these stories because I believe they can do something in the world. I tell these stories because I have been given the courage to tell by those who have dared to tell their own stories of trauma, abuse, loss, and grief, stories which undoubtedly left permanent marks on me.

To shift the metaphor, recounting our meetings with the wolves seems a necessary practice in not only making sense of the events for ourselves but, also, in providing a possibility for others to imagine their way through their own meetings with their own wolves, those creatures who have so frightened humankind that we have brought about their deaths in masses; those same creatures many of us have since come to feel protective dominion over. Writing on the ubiquity of the wolf in the Western imagination, Carla Freccero notes how wolves are "always in the forest, the space of romance; wolves occupy the genre of romance, or they are *unheimlich*, uncanny, 'homelike' yet not, and thus also occupy the genre of horror."[14] Wolves are literally and metaphorically the things we love though they frighten

---

13 Iron & Wine, "Bitter Truth," on *Beast Epic* (Black Cricket Recording Company/Sub Pop, 2017).

14 Carla Freccero, "Wolf, or Homo Homini Lupus," in *Arts of Living on a Damaged Planet: Ghosts and Monsters of the Anthropocene,* eds. Anna Lowenhaupt Tsing et al. (Minneapolis: University of Minnesota Press, 2017), M94.

us, or, perhaps, wolves frighten us because we love them. The encounter with the wolf is both familiar and frightening, so very uncanny, so akin to how I felt about my father as a child. I loved him though he frightened me. I was frightened of him because I loved him through all the sneers, snarls, and battings of paws.

We love the wolves as we fear them. The wolves are beautiful and horrific and uncanny, not unlike ghosts. The characteristics of monstrosity and ghastliness morph into one another. Wolves become a pivot point between monsters and ghosts. "I am also tracking wolves in their spectrality," Freccero writes. Though she admits to having originally written "in their integrity" — what could she have meant by that, she herself wonders — she does not say much more about landing on the word "spectral" other than accounting for wolves spatially and temporally in the imagination, an ever-elusive non-present presence.[15] But I cannot separate the wolf from the specter. I think it is because I chase the wolves just as I chase the ghosts. Ghosts. Wolves. Monsters. All beings with haunting qualities. They each metaphorically and literally stalk these pages. They each haunt in their own way.

So rarely do we actually happen upon literal wolves. It seems we must meet them metaphorically, whether the encounter is romantic, horrific, or an admixture of both. We still want to find them in the wood. We still imagine them roaming the forests. How romantic. How ghastly. And I am fully aware of my tendency to describe the wolves I meet in my writing as always in a snarl, teeth gnashing a threat to my being. Rarely do I recount them skulking away, tails between their legs or hiding amidst the trees in fear. I write as though the wolves stalk me, but, if I am to be honest, I am also stalking them. I like to believe I am describing my encounters with the wolves as I happen upon them in my walk through these thick woods, as if it is mere happenstance, as if I am not in search of any retribution but in search of something more akin to a resolution or an understanding of the conditions that made possible the birth and survival of these wolves in the face of their literal mass extinction.

15 Ibid., M93.

The truth is, I am seeking some combination of redress, solace, and comprehension here. I want to understand which are the creatures we preserve and protect and which are the ones we kill and why we do so. I want to imagine what it means to settle with and live amongst the dangers and within mutual fears. I am indeed searching. I am doing the seeking. I am chasing down the wolves even as I imagine them chasing me down. I am conjuring the ghosts even as I fear their haunting.

How do we live in the tensions between the chase and the pursuit? How do we live in the rough spots, rather than evening them out by getting even somehow? I prefer to think of my ghost stories as love stories, rather than acts of vengeance. In Qwo-Li Driskill's poetry collection *Walking with Ghosts,* Driskill calls forth and travels with ancestral ghosts from a lineage of Indigenous or queer spirits. In a poem reflecting on the AIDS Memorial Quilt in Washington, DC, Driskill writes, "And how can we ever / gather up all of our ghosts, / kiss each of them on the cheek / and say, / Everything's gonna be all right. / It's time to go home now, sugar. / It's time to go home."[16] Some of the ghosts I reach toward in this writing are the spirits of the dead, familial and queer ancestors whose cheeks I long to meet with my lips in a farewell send-off home or in a bringing home to me as I receive their message that perhaps everything's gonna be all right. But many of the ghosts who haunt these pages, the ghosts I choose to walk with most often, are the traces of people who still walk this earth. I want to reach toward them, through the pain and hurt, and imagine what it could mean for me to plant that kiss on the cheek, to forgive and to ask forgiveness, to settle into the ways they live with me and always will exist in some capacity in the home of my heart and body. A student recently asked me if the kind of writing I do demands forgiveness of those who have done harm. The question gave me deep pause. What fell from my mouth was, "absolutely not. Sometimes we write because we cannot forgive." This is to say, I want

---

16 Qwo-Li Driskill, *Walking with Ghosts* (Cambridge: Salt Publishing, 2005), 18.

these love stories to imagine capacities for forgiveness, but I also want to acknowledge that some acts of violence and harm may be unforgiveable. It doesn't stop me from wanting to find the love story, all the same.

* * *

In all my reckoning, I have found it to be true that most people are not purely evil. Those who have done harm have also brought joy and pleasure to my life, and, I imagine, to the lives of others as well. Indeed, there are reasons I loved them and perhaps still love them, despite it all. In Carmen Maria Machado's recount of her journey through an abusive relationship, she too ruminates on the tension between love and abuse. Machado reflects on the classic 1944 film *Gaslight,* the title of which has lent itself to the term "gaslighting," a deceptive and manipulative tactic in which the person being "gaslit" is made to question their own beliefs and memory. When someone gaslights another person, they might repeatedly insist that things that actually happened in fact did not happen, which causes the other person to feel so uncertain about the misalignment of memory that they begin to wonder if their own memory is unreliable, or, in some cases, they might begin to suspect that they themselves are "insane" or "going insane." For example, when someone gaslights another person, they might say something like, "well, I don't remember that, so what do you want me to do about it?" over and over again, such that the incongruence of memory causes the person who is remembering what the other person never remembers to wonder if they are inventing their memories or remembering falsely.

In the film, Gregory marries Paula and convinces her to move with him into the house she used to live in with her beloved aunt who was murdered in the home, her body left for young Paula to find. When they move into the home, Gregory places all of the aunt's belongings into the attic and seals it off to purportedly help Paula start a new life in the home without being surrounded by her aunt's memory or ghost. In their time together, Gregory hides items from Paula in an effort to convince her that she is forgetful and frequently loses things. By convincing her that she is moving items about the house with no memory of doing so, he succeeds in also convincing her that she is "ill" and "going mad." He then isolates Paula from her friends and social acquaintances under the pretense that she is too ill to go out or receive visitors. Gregory proceeds to leave the house in the evenings and tells Paula he is going to work in his studio. Instead, he doubles back and enters the house through a rear skylight where he spends the evenings rooting through the aunt's belongings in the attic in search of some crown jewels.

When Gregory is in the attic, he turns the gas lamps on to help him see by, which results in a perceptive dimming of the lamps in the house. Paula notices the dimming but has thus far been so "gaslighted" by Gregory that she believes herself to be imagining it. It would seem that Gregory has also gotten the house staff in on the charade, as they deny hearing his footsteps in the attic and claim not to notice the lamps dim as they insist no one has turned on the gas elsewhere in the house. As I watch the film, I think how curious that we have culturally clung to the dimming of the lamps to bring us to the term "gaslighting" when the much more intentional abuses and manipulations involve Gregory's movement of objects and his claims that Paula has forgotten information that was never actually relayed in order to convince her she is not only careless and forgetful but that she is also going mad.[17]

In Machado's reflection on the film, she notes how Gregory's torment of Paula has a clear motivation: a greedy desire to steal her jewels. This clear motivation, she reflects, is "a reminder, perhaps, that abusers do not need to be, and rarely are, cackling maniacs. They just need to want something, and not care how they get it."[18] Abusers are not necessarily "cackling maniacs"; they are not always pure evil. Yes, I think sometimes they want something or some things, and, somewhere along the way,

---

17 George Cukor, dir., *Gaslight* (1944; Metro-Goldwyn-Mayer, 2004).

18 Carmen Maria Machado, *In the Dream House* (Minneapolis: Graywolf Press, 2019), 94.

they have learned how to not care how they get it, or maybe they have learned to simply accept the hurt they have to cause to get it as some kind of necessary evil. (Are evils ever really necessary? What are the criteria that come to define that necessity?) But I also think of how Gregory so meticulously plotted his manipulations of Paula over years, carefully constructing a false reality that he knew would be her torment and would have been her end if not for the interventions of an astute detective. There seems to be something evil indeed in Gregory's scheming. There is such a fine line between evil and the lack of empathy for another human being who is expended for one's own personal gain.

I think of the abusers I have encountered in my own life, and I know in my bones that none of them are purely evil, though they may sometimes do awful, even evil, things. I think what it takes to get something at all costs is often derived from the survival skills a person might develop in the face of their own traumas. I know my father carries a lot of pain from his childhood, and addiction and anger are his outlets and his survival tools. I know I have also hurt people when I have lashed out in ways that might be traced to my own trauma-based survival skills or to my inability to develop healthy habits in response to pain, frustration, or upset. We cannot always know the hurt those who do harm are carrying, and, importantly, their hurt does not excuse the hurt they bring to others.

Rather, I am brought back to the complexity of writing these stories of pain and harm. I have been hurt because I have loved. I can ask these questions and raise these fears about moving into masculinity, injecting the powerful elixir of testosterone, and blasting the doors open because I have known abuse, but also love, at the hands of men. There is no doubt the writing of this book has been cathartic and healing for me. At this stage in my process, I also want to try to remember even those who have done harm for the times they made me laugh or softened my heart, when their embraces were warm and supportive, even if those moments of endearment were sometimes just a respite from the abrasions and fists, metaphorical and otherwise.

This book has been an endeavor in learning how to love, how to heal, and how to live with these ghosts. It has been a lesson in learning how to live with the anger and sadness while also recalling and reveling in joy, finding ways to breathe life back into something that had been left for dead, corpsed and haunted. "What we recall," Saidiya Hartman writes, "has as much to do with the terrible things we hope to avoid as with the good life for which we yearn."[19] Ultimately, these stories are my refusal to "get over it" and to move forward as though we can leave the past in the past and let bygones be bygones. Rather, this book is my attempt to tear open the wounds, to confront everything I am still not over and may never be, and to yearn, endlessly, for the good. I have moved and am moving still through the space-times of vignettes and memories that take up specific locations, that reach backward and forward in a search for my body, in search of a new order, an overture where there had been none.[20] To seek out the space(s) in which I long to find myself, to locate my desires to be, to become, to always have been, to be always becoming. This is to say that though this book is written, it is far from complete, stable, finished, or at an end. What the words have come to mean to me, what they might mean to you, and what they might yet come to mean to any of us is unstable and full of shifting possibility. As we grow, so the meaning of the words and stories and the movements of ghosts evolve and change. I invite you, in Alice Notley's words to "come with me amid this instability / permit me not to know what things mean yet."[21]

---

19 Saidiya Hartman, *Lose Your Mother: A Journey Along the Atlantic Slave Route* (New York: Farrar, Straus, and Giroux, 2008), 100.

20 Ibid. Hartman writes, "but when does one decide to stop looking to the past and instead conceive of a new order? When is it time to dream of another country or to embrace other strangers as allies or to make an opening, an overture, where there is none?"

21 Alice Notley, *Benediction* (Tucson: Letter Machine Editions, 2015), 4.

I Don't Know If This Is About Trans Stuff, or What

I'm not talking about fucking; I'm talking about intimacy. One used to fade into the other, and sometimes I forget I've learned the difference.

— Sarah Manguso, *300 Arguments*[1]

In many ways, healing from trauma is akin to creating a poem. Both require the right timing, the right words, and the right image.

— Mark Wolynn, *It Didn't Start With You*[2]

I am watching Cris Mazza's film *Anorgasmia,* which she dubs the "fictional sequel to her real-time memoir *Something Wrong With Her.*"[3] The memoir lives out her reunion with a boy from her past while interrogating her current experiences with "sexual dysfunction." The film, on the other hand, seems, to me, less about elusive orgasms and explorations in asexualities and more about gender. Of course, my worries over gender and the

---

1   Sarah Manguso, *300 Arguments* (Minneapolis: Graywolf Press, 2017), 39.
2   Mark Wolynn, *It Didn't Start with You: How Inherited Family Trauma Shapes Who We Are and How to End the Cycle* (New York: Penguin Books, 2016), 11.
3   "Film & Music," *Cris Mazza,* http://cris-mazza.com/projects/.

body circle back to sexuality, desirability, and desire. But gender, and its attendant dissection of body parts, is where we begin. Just about two minutes into the film, we see Cris on the floor of what looks like her basement, taking photos of herself in front of a mirror, when Mark walks down the stairs. Mark is the boy — now man — from her past, whom we first meet in the book. He has recently moved to the Chicago suburbs to be with Cris, after some thirty years estranged. Mark never stopped loving Cris; Cris, I think, is learning how to love Mark.

In this scene, Cris tells Mark, "I'm gonna do a transgender makeover. I'm gonna go transgender and do self-portraits that way."[4] I watch and rewatch this clip. "I'm gonna do a transgender makeover. I'm gonna go transgender... I'm gonna go transgender... I'm gonna go transgender...." The phrase echoes in my head. Mark looks perplexed if not a bit displeased. I am both perplexed and intrigued. I cannot help but think Mazza imagines transgender as some kind of mask or costume to put on. "I'm gonna do a transgender makeover. I'm gonna go transgender."

Throughout the film, Cris asserts that she does not like the word "woman," that she cannot apply it to herself, that she hates when Mark talks about her "femininity," and that she feels "not female" but maybe also not quite male. Accordingly, she wants to know "what it feels like to be looked at as something that's not female," thinking the experience might somehow be liberatory. So she embarks on what she calls a "transgender experiment," or what her friend Dan calls a "temporary transition," or what her colleague Chris calls a "costume switch." She also says to Chris, "hopefully it won't be *performing*; it will be *being... being* male." At which point does Cris shift from performing to being? When does the "costume switch" become something more than a change of clothes; when does it become a state of being, a "gender transition," perhaps? I think of Diane Torr, whose drag performances and "man for a day" workshops were de-

---

4   Frank Vitale, dir., *Anorgasmia: Faking It in a Sexualized World,* produced, written, and performed by Cris Mazza, 2015.

signed to draw out the complex ways we embody gender norms, to help women realize how they are often "giving their power away" through the performance of gender. Torr also used drag to memorialize and hold close the men in her life that she had lost. Her performances as a man for a day, or an evening, were always called "drag" and "performances," never "transgender."[5] One might do drag for a day, in a sense *be* a "man for a day," but how does one "do a transgender makeover" or "go transgender" for a day?

Cris cuts off her hair, buys men's clothing, and, dressed as "Dave," goes to her friend Dan's house to meet his family. The whole experiment goes "badly" by Cris's account, and the evening was "rather awkward" according to Dan's wife, Molly. Upon leaving the house and stepping onto the front porch, Cris overhears Molly speculating about whether or not "Dave" is transgender or asexual, seeming to not quite understand how vastly different the two identities are, slipping between gender and sexuality, from transgender to asexual, imagining the trans body as either undesirable or undesiring or both. After overhearing and absorbing Molly's slippage, Cris returns home and decides to do some research, first on asexuality. She comes to understand asexuality as an absence of a physical need or desire to have sex. She wonders if she might be asexual. Throughout the film, she grapples with this question as she tries to understand the differences between sexuality and gender and how to situate her potential asexual and agender identities. What, we might ask, does one have to do with the other? Does Cris's experience of being not female but not quite male have anything to do with her "sexual dysfunction," and what might the events of her past mean for both her gender and sexuality?

In this moment following her first transgender makeover, Cris also wonders how she could have been more "convincing" to Molly and her children. In her research, she also finds a

---

5   Stephen Bottoms, "Diane Torr Obituary," *The Guardian,* June 29, 2017, https://www.theguardian.com/artanddesign/2017/jun/29/diane-torr-obituary.

"transsexual" site on the internet. She tells Mark, "I was trying to figure out what I could have done that was more, that would have helped more to be convincing. Now, nothing on there says anything about how to act, what to say." At this point, I am not sure if Cris is looking for a guidebook on how to play a man or on how to play at trans. Mark replies, "I think that's because being a man isn't really inside you." While Cris resents when Mark calls her "feminine" or a "woman," she does not directly object to Mark's idea that being a man isn't really inside her. Cris articulates herself somewhere in the space between female and male, nonbinary perhaps. With this shift to the in-between spaces of gender, I wonder then what it means to "be convincing"? What does it mean for "being a man" to be "inside you"? What does it mean to be a man? What *is* a man?

* * *

I am four years old, living on a US naval air force base just outside of Memphis, Tennessee. My father, a naval airplane mechanic, returns home in the evening, his hands stained with grease, the smell of cigarettes and beer on his breath. I crawl into his lap, my shins pressed to his thighs, my hands on each of his cheeks, rubbing the scruff on his face. I reach my face up to his, to feel the scratch of his jaw against my baby-smooth cheek. I pull away and look into my father's eyes. "I want to be a boy like you," I say. He laughs. He tells me I shouldn't want to be a boy because being a boy means becoming a man. It's harder to be a man, he says, to have to find the courage to ask a girl out, to pay for the date, to support a family. He tells me I should be glad to be a girl, that I can just let a man take care of me. For my father, manhood is expensive. I thought I was willing to pay the fare. I spent those hot, southern summers running around shirtless, throwing a football in the yard, wrestling with the boys in the neighborhood. They all thought I was just a rambunctious little girl, a wily tomboy. I'm not sure what I thought I was.

Was a I boy; did I just want to be a boy; was I at all like a boy? Thomas Page McBee writes of the panic, a "new PTSD," that sets in when he encounters men who cannot see the man he is (or the man inside of him), menacing men who instill fear and threaten his safety and bodily integrity — the fear of entering gas stations in unfamiliar areas, the moments when his body says turn around, leave, run! He remembers how his first girlfriend compared him to other boys. "You're like a boy... but better," she said.[6] I read and reread these words: you're like a boy, but you're not a boy. You're like a boy, but you're better than a boy because you're not a boy. I am like a boy. I am not a boy. I am not like a girl, but am I a girl? I am not a girl. I am not a boy. I am like a boy. I am not like a girl. I am a boy. What am I? Is there a man inside of me?

Fast forward to just a couple weeks before my 34th birthday. *R* and I are hiking in Maine, and I am walking ahead of her on the trail. "You're like a guy," she calls out. Moments before, she told me she often questions whether she really wants to be queer. In response, I told her that sometimes I am afraid she is going to decide I am not the kind of man she wants, that I'm not really "man enough" for her, that I worry she would rather be with a "real man." It is after I say this, following a short period of silence, that she tells me I am like a guy. I am caught off guard, pause in my tracks. I turn to look at her; I am not sure what to say; I am uncertain I heard her correctly. "Huh?" I ask. She repeats herself, "you're like a guy. I mean... you even walk like a guy." After a beat, I simply say, "because I am a guy." I surprise myself with those words. We walk on in silence. Shortly thereafter, I tell her I have decided to stop using she/her pronouns. She nods her head, but continues to call me "she" right through the time we break up and for all I know, I am still "she" to her, will always be her "ex-girlfriend." *Like* a guy, but *not* a guy.

Almost a year later, I am driving through Oakland with *TT* as we head out to dinner. I have just come from a therapy session

---

6   Thomas Page McBee, *Man Alive: A True Story of Violence, Forgiveness and Becoming a Man* (San Francisco: City Light Books, 2014), 53.

in which I talked about how I wasn't sure if I should keep on the testosterone, maybe up my dose and become a (passable) man or stay somewhere in the middle space I currently occupy — *like* a guy, *not* a guy. It's not that I want to be more convincing; I just want to be me. But I am unsure what that means for how much testosterone, if any, I want to inject into my body. I tell *TT* how these questions weigh on my mind and body. I say I worry if I become a man then I won't become the man I imagine myself to be. What kind of man is inside me, I wonder. I joke: will I be too "faggy" and not the burly lumberjack of a man I aspire to be? But I also like the affects and sensibilities I embody, those that cause people to do a double-take, to tell me that I'm part gay boy, a little bit of a fag. At the same time, I carry a fantasy image of myself as another kind of man, a man whose wrist never goes limp, so to speak. And along with that fantasy, comes a fear of becoming the man my father is. What does it mean to be a man? Can I embody all these masculinities at once? Writing on the expansiveness and multiplicity of the testosterone molecule and how it exists within the body, Rebecca Jordan-Young and Katrina Karkazis claim, "T is flexible enough to accommodate multiple masculinities."[7] But is masculinity flexible enough? Marquis Bey writes, "we become men, and, consequently, we can, and must, unbecome the men we were told we have to be."[8] I can become and unbecome exactly the man I need to be. *TT* will later thoughtfully mark this conversation by giving me a card decorated with a lumberjack dressed in high heels. But in this moment, she turns to me and says, matter of factly, without missing a beat, "what do you mean 'become'? You are a man." My eyes pool. I nearly cry. Not "like a man." "You are a man."

How did I go from being like a man to being a man? Is being a man inside of me? Or is it in the eye of the beholder? I recall a moment earlier that summer before my 34th birthday, just a

---

7   Rebecca Jordan-Young and Katrina Karkazis, *Testosterone: An Unauthorized Biography* (Cambridge: Harvard University Press, 2019), 81.
8   Marquis Bey, *Them Goon Rules: Fugitive Essays on Radical Black Feminism* (Tucson: The University of Arizona Press, 2019), 78.

couple months before I headed off to the Maine woods with R. After years of space-taking and heart-mending, I am reunited with S in the chill of a San Francisco July. She is in town for the month from her current post abroad. We meet for a drink, and, sitting at the bar side-by-side, she wraps her arm about my waist, her hand coming to rest on that tender spot of self-consciousness, where the flesh always looks and feels a bit too curvy on my body, the point just above the hips some affectionately dub the "love handle." I tense a bit, and S, perhaps sensing my discomfort, gives me a squeeze and says, "there's nothing there. You are so solid." Leaning in closer she adds, "you really have become such a handsome man."

Why is it that S and TT see me as a man where R could only see me as being *like* a man? Just a couple months after that trip to Maine, R and I talk on the phone late into the night. This conversation will end up being the last one we have as a couple. We hadn't spoken in a couple of days. During that time, I went to my doctor to inquire about testosterone. My doctor wrote me a prescription and scheduled me for a return visit at the end of the week to learn how to administer the shot. I am terrified and excited, anxious and nervous, and eager to tell R about this. On the phone, I tell R that I am making a life-changing decision, but before I can say more, she cuts me off. "Look," she says, "I don't know if this is about trans stuff or what, but I'm trying to be really patient with you. You haven't given *me* compliments, like I love how you improvise, or I love how you take care of your dog. Something. Anything." We hang up the phone, both in tears — she because I won't compliment her at that moment, and I because she never asks to hear about my life-changing decision. I feel utterly alone in the journey I am about to embark upon. Later, S will remind me it is not that I am doing this alone but that I am doing it without intimacy. Togetherness and intimacy still fade into each other. I need to remember that I am learning the difference.

It will take me months to make sense of that phone conversation with R. But the next day, R and I break up. The day after that, I go for my first shot of testosterone. Three months later, I meet *TT*. Several months after that, *TT* tells me that she never saw me as anything other than a man. Is this about trans stuff, or what? Surely, it cannot be the testosterone in my body that allows *TT* to see me as a man where *R* couldn't. My dose is low. I have only told a handful of people that I am taking testosterone, and most people, especially those who don't know, cannot see or hear any change in me. Everything seems out of sequence: *S* tells me I have become a handsome man months before I even start testosterone. I meet *E* that same summer before I start testosterone, and he says, "I just don't get it. I don't see how anyone can see you as anything other than a man." But then, ten months on testosterone, I am sitting in a gay bar in Omaha with a friend. The bartender is curious about us: "what brings you ladies to Omaha? You ladies gonna sing some karaoke tonight? Can I get you ladies another drink?" My friend turns to me and asks, "why does he keep saying 'ladies'? Can't he see you're obviously a guy?" No. No, he can't. Most people can't — except the stranger at the bookstore who called me "sir" and "man" for the entirety of our interaction (on T), or the cashier at the grocery store who called me "man" and "bro" for that entire exchange (pre-T), or the man in front of me in line at the Space Needle in Seattle who turned to his wife and, gesturing toward me, said, "ha, did you hear what he just said?" (on T), or the woman who walked into a crowded women's restroom at the San Francisco Opera, saw me before she saw anyone else, and, in a panic shouted, "is this the women's room?!?" (pre-T). I could go on. Maybe the question is not how did I go from being like a man to being a man; rather, I might ask, when, where, and to whom am I like a man or simply a man? And does testosterone have anything to do with it?

* * *

I visit a psychic who tells me testosterone is like medicine for my body. I think she is right about this, but calling it "medicine" comes with its own set of complications. In *Testo Junkie,* Paul Preciado demarcates when the drug, testosterone, shifts from being medicine to being a substance to be abused. Such a differentiation also defines the psychosis of the user, that is, "I must choose between two psychoses: in one (gender identity disorder), testosterone appears as a medicine, and in the other (addiction), testosterone becomes the substance on which I am dependent."[9] Am I a self-medicating addict or am I being medicated for a psychiatric disorder?

When my doctor writes my prescription, I watch her update my medical chart. The diagnosis of "gender identity disorder" I received years ago when I sought approval for top surgery becomes a diagnosis of "gender dysphoria." Whichever we call it, I remain diagnosed and medicated. Preciado is on the other side, with no prescription for the testosterone gel he regularly rubs into his shoulder. He writes, "I would have liked to have fallen into a dependence, have the security of permanently and chemically clinging to something. Deep down, I was hoping that testosterone would be that substance. To be attached, not to a subjectivity, but to the change produced by the ingestion into my organism of a substance without will."[10] After my first shot of testosterone, my thigh is sore for days at the site where I plunged the needle into the muscle. Pushing my palm against that spot on my thigh becomes addictive. I become attached to the soreness. I begin to fantasize about administering my next injection, feeling the soreness again. I become attached to the point of pain that serves as the somatic reminder that this is where I am putting a substance into my organism that will someday, somehow change my body in ways I cannot know. The testosterone is both medicine and addictive substance. I am both a medicated subject of what Preciado calls the pharmacopornographic era and an addict. But am I addicted to the substance, the process, the changes it will produce, or the pain and soreness? What, exactly, am I addicted to?

---

9   Paul Preciado, *Testo Junkie: Sex, Drugs, and Biopolitics in the Pharmacopornographic Era,* trans. Bruce Benderson (New York: The Feminist Press, 2013), 257.
10 Ibid., 247.

I read and reread McBee's *Man Alive*. I make my students read it. I buy copies for my friends. I cannot quit the book. I am addicted to the tears it always brings — the quiet pools in my eyes that never quite spill over, the silent heaving of my chest. I cry in my silent way because McBee's anxieties — of stopping at restrooms in small towns, of fearing the man he may become or the man he already is, of running both from and toward the traumas of his past as he continues to become who he always was — are too familiar. They rattle around my chest, pick up crushing weight in my sternum. As I read, I feel the inevitability of needles in the thigh, cracking vocal chords and deepening voice, a 5-o'clock shadow, another puberty on the horizon. I am frightened, but I also want it so badly, enough to wonder if it is the only way I will continue to survive here. I always thought I would start the injections when I finally felt ready to run — to run away from my life, to start over somewhere alone as someone new. But I haven't run away. Instead, I run toward the past even as I am ever hurtling toward some unforeseeable future. And now, in this moment, I push my hand to my thigh which has become accustomed to the weekly injections, and I long for that mark of tenderness that only occasionally lingers after a shot.

* * *

There are so many ways to be marked. While reading Mazza's memoir *Something Wrong With Her,* I get stuck on one scene. I read and reread it. Mazza narrates a moment when, as teenagers, Mark pushed her onto a bed and got on top of her. She fled. Mark scolded her, "girl, you just don't give me enough, you don't put out." For a long time, she found ways to convince herself to endure sexual encounters with boys that felt unwanted, coerced even. But finally, her brain stopped chanting, "you're supposed to like this." Instead, in this moment with Mark she decides she is frigid. She writes, "it was the scolding that had penetrated me. I was marked."[11]

I am 17 years old, finishing my senior year of high school in a northeast Ohio suburb. It is St. Patrick's Day, and the boy I am dating invites me to a small gathering at his apartment. He is 19 years old and just moved out of his parents' house. Late into the night after many beers and whiskeys, he turns to me and says, "just sleep over here. We can share my bed." We go down to his bedroom, and as we fall into bed, we begin kissing. I am on my back. He is on top of me. His hands are all over me, his tongue in my mouth. I pull away. "Let's just sleep," I say. "You're such a tease," he says, just before he pins my hands above my head with one hand gripping my small wrists. With the other hand, he guides his cock into my mouth. "Keep it in your mouth," he growls. "Use your tongue," he pants, as he thrusts in my mouth. He comes quickly, in less than a minute. I am gagging on his come, spitting it out of my mouth. "Just swallow it," he snarls, as he lets go of my wrists and lets me up. I go to the bathroom to wash the come from my mouth and hair. The next morning, I go home and rinse my mouth over and over. I stand in the shower until my mother shouts at me to get out of the bathroom already. Later that day, he calls me and says, "I really like you. I had a great time last night. You didn't have to do that, you know, unless you wanted to." I quietly tell a lie back into the phone, "I wanted to." The next time I see him, he sticks his finger inside me. I feel pain at insertion, but otherwise I am numb. "Tell me when you're done," he says. "I'm done," I say. "My turn," he says. A year later, I move across the country and try my best to forget any of that ever happened. Sarah Manguso writes in *Ongoingness,* "nothing's gone, not really. Everything that's ever happened has left its little wound."[12] I was such a tease. I didn't give enough. He penetrated me. I am marked. I will remain numb. I

---

11 Cris Mazza, *Something Wrong With Her: A Real-Time Memoir* (Los Angeles: Jaded Ibis Press, 2013), 61.

12 Sarah Manguso, *Ongoingness: The End of a Diary* (Minneapolis: Graywolf Press, 2015), 32.

will choose to be celibate for years. And I will learn that everything leaves its wound.

In an interview in *The New Inquiry,* Megan Milks asks Mazza about her resistance to a narrative of trauma and victimization in telling her story. Mazza responds that to "cry victim" would make Mark one of the victimizers. "We weren't rapist and victim," she asserts, "we were two kids."[13] I think back to that night. We were two kids. I never thought of my 19-year-old boyfriend as a rapist; I still cannot call what he did rape. I think of Jeannie Vanasco's battles over whether or not to call her sexual assault "rape." A boy she also dubs "Mark" penetrated her without her consent. He used his fingers. He marked her. She lives in the aftermath; she lives with Mark's mark.[14] I live with my own marks. But I never thought my teenage boyfriend was responsible for my numbness or my celibacy. I cannot really know if I was already numb when he touched me or if his touch made me go numb. I cannot really know if I chose celibacy because of that experience with him or for some other unconscious reason. These are not the questions I am asking, nor the answers I seek. I think of Joan Didion: "we tell ourselves stories in order to live." I think of Hanya Yanagihara: "don't we read [fiction] exactly to be upset?"[15] I read and tell in order to be upset, in order to live. I gather the fragments that will never fit together to make a whole.

I want the trauma to be poetry, but I cannot find the right timing, the right words, the right image. Like Ann Cvetkovich, I want to explore how "traumatic events refract outward to produce all kinds of affective responses and not just clinical symptoms." I want to know if it is possible "to name a connection

---

13 Megan Milks, "Doing It Wrong," *The New Inquiry,* November 12, 2013, https://thenewinquiry.com/doing-it-wrong/.

14 Jeannie Vanasco, *Things We Didn't Talk About When I Was a Girl: A Memoir* (Portland: Tin House Books, 2019).

15 Joan Didion, *The White Album* (New York: Farrar, Straus and Giroux, 1979), 11; Hanya Yanagihara, "Don't We Read Fiction Exactly to Be Upset?," *The Guardian,* March 4, 2016, https://www.theguardian.com/books/2016/mar/04/hanya-yanagihara-a-little-life-what-is-brave.

while refusing determination or causality."[16] I ask how this constellation of events makes me — makes me desire or not desire, makes me desirable or undesirable, makes me like a man or a man. A question, a refrain in McBee's text hits me in the gut every time: *what are you running to?* With every step forward, I find myself turning back for answers. In *Tender Points,* Amy Berkowitz writes of the pain in her body, of rape, of her body's battle with fibromyalgia. She is searching for the key that unlocks the link between her trauma and somatic pain when she writes, "when the onset of this pain follows a traumatic event (as it often does), it's hard not to understand that trauma as a certain kind of key." So much of the advice doled out to the chronically ill, the chronically pained, the traumatized, is to "look forward, not backward. Focus on what you need to do to get better, not what caused your illness." Berkowitz cannot look forward. She needs to know the "tangled chain of events that got [her] here." "Looking backward," she writes, "is what I need to do to get better." I keep looking back in order to find myself here.[17]

* * *

I am 4 years old. I am sitting on my father's lap, my hands cupping his cheeks. I have just told him I want to be a boy. He tells me I do not want to be a boy because the costs are too high. "Fine," I say, "then I want to marry you." He laughs again. "You can't marry me. I'm your dad, and I'm already married to your mom." Ernest Jones, in his speculations on female sexual development, suggests that "identification with the father is thus common to all forms of homosexuality."[18] Seems easy and right enough to me, sometimes. Maybe I'm gay because I identified with my father. If I couldn't be him and if I couldn't marry

---

16   Ann Cvetkovich, *An Archive of Feelings: Trauma, Sexuality, and Lesbian Public Cultures* (Durham: Duke University Press, 2003), 19, 90.

17   Amy Berkowitz, *Tender Points* (Oakland: Timeless, Infinite Light, 2015), 74.

18   Ernest Jones, "The Early Development of Female Sexuality," in *Psychoanalysis and Female Sexuality,* ed. Hendrik M. Ruitenbeek (New Haven: College & University Press, 1966), 31.

him, then maybe I could be *like* him, meaning I could marry a woman like he did, which would make me gay. But if I want to (re)imagine myself as a boy, then my desire to marry my father would make me a homosexual. But if I was a boy who then grew into manhood, and if I am now seeking the love of women, am I still gay? If I was a boy and am a man, then to some extent, I am not gay. If I was a girl (and to some extent, I believe I was), but am not a woman, then I am not gay *and* I am gay. Maybe the point is not whether or not I am a homosexual but that my father left his mark on me: my identification with, my love for, my identification against, and my hate of my father have all this gender and sexuality stuff twisted for me.

The girl child, explains Sigmund Freud, upon recognizing the genital difference in the boy or man, "soon becomes envious of the penis; this envy reaches its highest point in the consequentially important wish that she also should be a boy."[19] But the wish to be a boy in order to have a penis is meant to be a phase the girl moves through in her infantile sexuality, as she fixates instead on her infatuation with her father. But I both wanted to be a boy and became infatuated with my father, or at least, I thought I wanted to marry him. On infantile object selection, Freud concludes that the sexual feelings a child has for the parents are differentiated by sex, such that the son is attracted to the mother, while the daughter is attracted to the father. But the incest taboo quickly alerts us to the need to reject such fantasies as we overcome our incestuous desires on the path to healthy, adult sexuality. However, Freud notes that many children can be detained at these different stations of development and some will "never, or very imperfectly, withdraw their affection from their parents." Of those who get held up at the station, so to speak, Freud claims, "they are mostly girls, who to the delight of their

---

19 Sigmund Freud, *Three Contributions to the Theory of Sex,* trans. A.A. Brill (New York: Nervous and Mental Disease Publishing Company, 1918), 57. Though James Strachey translated a revised version he titled, *Three Essays on the Theory of Sexuality,* published in 1962, I find Brill's pithiness and directness in the 1918 translation to be more poetically poignant for my purposes here.

parents, retain their full infantile love far beyond puberty, and it is instructive to find that in their married life these girls are incapable of fulfilling their duties to their husbands. They make cold wives and remain sexually anesthetic."[20] Freud might say, I, the daughter, upon recognizing my lack of a phallus, wanted to be a boy like my father, who has the phallus, so that I too may have the phallus. But soon understanding that I could not be a boy — but was I a boy? Was I a girl? — I decided I would rather marry my father in order to have the phallus, in order to take it from my mother.

But what if the daughter is actually a son who lacks a penis and wants to marry his father? Does this daughter, who is actually a son, remain stuck in the course of development, making for a cold and sexually anesthetic wife? But if the daughter is actually a son, does she then make for a cold and sexually anesthetic husband? Have I been sexually anesthetic because I wanted to be a boy and marry my father, or was it because my boyfriend told me I was a tease and penetrated me anyway, or was I always sexually anesthetic because some people just are? Was I ever a daughter or son; was I ever one or the other?

Even into adulthood, I long to become the man I always thought I would already grow up to be. I am nostalgic for the certainty of this fate even when I know of its impossibility. I reckon with simultaneous and contradictory feelings of alienation and belonging, displacement and longing. I hear my father's voice declaring that his white skin gives him power, that he pays a steep price to be a man. I am running both toward and away from a masculinity and a whiteness that cannot help but be complicit in the racist, sexist, and heterosexist ideologies that fuel this cruel world. How do I recode dominant masculinity? How do I become and unbecome? What do I become and unbecome? How do I take stock of what I am running to, given what I am running from? What does it mean that the very places I have spent my life running from, the places that house domi-

---

20 Ibid., 85–86.

nant masculinity (my father's lap, my teenage boyfriend's bed), are now the memories I am turning toward?

* * *

I have a scrapbook my mother put together for me shortly after my birth. The first page contains a photo of me as a newborn, swaddled in a white blanket, lying atop a blue sheet. This photo was likely taken in the hospital shortly after my birth. In the photo, I am looking directly at the camera with my right hand raised as if waving or grasping for something. I also have a faux-hawk. I still sometimes sport this hairstyle. Above this photo, my mother wrote, "K—'s Birth" and, below the photo, the date of my birth. Next to the photo, there are ten steno pad pages stapled to the scrapbook page. The heading on page one: "A letter from Mom." In the letter, she details her nearly thirty-two hours of labor, including the need for an episiotomy that eased my arrival into the world and her joy at the doctor's announcement, "It's a girl." She writes to me, "you were so beautiful to finally see and even though I had to work long and hard for you it was well worth it and I wouldn't trade you for the world. […] Your Aunts and Uncle and both your Grandfathers came to see you + me (but mostly you) in the hospital and they all fell in love with you, […] I'm glad you're here. I love you." Reading my mother's words unexpectedly turns me into a blubbering mess. I am not usually one to cry much, which has always been the case despite what they tell you about testosterone halting one's capacity for tears. I cry because I do not recognize the person who wrote this letter. I want to know her and to be the child in the letter who is beautiful and so loved that her mother wouldn't trade her for the world. The person who wrote this letter is not the mother I remember or the mother I know.

Not too long ago, after my top surgery and before I decided to start taking testosterone, I was visiting my family in Ohio. My mother asked me to sit on her back porch and drink a beer with her in the cold winter night, a space heater at our feet. When we sat down, she looked at me curiously. "I don't get it," she said, "are you gay? Are you trans? What are you?" I whisper back, uncertain, "I'm just me, mom. I'm just me." Reading and rereading the letter, I imagine what it feels like to be loved by my mother. I came into the world through her screaming. My mother had her vagina cut open to her asshole to make room for me. The first thing she wanted to know is if I was a boy or a girl. Today, she wants to know if I am gay or trans. When I tell her I am just me, she says, "all I know is that the Bible says it ain't right." I have learned to hate myself through all of her unwanting, even when she promised not to trade me for the world, even though she promised that everyone had already fallen in love with me.

* * *

"You have to let people love you," McBee's therapist says.[21] R says, "let me love you." "I see you," she says. But to her, I was her girlfriend who is *like* a guy. I tell her that all I have been asking is for her to love me, to see me. I tell her that I *am* a guy. I tell her that I am not "she." I tell my therapist that every time I try to confront R with my "bad" feelings, I feel bulldozed. My throat closes up, my heart pounds, my brain goes foggy. All I can do is say that I am sorry for having feelings; I am sorry for having needs; I am sorry. I tell my therapist I feel like a scared little girl again, waiting for someone to love her, or a scared little boy waiting for someone to see him and to love him. My therapist reminds me that what I am feeling is not what everyone feels when they remember being a child. She says this is bigger than R. She pinpoints early childhood imprints. She tells me I am experiencing complex PTSD symptoms that are likely activated by R. She suggests that I talk to R about this and that I ask her to form a strategy with me in which I can tell her I am experiencing these symptoms and she can hold space for me to breathe and gather my thoughts and feelings. R says, "yes, of course, of course." But, moving forward, when I cannot speak, she will tell me I am acting like a "petulant child"; when I finally find my

---

21 McBee, *Man Alive,* 125.

voice, she will tell me I need to learn to say something sooner; when I tell her I feel alone in our relationship, she will tell me I have abandonment issues; when I tell her I am hurt by something she said or did, she will say, "that is just the story you are creating," and she will tell me I need to "get over it already."

"Empathy is not just a shared emotion," Kristin Dombek writes, "but [it is] an experience of the place, the perspective, from which the other's emotions and actions come."[22] During one of those moments with *R,* I ask her to try to put herself in my shoes, to imagine how she would feel if I treated her exactly how she treated me, to put herself in my place, to imagine my perspective. "That's not helpful to me," she says. "Empathy," Leslie Jamison writes, "means realizing no trauma has discrete edges. Trauma bleeds. Out of wounds and across boundaries. Sadness becomes a seizure. Empathy demands another kind of porousness in response."[23] When *R* refuses my request for empathy, to make herself porous, I seize. I bleed from all the old wounds.

I remember one night holding *TT* in my arms as we talked about how we might best love each other and make space for each other's pain. She said, "sometimes the question we should ask is not 'what is wrong with you?' but 'what happened to you?'" In tracing the multiple ways we inherit trauma, Mark Wolynn explains that traumatic incidents disrupt our thought processes into a disorganized scattering, such that in the aftermath, we are not always able to connect certain memories to the originating incident. Instead, he explains, we store fragments of memory in our unconscious which can be activated in our bodies and memories. He describes this process of triggering as one in which we might imagine an "invisible rewind button" being pressed, "causing us to reenact aspects of the original trauma in our day-to-day lives."[24] The result is that we unconsciously find

---

22 Kristin Dombek, *The Selfishness of Others: An Essay on the Fear of Narcissism* (New York: Farrar, Straus and Giroux, 2016), 105.

23 Leslie Jamison, *The Empathy Exams: Essays* (Minneapolis: Graywolf Press, 2014), 5–6.

24 Wolynn, *It Didn't Start with You,* 15.

ourselves "reacting to certain people, events, or situations in old, familiar ways that echo the past."[25] The body's cache of original traumas might surface and split open at any given point.

The trigger, the reminder, the familiar, perhaps uncanny, sensation activates our compulsion to repeat, to react, and to relive. In *Healing from Hidden Abuse,* Shannon Thomas suggests that survivors of abuse and trauma develop a biochemical dependency on toxic relationships.[26] They become addicted to the highs and lows, the pushing and pulling. Thinking about Thomas's claims about biochemical dependency alongside Wolynn's observations about triggering, I wonder if our addictions make us *want* to push the rewind button, and if what Freud called the "repetition compulsion" is just as much biochemical as it is an instinct toward death or a psychic attempt at mastery. What if it is just as much about pleasure? Do I find myself, yet again, an addict, addicted, in a way, to trauma and abuse? Do I actually crave this odd familiarity and comfort, a certain pleasure in the pain maybe, brought on by the echoes of my past?

* * *

Before I start seeing my therapist, I tell R that my dynamic with her reminds me of the dynamic I have with my father. I am infinitely awaiting his apology. I spent two years waiting for an apology from R, and I am still waiting. R snarls at me, "I am *nothing* like your father. I resent that you would even say that." I tell her that I didn't say she was like my father. I said we share a similar dynamic. But in that moment, she is more like my father than she even realizes. The psychic tells me R is actually like my mother. She tells me my father was obviously mean and aggressively abusive. My mother, she tells me, is likely a narcissist and is emotionally abusive but with subtlety. I suddenly recall the

---

25 Ibid.
26 Shannon Thomas, *Healing from Hidden Abuse: A Journey Through the Stages of Recovery from Psychological Abuse* (Arlington: MAST Publishing House, 2016), 157.

last conversation I had with my mother. I tell her I cannot stay at her house when I am in town because of what she said to me the last time I was there. (*Are you gay? Are you trans? What are you? A new echo.*) "Like what?" she asks. I say, "that homophobic and transphobic stuff you said." "Well, I don't remember that," she says. And we leave it at that.

I remember one of the last conversations I had with *R*. I tell her that, about a month prior, I was hurt and felt demeaned by something she said to me in front of her friends. "I don't remember that," she says, then, "what do you want me to do about it now? You can't bring stuff up a month after the fact." We leave it at that. But *R* uses this line on me enough times that I sometimes do wonder if I am actually remembering incorrectly or if all her not remembering is designed to help me forget. What is it that R wanted bad enough that she didn't care how she got it? Control of the narrative, an erasure of all the ways she'd done harm and caused hurt? When it comes down to it, my therapist says *R* and my mother are wrong: if I am still having feelings about something, then I can bring them up. "Just because they don't remember it, that doesn't mean it didn't happen," she says. The psychic says, "thank Jay-sus you didn't shack up with her and have babies. It'd be like raising kids with your mother." The psychic is a little rough around the edges but a straight shooter. I nod. "Yes," I say, "yes."

"I see you," *R* says. In the end, I don't think *R* ever did see me, and I cannot be sure she ever even loved me. I realize that during the year I was with *R,* I couldn't really see her, which is to say I didn't really know her. But the people who cared about me could see right through her. *N* said *R* is a narcissist, and she worried that I am stuck in an emotionally abusive relationship. *E* said *R* seems incapable of loving me and that I seemed much happier before I started dating her. *C* said that *R* is a "total narcissist," and she hates to see me in so much pain all the time. *B* said he doesn't understand why I let *R* treat me the way she does over and over again. *D* said *R* is verbally abusive toward me and that a loving partner would never say the things she says, at least not without apology. *M* handed me a book by Sandy

Hotchkiss, *Why Is It Always About You? The Seven Deadly Sins of Narcissism*. The book will later shake me to the core. Everyone else could name what I could not. On the process of coming to know her abuser as an abuser, Carmen Maria Machado writes, "I didn't know her, not really, until I did. She was a stranger because something essential was shielded, released in tiny bursts until it became a flood — a flood of what I realized I did not know."[27] I didn't know *R,* until I did. Tiny bursts that suddenly became a flood of recognition.

Recognizing the abuse as abuse is something I will come to months after the relationship ends, but I will remain haunted by the possibility that I did actually see *R* and she did actually love me to the best of her capabilities. I am stirred by Dombek's interrogation of narcissism when she writes, "it is something you'll come to months or years later, if at all: the possibility that the way [she] was with you was real, and that it was love; […] You might understand this in the middle of the next time you fall in love with someone else, and find yourself, still, in love with [her]. You've just spread your love out in time, and [she] has spread it out in space."[28] Am I still spreading my love out over time, or is it just my wish to hold onto all the good I wanted in her? Machado continues, "afterward, I would mourn her as if she'd died, because something had: someone we had created together."[29] Was the *R* who actually loved me the one we had created together, the *R* she wanted me to see, the *R* I wanted her to be, the *R* who worked like a dam, trying best not to let the tiny bursts break through? Sometimes, I still want to believe in *R,* just like a part of me still wants to believe in my father.

* * *

---

27 Carmen Maria Machado, *In the Dream House* (Minneapolis: Graywolf Press, 2019), 77.

28 Dombek, *The Selfishness of Others,* 119.

29 Machado, *In the Dream House,* 77.

I go through a phase in which I decide to write poetry in a more frantic voice than I usually write in. I only realize now that all the poems written in this voice happen to be the only poems I have written explicitly about abuse, as if healing trauma is like writing a poem. I end up publishing those poems in a series. But I hold onto one.

How to Make Me Disappear

Step one: turn it
click doorknob jiggle jiggle.
He will yell — open
this door, missy, little lady, girl
you better now right this minute 'til
the count of ten
never never never
but you do

Step two: nails to the quick bite
if the screams try
to wriggle loose, inhale
lungsful throatchoke
tight tight tight

Step three: hold
it in. breath off. you do not
exist if he cannot hear you
whimper whisper wail wait
beltsnap lightsblack

Step four: rip
the beadeyes off all the dolls —
nobody sees a thing

Much of my life has been spent either trying to disappear or to become someone else. Becoming someone or something else is, I suppose, its own kind of disappearance. I cannot help but wonder how much of my desire to not be me is inflected by wishing I could be anyone but the "little missy" my father came after or by my efforts to hide all the abuse that shaped me in order to close the eyes of the world to it, right down to my inanimate dolls, until it all spilled onto the public space of these pages.

In "A Child Is Being Beaten," Freud writes of the phases of movement through the beating fantasy. In the third phase of the beating fantasy, the refrain goes, "my father is beating the child, he loves only me." The child being beaten, Freud reminds us, is almost always a boy.[30] I am being beaten. My father does not love me; he loves only me. I love my father; I want to marry my father, even though he beats me (or because he beats me?). The child being beaten is almost invariably a boy. I am the child being beaten. I am a boy. The girl becomes envious of the penis and wishes to be a boy. I am a girl. I wish to be a boy. I am a boy. (Was I ever a boy? Was I ever a girl? When did I become a boy? Did I ever become a man? When did I become a man? Am I becoming a man? Am I a man?) Freud might answer that my ideas about being a boy are a product of my masculinity complex, and, that if stuck in certain stages of development, when girls turn away from their incestuous love of their father, they want only to be boys. I loved my father. I wanted my father to love me, but he only loved me as a girl. I am a boy, so my father beat me. My father beat me because I was a girl. My father beat me because I am a boy. Why did my father beat me?

Reading Hanya Yanagihara's *A Little Life,* I return again and again to one scene. Jude, one of the main characters in the book, is a young boy, living in a monastery where he experiences multiple types of abuse at the hands of the brothers and the Father

---

30 Sigmund Freud, "'A Child Is Being Beaten': A Contribution to the Study of the Origin of Sexual Perversions," in *The Standard Edition of the Complete Psychological Works of Sigmund Freud,* Vol. 17: *An Infantile Neurosis and Other Works (1917–1919),* ed. and trans. James Strachey with Anna Freud (London: The Hogarth Press, 1955), 190–91.

(as in the priest, but the uncanny parallel we might draw to the father that haunts the psychoanalytical imagination is not lost on me here). In this scene, Jude has just spilled some milk, and after cleaning it up, he has been commanded to go to his room. As he runs down the hall to his room, he notices that the door to his room is closed. It is usually left open, unless one of the brothers or the Father is paying him a visit. He pauses in the hallway, unsure of what is waiting for him behind the door. But if he turns around, he will face the wrath of the brother who sent him to his room for spilling the milk. Frozen in the hallway, young Jude must make a choice: return to certain punishment or take his chances opening the bedroom door. He finally works up the courage and opens the door with a slam, only to find nobody else in the room, just his furniture and a newly placed bouquet of daffodils. He falls to the floor, engulfed in sadness.[31] As I read and reread this scene, the tension always builds. My breathing quickens. I feel the panic that fails to dissolve in the anticlimactic opening of the door.

I am 9 years old. I am standing at the end of the hallway, and my father is coming toward me with his hand raised. I am paralyzed with fear until I make the snap decision to run into my bedroom. I jump into the bed and pull the covers over my head. My heart is pounding. I cannot breathe. All my muscles are tensed in anticipation of the crack of a palm on my backside. I wait and wait in my panicked state, but the beating never comes. I cautiously pull the covers from my head and sit in the quiet. My father has retreated to the living room where he is smoking a cigarette, drinking a beer, and watching television. I cannot know why he did not hit me that day. I have wondered if seeing my fear of him shook something deep inside him and he relented, or if he just didn't feel it was worth the chase. I am haunted more by the silence and stillness, the empty room, than I am by the crack of a belt and the memories of red, stinging flesh.

---

31 Hanya Yanagihara, *A Little Life* (New York: Doubleday, 2015), 172–73.

I am 34 years old. I am standing in R's hallway. I am collecting my things that she held onto after our breakup. She leaves
them in a box outside her apartment door. Against my better
judgment, I knock on her door. To my surprise, she opens the
door. "What do you want?" she sneers. My heart is pounding,
my throat is closing up. I am not sure why I knocked. I am not
sure what I want, really. Some short discussion follows, and, by
the end of it, I have backed away toward the building exit. She is
coming at me down the hallway, her finger in the air, gesturing
and shouting at me. I am growing small against the exit door. I
am that shrinking, frozen little child again. Peter Levine suggests
that the precondition for the development of PTSD is that the
trauma experience causes both a sensation of being frightened
and a sense of being trapped, bringing together both intense
fear and immobilization. This coupling of fear and immobility
not only occurs in the formation of trauma, but it maintains it
and is necessary for deconstructing and transforming it. In fact,
much of Levine's treatment modality in transforming and releasing trauma from the body involves literally moving the body
in ways that revisit and unleash the trauma from the sites it has
been stored in the body. And if not to release it, then to at least
help the traumatized subject create a safe "container" for such
sensations in states of hyperarousal. Levine writes about how,
in treatment, some of his patients literally need to get their legs
moving, as if to run.[32] Away or toward, I am not sure. Perhaps
both.

In that moment in R's hallway, I feel both frightened and
trapped. My legs are frozen as I shrink against the building's
exit door. Levine suggests that many people, after experiencing
trauma, manage to continue living in what he calls a "functional
freeze," in which they are able to maintain work, family, and
social life, but are severely limited in their enjoyments of life.
He writes, "while traumatized humans don't actually remain
physically paralyzed, they do get lost in a kind of anxious fog,

---

32 Peter A. Levine, *In an Unspoken Voice: How the Body Releases Trauma and
Restores Goodness* (Berkeley: North Atlantic Books, 2010).

a chronic partial shutdown, dissociation, lingering depression, and numbness."[33] I am curious about all the ways in which trauma lingers and repeats itself, numbing, depressing, and dulling one's life experiences. But in reflecting on this particular moment with R, I am especially interested in trauma's return in the chronicity of the freeze or the partial shutdown. I am stuck in place, and a fog covers my brain as I can no longer make out R's words as she moves toward me, her face hot and seething, her mouth an open yaw of screams and snarls.

Levine describes trauma response as much more complicated than "fight or flight"; instead, we might move through stages of "arrest," which entail vigilance and scanning, to a stage of assessment of the situation to any of the stages of flight, fight, freeze (or fright), and fold, a collapse into our helplessness.[34] I am on the verge of folding at the end of the hallway. And I know all I must do is remember to move. Somehow, in a moment, I find the capacity to move my legs again. I feel as though I am running in place before I turn and hurriedly shove the door open. I quickly walk away and feel on the verge of a sprint as I let the door slam on her shrill words. This is the last time I see R, my last memory of her, of us, that I hold: her face, twisted in anger as she shouts and gesticulates, moving toward me as I shrink away like a frightened child. In this moment, she is more like my father than she even realizes. But, this time, instead of hunkering down in anticipation of the beating, I walk away from it.

I wish I could tell you that was the end of it, that I was the one to walk away and never turn back. But it is not the case. Just hours after I walked through the doorway, I wrote and sent via email a letter of apology and a plea yet again for R to respond to the ways I had recounted being hurt by her, again desperately seeking from her the apology I would never receive. She ignored that email. I never heard from her again. She erased me from her life and lingered in mine as a ghost, or as the wolf stalking me through the forest, interrupting my sleep. Berkowitz writes,

---

33 Ibid., 52.
34 Ibid., 48.

"I have a wolf in my story. But he will not interrupt my walk through the forest. Which is to say he's already interrupted it: He's the reason I'm here, sorting out the aftermath. Which is to say the wolf is eternally interrupting my walk through the forest: emerging from behind the same tree again and again to block my path."[35] There are many wolves and many paths in my story. My father, the boy who pushed himself into my mouth, my mother, R, the diagnosis, the drug, the man I am like, the man I am, the PTSD symptoms themselves. They all repeat. They all either block my path or reroute me onto new paths. "But to solve this kind of mystery, it seems," according to Berkowitz, "you need to walk alone into a forest. You need to walk until you meet a wolf."[36]

If my therapist tells me my partner is activating my PTSD responses that come from the emotional abuse I experienced as a child, does that mean my partner is emotionally abusive? I cannot name it. I cannot say it as I imagine R's teeth bared like a wolf. I hear R's voice still echoing in my head, "don't you see that's the story you created?! Don't you see that's the story you choose to tell?! Can't you see that's just your version? That's not really what happened! Just get over it!" But her voice is not the only one that reverberates. The echoes of my past ring, "come here right now, little missy. What are you? I don't remember that. That didn't happen. You're such a tease." I will remain in denial for months, for years, for what seems like a lifetime. Only now, as I write this, do I finally dare to name it: My relationship with R was emotionally abusive; I was sexually assaulted at the age of 17 by my boyfriend; my parents are emotionally abusive; I developed a patterned response to abuse, grew attached to it (addicted, maybe); I have been numb, and I have been celibate, but now I am not; I inject testosterone into my thigh every week, but I am not sure if I am a man or ever will be; I am unsure of how or if all these things connect; I am still walking through the forest, and the wolves are still emerging from the trees.

---

35 Berkowitz, *Tender Points,* 17.
36 Ibid.

* * *

I return to Cris, sitting on her basement floor, picking herself apart. After she tells Mark she is "gonna go transgender," she dissects her body into pieces of meat and bone. "Every single part of me, there's something wrong," she says. She describes her thigh as a ham but not a very good one, her knee as a discolored, scabby circle.[37] I know the drill. I have picked my body apart in so many ways: the breasts and the scars that mark where they used to be, the curves of my hips, the budding hairs on my chin, and the muscles of my shoulders. Even the parts that are supposed to feel right still feel wrong. Maybe Cris and I aren't really all that different. Maybe Cris is not actually trying to be convincing to anyone else. Maybe we are both trying to convince ourselves that we can be at home in our bodies, that we can heal our grief, that we can make peace with the wolves, that making contact with the ghosts will change something for us somehow, that we can collect the fragments and let the wounds, big and small, scab over.

---

37 Vitale, dir., *Anorgasmia.*

2

An Unmistakably Masochistic Character

I no longer believe it is bad
I only believe it is suffering
  — Brian Teare, *The Empty Form Goes All the Way to Heaven*[1]

I live in my suffering and that makes me happy.
Anything that keeps me from living in my suffering is
unbearable to me.
                              — Roland Barthes, *Mourning Diary*[2]

I step off the subway and emerge at the corner of a busy inter-section. I pull my phone from my pocket and dial the number as instructed. Amidst the traffic noise, I can just barely hear the woman on the other end give me the exact address where I am to meet her. I make my way to the building a couple blocks over. At the exact appointed hour, I call up, and she buzzes me in. I climb several flights of stairs and just as I reach the door, it opens. The mistress greets me with a warm smile and a tight corset. I step

---

1   Brian Teare, *The Empty Form Goes All the Way to Heaven* (Boise: Ahsahta Press, 2015), 60.

2   Roland Barthes, *Mourning Diary,* ed. Nathalie Léger, trans. Richard Howard (New York: Hill and Wang, 2010), 173.

inside, remove my shoes, and take a seat on the couch. We begin our negotiation. I want to be spanked. I want to be flogged. Light bondage is good. I don't mind being slapped in the face; I welcome it. Yes, I am a boy. Yes, it feels good to have my masculinity affirmed. No visible marks please, but marks that will be concealed by clothing are perfectly fine, desired even. No, I will not masturbate. No, I do not want sexual genital contact. Yes, I want to cry. Yes, I want her to have power and authority over me. "Red" is the safe word. She leads me into the dungeon.

* * *

In the essay that begins this book, I wonder if the complex constellation of events that range from sexual assault to childhood abuse have any bearing on how I move through an ever-evolving practice of gender and sexuality. As I become addicted to the ritual of piercing my thigh muscle weekly with a needle connected to a syringe loaded with testosterone, I wonder if I am not also biochemically destined to repeat trauma and its attendant patterns. Do I cling to emotionally abusive relationships because they feel like home? Do I like being pinned down in sexual play because I'm trying to reclaim something from the time my boyfriend pinned me down when I was 17? Do I pay someone to beat me because it feels like the love of my father? I cannot help but wonder if pleasure may find some roots in trauma, if it might also arise from pain — psychological pain, somatic pain, or psychosomatic pain.

In the vein of Ann Cvetkovich, I have long been invested in making sense of depathologized trauma in queer lives.[3] In particular, I have been focused on calling attention to the asexual community's aversion to trauma narratives for fear such experience may cancel out their fight for a "normal," nonpathological, natural, "born this way," asexual identity or orientation. I have instead called for a space to narrate trauma in conjunction with

---

3   Ann Cvetkovich, *An Archive of Feelings: Trauma, Sexuality, and Lesbian Public Cultures* (Durham: Duke University Press, 2003).

(a)sexuality and to be able to talk about one's lack of interest in sex alongside one's experience with trauma and abuse; not necessarily as causally related but as, perhaps, correlated or at least part and parcel of a life story that need not be diagnosable.[4]

But I have also wondered about the value of diagnosis. Diagnosis often means access to treatment and cure, as complicated as that may be. We don't always want to or need to be cured or treated, but sometimes we do. In *Brilliant Imperfection,* Eli Clare urges us to consider what diagnosis does, that it not only names and describes but also shapes the way we are understood in the world and how it therefore informs how the world treats us. As Clare asserts, some diagnoses make violence thinkable and doable. They make space for cures to function ideologically as sites of erasure or eradication of difference founded on racist, ablest, hetero- and cis-sexist motives. But for some, diagnosis can provide information, knowledge, or answers to the question of what is happening to the body and why. For some, diagnosis is manipulable, providing pathways to the medical technologies one may want to access.[5] But I am also aware that for many, the violent treatments that follow diagnosis leave no room for manipulation, no room for spinning the diagnosis to one's advantage. For me, a diagnosis of gender dysphoria means my insurance company covers the costs of top surgery and hormones. A diagnostic code indicating unspecified reactions to severe stress means my insurance company covers the costs of therapy. A diagnosis of gender dysphoria means I am distressed, conflicted, and uncomfortable with my body. A diagnosis of severe stress reaction linked to symptoms of complex PTSD means I may experience depression, anxiety, or dissociation. I am diagnosed, which means my body and mind are made available to treatments which may prove to make my life more survivable, even livable. At the same time any of these elements of diagnosis may

---

4   KJ Cerankowski. "Illegible: Asexualities in Media, Literature, and Performance," PhD Thesis, Stanford University, 2014.

5   Eli Clare, *Brilliant Imperfection: Grappling with Cure* (Durham: Duke University Press, 2017).

be used to explain away my gendered and sexual practices or nonpractices as treatable symptoms rather than complex and intimate affects.

In this ricochet between diagnosis and treatment, I want to know where trauma meets pleasure meets pain. In *An Archive of Feelings,* Cvetkovich turns to Dorothy Allison's work in order to explore the connections between sexual trauma and pleasure. If I am to be honest, I often attribute Allison's writing as a kind of salvation, a rescue net for me, a poor, queer, white-trash kid who hadn't yet understood such a life to be survivable. In an essay entitled "Notes to a Young Feminist," Allison recalls how she came to feminism through authors like Rita Mae Brown, Judy Grahn, Adrienne Rich, Alice Walker, and Audre Lorde. She says of reading their work, "what made me a feminist were occasional glimpses of my real life on the page."[6] Like those authors, Dorothy Allison, too, gives me glimpses of my own life on the page. I remember clutching a worn library copy of *Bastard Out of Carolina,* reading furiously through the pages as if — no, because — my life depended on it. I cried for Bone as a way of crying for myself.

Bastard Out of Carolina is canonical in queer trauma literature, if such a canon exists, weaving a complex and tangled narrative of abuse, trauma, pain, and pleasure. The novel follows a young girl, Ruth Anne Boatwright whom we come to know as "Bone," as she endures the physical and sexual abuses of her stepfather Daddy Glen, along with the betrayal of her mother Anney, who ultimately chooses her husband over her child. Through it all, Bone grows into her sexuality, even working through some of her trauma in her masturbation fantasies. She also spends time with and develops an attachment to her Aunt Raylene, who later becomes her guardian and caretaker. We learn from Bone that Aunt Raylene was "different" from the rest of her Boatwright sisters, and later Raylene confesses to Bone her past love of a woman. Bone is intrigued and fascinated by

---

6   Dorothy Allison, "Notes to a Young Feminist," *In These Times,* April 27, 2004, https://inthesetimes.com/article/notes-to-a-young-feminist.

Raylene's proclivities, and the narrative ends with Bone's assertion, "I was who I was going to be, someone like her [Raylene],
like Mama, a Boatwright woman."[7] With these final words, we
are given the sense that there is a potential queerness in Bone, a
likeness to Raylene, thus offering space in the narrative to com-
plexly hinge experiences of sexual trauma and abuse to queerness and sexual pleasure. As a teenager reading the novel, I held
onto that possibility of being who I was going to be, as a future
yet to come, becoming who I was going to be, not simply being
who I am.

While reading and rereading the novel, I am pushed unexpectedly into territory in my own psyche I hadn't yet confront-
ed. Bone's fantasies of pleasure in pain force me to ponder my
own fantasies and desires and their links to my own traumatic
hauntings. In her reading, Cvetkovich, like me, is interested
in Bone's masturbation fantasies in which she orgasms to the
dream of fire as Daddy Glen beats her. In some of the fantasies,
Bone reclaims her power over Daddy Glen as she successfully
defies him in front of an audience who cannot look away. They
must watch her reign triumphant over him. Cvetkovich writes,

> out of the pain and shame of being beaten, Bone is able to
> salvage the pride of pleasure in her fantasies and orgasms.
> To call these fantasies masochistic in a simply derogatory
> sense, or to consider them the "perverse" product of sexual
> violence, is to underestimate their capacity to provide not
> only pleasure but power. [...] Neither wholly a source of
> shame nor a source of pride, Bone's sexual fantasies are in-
> distinguishably both. The pleasure they produce cannot be
> separated from the trauma to which they are also connected.[8]

If it is not apparent by now, I am less interested in the climactic,
orgasmic pleasure of the beating fantasy and more interested

---

7   Dorothy Allison, *Bastard Out of Carolina* (New York: Penguin Books,
    1992), 309.
8   Cvetkovich, *An Archive of Feelings*, 103.

in the imbrication of trauma and the phantasmatic production of pleasure and power through the fantasy of being beaten; or, even, the inseparability of the pleasure produced from the trauma.

Let us return to Freud's "A Child Is Being Beaten." In phase two, "the phantasy is accompanied by a high degree of pleasure, and has now acquired a significant content [...]. Now, therefore, the wording runs: '*I am being beaten by my father.*' It is of an unmistakably masochistic character."[9] Freud claims this second phase is most important and most momentous, but it never succeeds in becoming conscious. But my own beating fantasies haunt my conscious mind. They come to me in waking life, rarely in the dreams of deep REM sleep like they do for Bone. And with these fantasies, my memories haunt me. My father's voice echoes in my head, "listen here, young lady; get over here now, little missy." A belt removed from a waistband, a snap-snap for good measure, anticipatory punishment, a bending over the knee, and a pulling down of drawers. Leather to flesh. I am being beaten by my father. I am of an unmistakably masochistic character.

I wonder if I am stuck in this second phase, somehow made conscious against Freud's supposition that the masochistic pleasure in the beating fantasy never makes it to the conscious realm. But when we move on to the next phase, recall, the fantasy becomes, "my father is beating the child, he loves only me."[10] The child being beaten is almost invariably a boy. Maybe I am not stuck in the second phase, after all. The pleasure in the beating fantasy for me relies upon me being a boy. I am being beaten. That familiar refrain echoes again: My father does not love me; my father loves only me. I am the child being beaten. I am a boy. I wanted my father to love me, but he only loved me as a girl. I

9   Sigmund Freud, "'A Child Is Being Beaten': A Contribution to the Study of the Origin of Sexual Perversions," in *The Standard Edition of the Complete Psychological Works of Sigmund Freud*, Vol. 17: *An Infantile Neurosis and Other Works (1917–1919)*, ed. and trans. James Strachey with Anna Freud (London: The Hogarth Press, 1955), 185.

10   Ibid., 190.

am a boy, so my father beat me. My father beat me because I was a girl. My father beat me because I am a boy. Why did my father beat me? Freud also claims this phase of the fantasy has become a sadistic one: "but only the *form* of this phantasy is sadistic; the satisfaction which is derived from it is masochistic."[11] To call these fantasies masochistic in a simply derogatory sense is to underestimate their capacity to provide not only pleasure but power.[12] I am of an unmistakably masochistic character. Am I my own sadist, delivering pain to myself through the repetition of the beating fantasy in search of a masochistic satisfaction? If I am the child being beaten, am I a boy or a girl?

* * *

As I step into the dungeon, the mistress grabs me by the hair and pushes her forehead against mine. "You have been a very naughty boy," she says, her breath hot across my lips. She smells of marijuana and lipstick. "And now," she says, "you're going to get what you deserve." I cannot help but grin. She quickly smacks the grin off my face and commands me to remove my clothing. I strip down to my jock; I am packing. Yes, I have been a very bad boy. In my head, my father's voice echoes with a difference, "listen here, young man; get over here now, little mister." She grabs my wrists and places me in a set of leather cuffs. She directs me to the cage, commands me to raise my hands above my head where she clips the cuffs to the bars. She spreads my legs just a little, grabs my ass cheeks, and begins administering the spankings. The cold flesh on flesh stings; we are just getting warmed up.

In *The Body in Pain: The Making and Unmaking of the World*, Elaine Scarry suggests that pain achieves what it does through its unsharability, which is made possible through its resistance

---

11 Ibid., 191.
12 Cvetkovich, *An Archive of Feelings*, 103.

to and destruction of language.[13] Pain has no language. It is a series of grunts and moans and cries. In the dungeon, I lose my language. I can barely mutter a "yes, ma'am" or "no, ma'am" when it is required of me. In the *New Bottoming Book,* a beginner's guide to the ethics of bottoming, Dossie Easton and Janet W. Hardy warn that it can be rude to faint during a scene, they warn that the bottom must let the top know when they are feeling dizzy or nauseous.[14] The spankings continue, I am warming up to the pain, but I am feeling lightheaded. My language is reduced to gasps, sighs, and grunts. I am a rude bottom. Before I can recover my tongue to utter the safe word, I lose consciousness.

* * *

In his study of pain and suffering, Patrick Wall asserts that "no ordinary person ever experienced a pure pain that was not accompanied by unpleasantness."[15] When I read this, I wonder if the unpleasantness of pain forecloses pleasure or if pleasure can also be tinged by a touch of unpleasantness. I wonder, if a person finds pain to be pleasant and pleasurable, with no accompanying unpleasantness, does that make that person no longer ordinary? Do they become extraordinary? In my pondering, I misremember a line from Heather Love's book, *Feeling Backward: Loss and the Politics of Queer History.* I think she wrote that queer love is somehow juxtaposed with "ordinary" love. How pleasantly queer, I think, to be extraordinary in one's pleasure derived from pain, to be in love with pain in that way. I pull the book off my shelf, flip through the pages, and find that I got it all wrong. Love writes, "same-sex desire is marked by a long history of association with failure, impossibility, and loss. I

---

13 Elaine Scarry, *The Body in Pain: The Making and Unmaking of the World* (Oxford: Oxford University Press, 1985).

14 Dossie Easton and Janet W. Hardy, *The New Bottoming Book* (Emeryville: Greenery Press, 2001), 125.

15 Patrick Wall, *Pain: The Science of Suffering* (New York: Columbia University Press, 2000), 29.

do not mean by this that homosexual love is in its essence failed or impossible, any more than regular love is."[16] The operative word is "regular," not "ordinary" — but what is the difference? For Love, all love is possibly impossible, but homosexual love is not "regular" (usual? normal? on schedule?), and for Wall, "ordinary" (regular? usual? plain?) people always experience pain with unpleasantness. All I can think is how irregular and extraordinary I must be. How queer. How uncanny.

* * *

Anna Moschovakis wrote a collection of poems entitled *You and Three Others Are Approaching a Lake*. In that collection, she lifts the words of other authors, borrowing language from everything from Craigslist ads to dense scientific texts. My favorite poem in the collection starts with a list:

It began:
1. Life is not fair
2. How can I be happy while others suffer
3. How can I not be happy while others suffer
4. Others will suffer whether or not I am happy
5. It is not the suffering of others that causes my happiness
6. It is not the not-suffering of others that causes my unhappiness
7. The not-suffering of others would not prevent my happiness
8.   [17]

Moschovakis juxtaposes suffering to happiness, moving between the individual and the collective. We are left with a final point of blankness, a heavy silence incapable of resolving the

---

16 Heather Love, *Feeling Backward: Loss and the Politics of Queer History* (Cambridge: Harvard University Press, 2007), 21.

17 Anna Moschovakis, *You and Three Others Are Approaching a Lake* (Minneapolis: Coffee House Press, 2011), 35.

tensions between our own happiness and the suffering of others and our own suffering and the happiness of others. There is no mention of pain or pleasure. But I draw my own connections between suffering and pain; pain becoming pleasure becoming happiness. What would it mean to be happy living in one's suffering or in that silence of resolution, for the pain or the unbearable thing to be not the suffering itself but the inability to live in it?

The suffering is not good or bad. It is only suffering. The same can be said of pain, pleasure, and happiness. We desire them in different ways, neither good nor bad but just as they are. It is perhaps in following that desire for living in suffering that we might awaken our own happiness. To bear the suffering as it bears on happiness or to let the happiness bear on suffering to make it bearable. Still, I do not want to suffer, even if I desire to continue to live in the suffering I must bear. I borrow Mochovakis's borrowed words and rewrite them into my own poem about the curved scars on my chest, the desire for the touch of a lover on the ridge of tissue, about the pain and suffering of becoming and loving. I want to imagine what it might mean to share suffering through the proximity of two bodies in love.

If I am to be honest, I actually wrote that poem not after reading Moschovakis but after reading Ely Shipley's *Boy with Flowers*. In the title poem, he writes of his lover tracing the scars on his chest, the scars reimagined as naked, thorny stems. He then writes in "hair & dream" of a memory of a dream, of cutting hair, of how quiet the hair is, of how it remains long after someone.[18] After my lovers leave, I spend the mornings sweeping hair from the corners of my room and from around the feet of the bed. Their hair goes on in the quiet of their absence. Months before *R* left me, I already anticipated the end. I wrote a poem that begins,

---

18 Ely Shipley, *Boy with Flowers* (New York: Barrow Street Press, 2008), 8–9, 23.

I spent the morning losing you, washed the last
stains of you from my sheets, gathered your hair
from cobwebbed corners, dropped dark spider
strands into wastebasket into dumpster, knowing
I will find stray hairs between my sheets, along
floorboards, in folds of clothes and skin
for months to come

Hanif Abdurraqib, too, writes of the lingering stray hairs of a lover he has lost: "miles away from here, in my Ohio apartment, there is still hair on a pillow from a woman who hasn't slept in my bed in two weeks, and likely never will again, after a year of doing it. Before I boarded the flight here, I pulled one of her long, black hairs off of a sweater and held it briefly to the light."[19] He holds the hair up briefly, taking it in as a kind of remembrance, a moment to grieve those quiet pieces that follow us. He continues, "not enough people face the interior of separation in this way. What it is to find small pieces of a person who you know you'll never get to wholly experience again. It feels, almost always, like piecing together a road map that places you directly in the middle of nowhere."[20] How is it we piece together our own paths with the pieces of others? How do we go on and collect ourselves in the break?

When I was still seeing *R*, she would occasionally sleep in my bed. After she would leave, feeling almost certain I was ready to leave her, I would strip my bedding and throw everything into the wash, as if I could wash away all traces of her. I hate to admit now that I carried out this ritual for months. But the point is, upon every leaving came a laundering. Still, I found the stray hairs for months. I believe I even found one of *R*'s hairs a full year after the end of our relationship, after any hope of ever experiencing the wholeness of her had expired. I am currently still pulling *L*'s hairs from the folds and corners of my home,

---

19 Hanif Abdurraqib, *They Can't Kill Us Until They Kill Us* (Columbus: Two Dollar Radio, 2017), 45.

20 Ibid., 45.

my clothing, my body. It is soon approaching a year since she stepped foot into my Ohio apartment. Yet her pieces remain. I remain in pieces, broken down in the middle of nowhere. How much more upsetting to pull one of those long hairs you recognize from the fibers of your clothing than to pull the hair of a stranger from your plate of food. Or maybe the upset is just different. One is grief; the other, disgust. Maybe. Or one is simply more uncanny than the other.

Why do all the poets know how quiet hair is? How it leaves us and we leave it. How we listen for it anyway after the loss. How we can sometimes hear it still in its stillness. How we sometimes search for it still in the corners and folds. Aracelis Girmay writes, "Sometimes you leave your hair at the bus station / & get on the bus."[21] Ocean Vuong writes, "I see it: the strand of hair lifting / from her face… how it fell / onto the page — & lived / with no sound. Like a word. / I still hear it."[22] How easily the hair pricks and wounds us.

An anecdote, a grievance:

I once walked around with a deep aching pain in my big toe for days. When I looked at my toe, I could see no visible wound causing the pain, but every time I took a step, it ached so badly. After a few days of this, I shone a flashlight on the toe for closer inspection and found a small gray hair (that of a dog, perhaps; *R*'s dog, maybe) lodged in my big toe. I carefully removed it with tweezers and the pain was immediately gone. I later learned this is called a "hair splinter." I had no idea hair could wound us so or that its removal could bring such im-

21 Aracelis Girmay, *Kingdom Animalia* (Rochester: BOA Editions Ltd., 2011), 56.
22 Ocean Vuong, *Night Sky with Exit Wounds* (Port Townsend: Copper Canyon Press, 2016), 25.

mediate relief. Usually. Sometimes we remove the hair, but its ghostly ache lingers.

But the point is not the hair (or is it?). The point is that we continue to find dead pieces of each other but not the living wholeness of someone after their leaving. The point is that the pieces are remnants are ghosts. The point is that the body both leaves us and continues on. We leave the body and continue on. Claudia Rankine writes, "and despite everything the body remains."[23] The point is we remain when we leave. The point is the pain remains even after the one who has inflicted it leaves. The point is loss and the quiet suffering that continues with and without someone. The point is the pain we cause each other. The point is the poem I wrote after reading Ely Shipley's poems while thinking about Anna Moschovakis's poem.

---

23 Claudia Rankine, *Citizen: An American Lyric* (Minneapolis: Graywolf Press, 2014), 69.

The Quiet Goes On Even After Someone

I fell asleep with *Boy*
with Flowers clutched to my chest.

I wanted to press our scars together long enough, hard
enough to feel each other's heartbeat. To press thorns
to thorns until we were nothing but naked
stems, bloodied and sutured.

I wanted to rip off our dresses and pull
those boys, those girls into my arms as if the future
could hold them better.

I wake wanting her fingers. Pressed to my chest. She
dances around ridges of tissue where fear
and absolution meet. Her touch tentative, delicate
as if too much, too close will bring pain to either or both
of us.

The suffering of others has no bearing
on my happiness. My suffering has no
bearing on her happiness. Her suffering
is more than I can bear. My suffering is
barely bearable.

The point is I am no longer sure what I am becoming and what I can bear.

* * *

After another dispute with *R,* I spend a lonely afternoon reading in a fluorescent-lit laundromat while my clothes tumble *ker-chunk ker-chunk* in the dryer nearby. I am weeping silently while a man folds his clothes and packs them into a drawstring bag. He glances up at me once, briefly, then returns to his own business, seeming a bit embarrassed by my suffering and wanting it to have no bearing on his own state of happiness or unhappiness. For a moment, my chest becomes so full, I think I may have to toss the book I am reading aside and run until my lungs burn and my heart finally bursts. I am again working through the fight, flight, freeze/fright response. I swallow the pain and the fear down, and I sit with the whir of washers and dryers, anxiously bouncing my legs. With the urge to run, I am reminded of the refrain in Thomas Page McBee's *Man Alive: A True Story of Violence, Forgiveness and Becoming a Man.* "You have to let people love you," McBee's therapist says. "What are you running to?," his therapist asks.[24] The words always hit me in the gut. How can I let anyone love me? What am I running to?

My therapist suggests maybe *R* holds my disappointment better than I hold hers. That for me to inflict suffering on another is unbearable, and, that for her, it has no bearing. As I reread my poem, I think I already know this. I have written it plainly enough: my suffering has no bearing on her happiness. Instead, I say to my therapist that perhaps I have compassion and empathy, where *R* has none. I take in the philosophies of Thich Nhat Hanh as lessons in how to love with loving kindness, compassion, joy, and equanimity. He teaches that when we truly love according to these four elements, the suffering of others becomes our own. It is impossible to dismiss the pain or

---

24 Thomas Page McBee, *Man Alive: A True Story of Violence, Forgiveness and Becoming a Man* (San Francisco: City Light Books, 2014).

suffering of the other.[25] It would therefore be impossible to say, "that's your problem," one of R's favorite refrains, her reminder to me that my problems are mine alone, not hers, and that my feelings of pain are just a product of the story I choose to tell. In *The Problem of Pain*, C.S. Lewis begins by imagining what his atheist self would have to say about being in pain in the world. His imaginings seem quite simple and straight-forward, and, for me, much preferable to the Christian maneuverings that occupy the rest of the work. "The creatures cause pain by being born, and live by inflicting pain, and in pain they mostly die."[26] We are the creatures. We bear on each other as we bear each other. We are all in pain, inflicting pain on one another. It is always our problem, never yours, never mine. Ours.

* * *

I am falling. I am screaming. I think I hear somebody ask me if I'm going somewhere. I come to with my hands cuffed over my head. "Red! Red!," I cry out. "I think I passed out," I say. The madam pulls me down from the cage and cradles me to her breast. She brings water to my lips, touches me gently on the shoulder. I settle into her embrace. I feel nurtured. When I am ready, she says she will take even better care of me. I rise, and she bends me over her desk. She begins flogging me, alternating between my ass and my upper back, along the shoulder blades. The beatings come harder and faster, harder and faster. She tells me she likes the way my body jumps with each strike, the way my back muscles flex and flinch as the leather pounds them. My suffering has every bearing on her pleasure. Her pleasure has every bearing on my suffering. My suffering is becoming pleasurable. How irregular. How extraordinary.

I shuttle between the bearable and unbearable, between pleasure and pain. I shuttle between presence and a desire to

25 Thich Nhat Hanh, *How to Love* (Berkeley: Parallax Press, 2014).
26 C.S. Lewis, *The Problem of Pain* (New York: The Macmillan Company, 1948), 2.

invoke my deeply developed skill of dissociation. Judith Lewis Herman suggests that children who experience ongoing abuse, or what Bessel A. van der Kolk would call "complex trauma," develop three major forms of adaptation: the first, a dissociative defense; the second, a fragmented identity; and the third, a pathological relationship to emotional states that make survival possible in ongoing and chronic abuse scenarios.[27] Similarly, Robert Stolorow, describes trauma as "unbearable affect," suggesting that developmental trauma is intersubjectively formed through "a breakdown of the child-caregiver system of mutual regulation," which then "leads to the child's loss of affect-integrating capacity and thereby to an unbearable, overwhelmed, disorganized state."[28] Basically, what this means is that when a child feels bad or experiences trauma, and the parent is not there to mutually regulate the trauma as the parent might be the one inflicting the trauma or abuse, then the child does not learn how to regulate their own painful affect. Instead, the child experiences what Stolorow calls a "severe constricting and narrowing of the horizons of emotional experiencing."[29] Or put even more simply, we might ask, how can one know one is suffering if the figurehead of love does not recognize the suffering? How can one know what one feels when one is having their feelings beaten into or out of them? That is to say, pain becomes confused with pleasure, and, perhaps, pleasure becomes confused with pain. The emotions are stored in the body. The affective trauma has somatic effects that one must learn to bear. According to Herman, such a result may comprise a pathological relation to emotional states. Feelings are confused and disordered.

---

27 Judith Lewis Herman, *Trauma and Recovery: The Aftermath of Violence from Domestic Abuse to Political Terror* (New York: Basic Books, 1997), 110; Bessel A. van der Kolk, "Developmental Trauma Disorder: Toward a Rational Diagnosis for Children with Complex Trauma Histories," *Psychiatric Annals* 35, no. 5 (2005): 401–8.

28 Robert Stolorow, *Trauma and Human Existence: Autobiographical, Psychoanalytic, and Philosophical Reflections* (New York: Routledge, 2011), 3.

29 Ibid.

The emotional states overwhelm. They become unbearable. How to survive it: dissociate.

* * *

I am reading Alice Notley's much anticipated *Benediction*: "i didn't choose my father yet something about him tears me up. i keep trying to choose my family because we're already demons together."[30] In the dungeon, I am bent over her desk. I am bent over her knee. I am remembering the way my father removed his belt and bent me over his lap, bare-assed and shaking. This is how my father stole my body. This is how he tears me up. With each lashing, if I cried out, he would tell me to stop crying. If I held my silence, he would tell me he would hit me until I cried. He constricted the horizons of my emotional experiencing. How would I know what I am feeling if my feelings were beaten back into me? My emotions were slammed so deeply back into my body, they could only be pulled out again by force. Eventually, the emotional states will overwhelm. There was no winning this game. Whether or not I cry, whether or not I choose him, my father tears me up. I am tearing up in her lap. She is beating me. My father is beating me. I am of an unmistakably masochistic character. We are demons together.

The madam lifts my body and pulls my face into hers. "Look at those little tears in your eyes," she says. Stolorow claims, "trauma is constituted in an intersubjective context in which severe emotional pain cannot find a relational home in which it can be held."[31] She cannot hold my pain, but she can pull it out of me and let it spill all over her dungeon. She recognizes my tears, which is another way of saying she recognizes my suffering in tears of pain, tears of pleasure. I try to stay with her through it all. I try to stay in my body, to feel the pain and pleasure, to let it all spill out of me. Making demons out of ghosts; making ghosts out of demons. I am paying her for the pleasure through which

---

30 Alice Notley, *Benediction* (Tucson: Letter Machine Editions, 2015), 22.
31 Stolorow, *Trauma and Human Existence,* 10.

I am trying to reclaim my body that had been stolen through pain. The pleasure produced from the pain cannot be separated from the trauma to which it is connected.

* * *

I am in Seattle, sitting in a circle with a bunch of guys talking about hysterectomies; advice from those who have had them, questions from those who want them. I feel myself unraveling. I think about testosterone. I think about hysterectomies. I think about becoming a man. I think about my father. I think about the man I want to be. I think about the man I don't want to be. I think about testosterone. I think about desire. I want the T; I don't. I want a hysto; I'm scared. I want a hysto; I don't want the T or my ovaries either. I don't want ovarian cancer. I don't want cervical cancer. I don't want periods. I want a hysto; I want T; I don't want a hysto; I don't want T. This could go on forever.

I leave the circle and text S. I wish I had brought the "gender magic elixir" she gave me, a gift procured from Dori Midnight, intuitive healer and apothecary. The elixir is designed for "transcendence, transformation, + self-determination" as one exists "between the worlds."[32] In this moment of hysterectomy panic, I think I should drop some of the potion under my tongue for transcendence and transformation. I text S because she is the one who sees me. After all, she gave me the elixir, and I need her. I know she will tell me that I am beautiful, that I am magic, that I am loved, that this is hard, but that I am everything I need to be. She says all of these things. It is enough and none of it is enough. We are no longer lovers, but I am finally ready to let her love me. This is unfair to her. I am no longer sure what I am running toward and what I am running from.

When I return home from Seattle, I meet M for a drink at a bar in the Mission District of San Francisco. He heard me read once in Tucson about suffering and wanting and not wanting

---

32 "Between the Worlds," *Dori Midnight,* https://dorimidnight.com/apothecary/between-the-worlds/.

testosterone. He says he knows those feelings. He says it is all too familiar. He shares my suffering. *M* says when he is on T, he is quicker to anger and finds it harder to cry. I think of T Cooper's *Real Man Adventures*. Cooper makes a list of the new truths on his journey to becoming a man, even if, he admits, they are also stereotypes:

1. I don't cry as much as I used to. Or: It takes way more to make me cry.
2. I am angry more frequently. Or: It takes way less to make me blazing mad.[33]

The list goes on, but these are the two points I think about while talking to *M*. I know that hormones have a powerful impact on the body, even while I want to resist these stereotypes that chalk masculinity up to physiology and endocrine systems. "The big mistake," Cordelia Fine writes, "is to confuse the persistence of the status quo with the dictates of testosterone."[34] In other words, I feel like Fine is saying to me, "you probably think the testosterone does this to you because everyone says it does."

Fine works to debunk the myth of the so-called "Testosterone Rex," the ferocious roar of a hormone that places masculinity into the realm of risk-taking, competition, and violence. Sex and testosterone, Fine asserts, are obviously so much more complicated: "far from being a pure biological measure of hormonal sex, T *responds* to contexts and situations, meaning that whatever influence T has on the brain and behavior can't simply be chalked up to 'testosterone,' a purely biological factor."[35] One's experience of testosterone is indubitably subjective and connected to one's own history. Testosterone has some common effects, but we know that everyone will have a slightly different experience with the drug, its emphases, and its results.

---

33 T Cooper, *Real Man Adventures* (San Francisco: McSweeney's Books, 2012), 23.
34 Cordelia Fine, *Testosterone Rex: Myths of Sex, Science, and Society* (New York: W.W. Norton, 2017), 150.
35 Ibid., 143.

Quicker to anger. Harder to cry. The words linger. I turn to *M* and tell him that I have always found it difficult to cry, and I have worked on my anger over the years, though I've always taken my time with it, bottling it, never knowing how or when to release it. I have been so careful about when and where I let it spill. How do I separate the anger from the pain from the trauma? Despite all the uncertainties, after this talk with *M*, I call my doctor and make an appointment for the following week to discuss starting on testosterone.

* * *

Scarry asks, "how is it that one person can be in the presence of another person in pain and not know it — not know it to the point where he himself inflicts it, and goes on inflicting it?"[36] As I read this, I think of *R*. I need to stop thinking of *R*. She said she can no longer be with me because she is tired of feeling bad. I tell her I am tired of feeling bad too. We have this conversation when I stop by her place on the way to the pharmacy where I was headed to pick up my needles and syringes and the small vial of testosterone that I will begin injecting into my body the next day. *R* does not even know this about me. She has been too preoccupied with her own suffering or her own pleasures. I cannot be sure which. She likes herself, she says, and I make her feel like a bad person. I tell her I think she is a good person, but she brings me too much pain. She says that she is sorry she has to break up with me and that it upsets her so much that she needs me to hold her and comfort her. I do. She says she is sorry we can't make it work. I hold her. I say nothing. She cries. I hold her. I leave.

When I walk into the doctor's office the next day, I am nervous and scared. I take a seat in the waiting area. They are running behind schedule, so I have a full hour in which to contemplate walking out the door and never looking back. But I wait. When they finally call me back, the nurse shows me how

---

36 Scarry, *The Body in Pain*, 12.

to clean the area of my upper thigh with an alcohol swab, how to draw the testosterone into the syringe, and how to plunge the needle into the muscle and push the drug into my body. When it is over, it is anti-climactic. I leave the clinic feeling like I am leaving another routine visit; a simple shot, and we move on. No big deal. Until I feel utterly alone in this process. In the depths of my loneliness, I miss *R* more than I can handle. I have to fight every impulse in my body to run to her, to beg her to come back and hold me while I toss myself into this vortex of uncertainty. I call *S*. She says it is not that I am alone, but that I am doing this without intimacy, familial or romantic. These words will haunt me. It is true. Intimacy has become something I have now only when I pay for it with my therapist, with my dominatrix.

* * *

As I wonder about *R*'s possible unobserved or unknown inflictions of pain, I think also of my father's inflictions. Surely, he knew it and went on inflicting it anyway. He raised his hand after each time he slammed it against my bare flesh and brought it down again, often harder than the last time. Eli Clare asks, "how did my father's violence, his brutal taking of me over and over again, help shape and damage my body, my sexuality, my gender identity?"[37] I wonder about my own father's violence. How did he shape me? How did he damage me? How many wounds has he left gaping open? How does my father's violence continue to haunt me? Am I running from it or toward it? What am I afraid of when I think about injecting testosterone into my body? Am I afraid I will become my father, drunk and angry like him? Or am I afraid I already am him, beating myself out of my own body?

On dissociation: this morning, I inject testosterone into my thigh muscle. As I plunge the needle into my skin, I cannot imagine this body as my own. I cannot be sticking myself with a

---

37 Eli Clare, *Exile and Pride: Disability, Queerness, and Liberation* (Cambridge: South End Press, 1999), 147.

needle. I cannot be injecting a hormone into my endocrine system that will modify my body in unknowable ways. I cannot be blasting these doors open. This is not me, I think. I am floating above myself. I am alone and terrified. I think of *M*'s words: quicker to anger, harder to cry. Harder to cry. It has always been harder to cry. But all of this is precisely why I went to the dungeon, precisely why I want to cry. "Tears of grief, tears of joy," Easton and Hardy write. "Sometimes what you want out of a scene is a purging, to go into overload and let it all out."[38] I want to purge the tears, the grief, the joy, the pain, and the pleasure. I want to earn new scars, invisible and emotional. I want the marks, even if temporary, to show for it.

My thigh is sore at the injection site. It is in this instant sting and lasting dull ache that I return to my body. Likewise, after my session with the dominatrix, my backside is black and blue, purple and yellow from the beatings. As long as the bruises last, I find a quiet joy in leaning against a wall or the hard back of a chair. There is a pleasure in the discomfort of placing pressure against the tender flesh. The marks, the pain, the wounds, the scars are all a somatic reminder of the journey I am on. They keep me in my body. I find myself bringing my fist to my thigh several times throughout the day, pressing just enough to feel the soreness at the injection site, to remind myself exactly where I put testosterone into my body. That is where I am making something happen to me that I cannot yet know or understand. It is not unlike the way in which I still, years after my surgery, run my fingers across the scars on my chest, the puckered flesh a gathering point of fear, forgiveness, pain, and pleasure. These wounds and sutures are the sites where my body is becoming my own.

* * *

I am face down on the floating table in the dungeon, receiving repeated lashings across my back. "Cry for me," she shouts, "go

---

38 Easton and Hardy, *The New Bottoming Book,* 86.

on and cry." And I obey her command. The tears in my eyes spill
out and my body shakes and trembles as I come apart. Easton
and Hardy warn the aspiring bottom who is also a survivor of
abuse to avoid any play that may trigger memories of the abuse.[39]
But all I want is to call up those somatic and affective memories
that haunt my pains and pleasures today. I am in the process of
reclaiming and marking the borders of my own body, what it
wants, what it can take, and where it belongs. This is my wounding. She holds the weapon. The wound, as well as the weapon,
according to Elaine Scarry, provide the means by which we as-
sociatively express pain. The wound and the weapon make pain
recognizable in the body. To lose them would be to lose the object of pain. To lose them, might mean to lose the self.[40] I have
lost my body, my self, my ego to pain. Now I am recovering my
body, my self, my ego through the same. The problem with our
defense mechanisms, Herman notes, is that the child grown up
finds their defenses formed in childhood to be increasingly mal-
adaptive in adult relationships. In fact, Herman claims, "eventually, often in the third or fourth decade of life, the defensive
structure may begin to break down."[41] I am halfway through my
fourth decade of life. Here I am, already breaking down.

When it is over, I lie prostrate in the smear of my tears on
the vinyl. It is over not because of any climax but because I am
paying for this intimacy for a predetermined amount of time.
It is the clock which forces an ending to this exchange rather
than a culminating peak of pleasure from which we must come
down. I could have, in fact, kept on weeping. She could have, I
know, kept on with the beating. These pains and pleasures are
durational, chronic, and cyclical with no demand for an end in
and of themselves. These wounds will soon form their own little
closures, tiny temporary sutures holding the pain in place for
now. The bruises will soon fade. The tears will sink back down
into my throat, until I tear open the wounds again.

---

39 Ibid., 138.
40 Scarry, *The Body in Pain,* 16.
41 Herman, *Trauma and Recovery,* 114.

When I am ready, I sit up on the table, and the mistress sits beside me. She pulls me to her breast and holds me. She thanks me for trusting her with my body, my fear, and my pain. I thank her for breaking me open.

As I leave the dungeon, I turn to offer my gift of appreciation — an assortment of dark chocolates — and the payment. She tells me the session was so hot, it made her hot. She tells me she wants to play with me again, and she would even lower her rate and give me more time for the opportunity to do so. Is this her business model, or is she sincere? I cannot be certain, but she almost forgets to take my payment. The monetary transaction is just as impactful for me as the session itself. I am engaging in the economy of sex work. But I am essentially seeking asexual services in this economy, as I am paying for intimacy without sex. I am seeking sensual pain and pleasure without sexual stimulation and climax. It is a fine and sometimes blurry line, but it is there for me.

Still, she made me feel sexy. I am not turned on, but I have purportedly turned her on. Beata Stawarska takes us on a journey through Maurice Merleau-Ponty's understanding of the intrasubjective experience of the body as the paradigm for intersubjective relations with other embodied subjects: I can touch my right hand with my left hand, which means my left hand is also touching my right hand. Therefore, I can touch the hand of another, and the other's hand is also touching me. As Stawarska explains, the reciprocity of this exchange brings about "a co-presence of touching and of being touched, a possible reversal between active and passive modes of tactility. [...] it is always possible that the hand that actively explores the other turns into an object being touched by the other hand; either hand can be both touched and touching."[42] She was beating me, so she was

---

42 Beata Stawarska, "From the Body Proper to Flesh: Merleau-Ponty on Intersubjectivity," in *Feminist Interpretations of Maurice Merleau-Ponty*, eds. Dorothea Olkowski and Gail Weiss (University Park: Pennsylvania State University Press, 2006), 93.

touching me, but I was touching her as I received her beating. My touch has turned her on. Her touch has turned me.

* * *

A piece of Bianca Stone's "Elegy" from *Someone Else's Wedding Vows* comes to mind: "I realize grief wants me to stay / a child, negotiating a stream of atoms, / picking flowers. Grief wants me in good condition. / Grief wants me to remember everything. Imperfect. Clear."[43] I am grieving for the child who never held the flowers. I am grieving for the child who never was in good condition. I am grieving for my inability to remember everything, imperfect and clear. Grief does not want me to stay a child. Grief wants me to learn how to be an adult, to mourn and heal the wounds. But how do I heal? As Eli Clare writes, it is "harder to express how that break becomes healed, a bone once fractured, now whole, but different from the bone never broken. And harder still to follow the path between the two."[44] Healed fractures are always more vulnerable to another crack. Stitches risk bursting open. Scar tissue bears a different tactility from flesh never cut or rent. To reclaim the stolen body is to walk the path between the wounding, the weapon, and the healing. To bear the suffering with the pleasure. Clare asks, "how do I mark this place where my body is no longer an empty house, desire whistling lonely through the cracks, but not yet a house fully lived in?"[45] My father broke me open. *R* broke me open. The mistress broke me open. If I break myself open, will I be able to place the pieces anew, to rebuild the home of my body? The cracks are wounds. Here they have been sutured. Here they have been covered up. Here they gape. The desire whispers through.

---

43 Bianca Stone, *Someone Else's Wedding Vows* (Portland: Tin House Books, 2014), 15.

44 Clare, *Exile and Pride,* 153.

45 Ibid.

3

The Time of Pain, A Hauntology

What does it mean to follow a ghost? And what if this came down to being followed by it, always, persecuted perhaps by the very chase we are leading?

— Jacques Derrida, *Specters of Marx*[1]

The whole essence, if you can use that word, of a ghost is that it has a real presence and demands its due, your attention.

— Avery Gordon, *Ghostly Matters*[2]

As I write this, I sit in pain, teeth clenched. I want to cry, not from the pain itself but because it persists. At least, I think that is why I want to cry. I cannot be entirely certain because I find my eyes welling with tears with unusual frequency lately, which doesn't make sense if you believe everything they tell you about testosterone and emotion. And by "they," I am not even sure who exactly I mean. Is it my friends who tell me they haven't cried since they started taking testosterone or the people who believe "real men" don't cry? I inject testosterone into my body every week; I still want to cry all the time; I still cry a lot of the

---

1   Jacques Derrida, *Specters of Marx: The State of the Debt, The Work of Mourning, and The New International,* trans. Peggy Kamuf (New York: Routledge, 1994), 10.

2   Avery Gordon, *Ghostly Matters: Haunting and the Sociological Imagination* (Minneapolis: University of Minnesota Press, 2008), xvi.

time. Right now, I am almost certain my eyes are blurry with tears because I know the pain I am feeling at this moment will not end for some time. I know I have again entered the time of pain. But, really, I know I never left it. My pain, my knowledge of its persistence and the fear that it may last forever, leaks from my body through my tear ducts. I cry because I am both angry and sad that it persists in the throbbing that creeps up my arm, in the piercing that shoots down my leg, in the sharpness that screams from my hip.

I feel so cliché, like I have been hit by a truck. Really, I was bowled over by a charging dog running wild through the brush. I was strolling with a friend and her dog through the humming thick of a verdant, Ohio springtime. She unleashed him into the tall grasses as she recounted the story of her first encounter with her animal companion, how he emerged from a sorghum field in northern Minnesota, mangy and wolf-like. She fancies her dog a cousin of the wolf, with the deep desire to run wild, to be rewilded and to rewild her, even as she dewilds him. But shortly after releasing him to run free through the thicket and bramble, she called him back, afraid to let him be too free or too wild.

Hearing her whistle, he blasted through the trees. From behind me, I heard her call, "Watch out!" As I turned, I saw the dog, in a blur, charging down the path directly toward me. I stepped to the side at the same moment he veered off the path. We collided, or, really, he barreled through me, causing me to twist, popping the previously damaged tissue of my ankle and extending the tendons of my arm as I caught my fall on an already damaged wrist joint, fresh out of a cast. The pain exploded in me. I jumped up immediately because the tumble had planted me in a patch of poison ivy. But as soon as I stood, my knees buckled. I knelt on the path, out of the ivy. A cold sweat broke across my forehead, down my neck, and over my body. My vision blurred, and my stomach lurched into my throat. But I said nothing. I quietly pleaded for my body to remain conscious with each exploding pang. I remained silent as my friend laughed at the scene. She did not realize I was injured or in pain because of my stoic hush. Such is how I learned to hold pain—in dammed tears and squelched groans.

Most of the time, no one can know I am in pain, unless I say so. I hold the throb in a quiet sobriety I learned, ironically enough, from my alcoholic father. His voice rings through my memories of his hand or a strop of leather coming down on my backside: "stop crying and I'll stop!" Or on other occasions: "I won't stop until you cry, until I can see how sorry you are." I cry; I am beaten for crying. I hold the tears; I am beaten until I cry. "The problem of pain," Eula Biss writes, "is that I cannot feel my father's, and he cannot feel mine. This, I suppose, is also the essential mercy of pain."[3] My father cannot feel my pain. He can only tear me up as he watches for the tears he either coaxes forth or shoves back into hiding. There is no mercy. Recall, Elaine Scarry writes of the unsharability of pain and the sharing made impossible through pain's resistance to and destruction of language.[4] Pain has no language. It is a series of grunts and moans and cries, and here I add, silences. Pain is a series of silences.

Some of my pain is in my joints, but pain also throws time out of joint. "The time is out of joint," Derrida begins *Specters of Marx* with this epigraph from Shakespeare's *Hamlet.*[5] For Derrida, it is in haunting where we find time out of joint. Haunting is historical, of a past, but it is not dated and not specifically located. It is the time of ghosts, the time between life and death, the time after life, after death, before life. The time of "learning to live" can happen only between life and death. "The time of the 'learning to live,'" Derrida writes, is to "learn to live *with* ghosts."[6] Pain is in the moans of a throat opening, in the silences between the moans, in the listening, in the living, and in the learning to live. All of it done between life and death.

But we must understand the substance of ghosts in order to learn to live with them. For Derrida, the ghost and the haunting

3   Eula Biss, "The Pain Scale," *Creative Nonfiction* 1, no. 32 (2007): 80.
4   Elaine Scarry, *The Body in Pain: The Making and Unmaking of the World* (Oxford: Oxford University Press, 1985).
5   Derrida, *Specters of Marx*, 3.
6   Ibid., xviii.

are both defined by repetition, reapparition, and the confusion of time: "repetition *and* first time, but also repetition *and* last time, since the singularity of any *first time* makes of it also a *last time.* [...] a first time is a last time." The first is the last, one and the same. Then. Now. Again. And Again. Again. "Let us call it a *hauntology,*" he proclaims.[7] An ontology of being haunted. Over and over. Again and again.

In the previous chapter, I suggested revising the temporalities of pleasure, imagining pleasure as existing in a temporal frame of repetition or ongoingness rather than finality, derived from and concurrent with pain; to be beaten to an end that lacks climax, an end that must arrive simply because life must continue. It would be an error to imagine pain as pleasure's opposite, as a discrete counterpart. Rather, pain and pleasure are sometimes inseparable. Pleasure may be derived from pain. Though also, pain reveals its own pleasures in telling, its own addictions in revisiting and revising the sites of wounding. Part of the pleasure in pain is its return and our return to it. Repetition. Reapparition. Knowing this, I want to explore the temporalities of pain and suffering.

* * *

I find myself both seeking out writing about pain and illness and more frequently stumbling upon it by chance. I pick up Martha Grover's *The End of My Career* because I saw a funny quote from the book, one that had nothing to do with illness or pain, on Twitter. I pick up Amy Berkowitz's *Tender Points* because it is a featured staff pick on the shelf at my local bookstore. I pick up Leslie Jamison's *The Empathy Exams* because someone mentions it in a post about ultramarathons on Facebook. I pick up Brian Teare's book of poems *The Empty Form Goes All the Way to Heaven* because it is the only book of poetry sitting on the new LGBT literature shelf at my local library. My friend gives me a copy of *Diving Makes the Water Deep* by Zach

---

7   Ibid., 10.

Savich because, she says, my writing reminds her of his, though I have not shared any writing with her about pain or illness. The list goes on, but my point is that my obsession with pain and illness is both purposeful and accidental. It follows me as much as I follow it.

In my quest to read and write pain, I became interested in how people living with pain share their experiences through visual art, a medium that doesn't require spinning pain into words. In my explorations, I ran across a community-curated website, PAIN *Exhibit,* featuring artwork by people living with chronic pain. As I clicked through the images, I found myself drawn again and again to a photo entitled "Rockville Centre Parking" by Bob Axel. The photo is rather mundane: a parking meter at the left of the frame on an empty stretch of sidewalk. There is a window at the right of the frame, with one of the vertical blinds slightly askew as if someone who is no longer present had been peeking out onto the street. Axel writes in his artist statement, "loneliness can be the heavy emotional toll of a chronic illness and resulting pain. In my work I am trying to find some beauty in painfully lonely images. That beauty could be the hope in a hopeless situation or the search for the serenity of accepting the way things are. For even if there is no life in this image there is the potential that something is going to happen, that life might get better."[8] The street, devoid of people or action, certainly evokes loneliness, but I am less concerned with the idea that anything might get better and more taken by the idea that something might *happen.*

The inactive street conjures potential for happenings that are yet to come. I am particularly fixated on the parking meter, a device for measuring time. The meter sits idle, but its presence serves as a reminder of the constant meting out of time. The meter is fed, or, time is paid for. The meter ticks down minute by minute; the meter expires. Time passes. The meter remains;

---

8   Bob Axel, "Rockville Centre Parking," PAIN *Exhibit: A Non-Profit Art Exhibit,* http://painexhibit.org/en/galleries/isolation-and-imprisonment/ ago4_axel/.

the pain remains. For me, this image evokes all the possibilities in the allotment of time—the past, present, future, future-past, past-future of time all at once. The first time and last time. The has happened, is happening, and might happen. Axel writes that there is no life in the image, but I find it to be full of life, exemplifying all the living that happens in the silences, in the aftermath of what has been and in the waiting for what might happen.

Claudia Rankine writes, "all living is listening for a throat to open—The length of its silence shaping lives."[9] Which is to say, we do a lot of living in the silences, in the gaps, in the wait for the opening of a throat to release the moan or wail. We wait, I think, in the time of ghosts. Which is another way of saying, the photograph, too, is haunted. Roland Barthes writes of "that terrible thing which is there in every photograph: the return of the dead."[10] Maybe the point is not to see pain in the image, but to feel the pain in the wait, in the haunt, in the return of our own ghosts. To wait with them, to share in the waiting, to share in the suffering. In the photograph, we are all made still.

I am taking stock of the way stillness and silence shape and have shaped my life as much as or more so than things said and done. I am learning that sharing pain can seem impossible. I know the pain is always greatest to the one who bears it directly. Zach Savich writes, "the pain I feel is worse to me than any other, because it is mine. And yes, during any moment of suffering, I also know that your (somebody's) suffering is worse. Each pain reveals another depth of pain I can't imagine, each pain reveals only itself."[11] I know my own pain. I know my own suffering. I know yours may be worse, much worse, so much more that I cannot even fathom it. It is not bad; it simply is. Sometimes pleasure. Sometimes hurt. Sometimes quiet, quiet as hair.

---

9   Claudia Rankine, *Citizen: An American Lyric* (Minneapolis: Graywolf Press, 2014), 112.

10 Roland Barthes, *Camera Lucida: Reflections on Photography,* trans. Richard Howard (New York: Hill and Wang, 1981), 9.

11 Zach Savich, *Diving Makes the Water Deep* (Chicago: Rescue Press, 2016), 58.

* * *

Pain can sometimes endure seemingly without end. With the endurance of pain can come the hope of cessation or the cessation of hope. To hope is to imagine an end of suffering. Sometimes, it seems that pleasure may only be derived from pain when we know it is not forever, when we know it has a telos. I experience pleasure when my dominatrix beats me because I know the beating will not last forever. I know the bruises will heal and the tenderness will subside. When my father beat me, my child brain could not deduce or anticipate its ending. I could not be sure that I would be healed before the next beating would come. There was no pleasure in that threat of pain's ongoingness. I experience pleasure when I prick my thigh muscle with a syringe because the pain is momentary. It stings and is tender for a day or two. I do not experience pleasure in the pain of my aching joints or when my sternum feels like it is collapsing into my heart because I never know if or when the pain will end. So often, whether pleasurable or insufferable, we want the cessation of pain. But, so often, it endures.

The greatness of pain in a moment is often overshadowed by the suffering of its endurance, by the uncertainty of how long it will haunt us, and the different ways in which it haunts us. In such uncertainty, it is difficult to resist becoming hopeless. David C. Roberts writes of his "secret life" of pain in which he joins "the other no-hopers" at Mayo's pain clinic. At the clinic, he recounts how chronic pain, unlike acute pain, "was treated as a malfunction in perception, whether or not an ongoing physical cause had been identified." The doctors at the clinic believe the brain becomes addicted to "dramatizing pain," which seems like another way of saying we are addicted to telling the stories of pain, which seems like another way of saying we become addicted to suffering. The doctors there argued that if one could learn not to dwell on the pain in such a way, then eventually the mind would let it go, no pills or pain treatments needed.[12]

Some of us, it would seem, are addicted to the drugs used to treat pain. Some of us are addicted to the suffering. Some of us may even be addicted to the pain itself. If we are so addicted, then how can the mind simply let go? Visibly, invisibly, individually, and intersubjectively, pain haunts. We are addicted to its ghosts. We suffer its haunting. How then do I write a hauntology of pain without also writing of my addictions? I don't. I can't. How do I distinguish the pain I am feeling in any given moment from the pain I am feeling at the potential for pain's endurance? I can't. How do I even distinguish pain from suffering?

* * *

I have heretofore let pain and suffering bleed into one another, without discrete edges. But there is a distinction to be made. Patrick Wall wants to understand pain through what he calls a "science of suffering," a science that makes suffering the tool and pain its object. Wall recounts how a group chaired by psychiatrist Harold Merskey was asked by the International Association for the Study of Pain to provide a definition of pain. The group described pain as "an unpleasant sensory and emotional experience associated with actual or potential tissue damage or described in terms of such damage."[13] Wall adds, they also tacked on this crucial note: "pain is always subjective. [...] This definition avoids tying pain to the stimulus."[14] Pain is both actually and potentially in the tissues of the body. Pain is the physical sensation as well as the mental and affective knowledge of the potential for pain. It may or may not be directly tied to a certain stimulus. The heart is composed of tissue. Hearts can be

---

12 David C. Roberts, "The Secret Life of Pain," *The New York Times,* August 1, 2017, https://www.nytimes.com/2017/08/01/well/live/the-secret-life-of-pain.html.

13 Patrick Wall, *Pain: The Science of Suffering* (New York: Columbia University Press, 2000), 27.

14 Ibid.

broken, which is another way of saying heart tissue can be damaged, even if metaphorically. Pain is the emotional experience of knowing that one is in agony, of feeling hurt itself, of understanding pain's persistence, of knowing that others are aching, of feeling into the pain of others. They describe pain as unpleasant. But sometimes pain is pleasant or, even, pleasurable.

If pain can be pleasurable, can suffering then be too? How do each relate to one another? Frank T. Vertosick, Jr. creates the analogy, "pain is to suffering what sex is to romance."[15] Vertosick imagines pain to be the embodied stuff of suffering and sex to be the embodied stuff of romance, whereas the suffering and the romance are the emotional/intellectual experiences of the materiality of the pain and the sex. I cannot help but wonder if it is possible to have suffering without pain, as I believe it is indeed possible to have romance without sex. However, pain can also be emotional; hearts are broken, after all. Eula Biss cites the Reverend James Chase, "pain is the hurt, either physical or emotional, that we experience. Suffering is the story we tell ourselves of our pain."[16] If suffering is the story we tell about pain, does this mean romance is the story we tell about sex or the way we turn sex into love into suffering? Julia Kristeva describes narrative as "the recounting of suffering: fear, disgust, and abjection crying out, they quiet down, concatenated into a story."[17] We suffer not from the pain itself but from how we make sense of it and how we tell its story. We tell the story in order to quiet the pain and the fear, its own kind of pleasure in pain, as we cull the abject tears into a hushed, whimpering yarn.

Or, we want the stories, all the same. In detailing the stages of healing from trauma, Judith Lewis Herman describes how in the second stage of recovery, the survivor needs to tell the story of the trauma in depth and in detail in order to transform the

15 Frank T. Vertosick, Jr., *Why We Hurt: The Natural History of Pain* (New York: Harcourt, 2000), 8.

16 Biss, "The Pain Scale," 22.

17 Julia Kristeva, *Powers of Horror: An Essay on Abjection,* trans. Leon S. Roudiez (New York: Columbia University Press, 1982), 145.

traumatic memory and integrate it into one's life story.[18] Healing trauma, then, is in the ability to suffer through or endure its telling. Dori Laub describes the narration of trauma as "a therapeutic process—a process of re-externalizing the event," which necessitates one's ability to "*transmit* the story, literally transfer it to another outside oneself and then take it back again, inside."[19] In other words, storytelling, too, demands a porousness, moving through another and back into ourselves. Along similar lines, Herman also argues that the narrative process has physio-neurological results that bring relief of PTSD symptoms: "the physioneurosis induced by terror can apparently be reversed through the use of words."[20] Pain is felt in the body, and trauma is held in the body, often manifesting as pain. The process of suffering, the creation of stories, the formation of words from silences, moans, and sighs can actually heal the terror-struck body.

After Roland Barthes's mother died, he cataloged his pain and suffering on bits and scraps of paper that later came to be assembled and published as *Mourning Diary*. In the collection of fragments, I am struck by Barthes's meditation on literature when he writes, "I cannot read without pain, without choking on truth."[21] That I cannot read his words without pain, without also choking on truth. Many nights I fall asleep with the diary pressed to my chest, the pages warped by my own loose tears. Each reading and rereading always (painfully) a surprise. Barthes writes, "always (painfully) surprised to be able—finally—to live with my suffering, which means that it is literally *endurable*. But—no doubt—this is because I can, more or less […] utter it, put it into words. […] My suffering is *inexpressible* but all the

---

18   Judith Lewis Herman, *Trauma and Recovery: The Aftermath of Violence from Domestic Abuse to Political Terror* (New York: Basic Books, 1997), 175.

19   Dori Laub, "Bearing Witness, or the Vicissitudes of Listening," in *Testimony: Crises of Witnessing in Literature, Psychoanalysis, and History*, eds. Shoshana Felman and Dori Laub (New York: Routledge, 1992), 69.

20   Herman, *Trauma and Recovery*, 183.

21   Roland Barthes, *Mourning Diary*, ed. Nathalie Léger, trans. Richard Howard (New York: Hill and Wang, 2010), 177.

same *utterable,* speakable."[22] I think back to Scarry's suggestion that pain not only eludes but destroys language, to how Claudia Rankine listens for the silences of what gets caught in the throat. To live is to endure. To endure is to live with our suffering, to live in our suffering, to make it endurable. It is to come to terms with its inexpressibility. It is not languageable, but it is utterable and speakable. By groaning out its very intolerability, we learn to endure in it, even as we choke on its truths.

I want to understand how the suffering in our stories and in our bodies is both individual and collective, how unspeakable and unsharable pain is coupled with pain and trauma in the body politic, or the collective body, making pain and suffering necessarily shared, thus creating a story that must be told. I am preoccupied with why I tell the story, even as I try to tell it. How do I tell the story of my pain if pain is also reduced to moans and silences that I can only understand as my own? How do you share my pain? How do I share yours? How do I understand the pains and suffering of others with which I have no direct experience? How do we all share the pain of the world? Why do I feel compelled to tell these stories and to suffer through them? I write and read exactly to be upset, after all. Savich, again, writes, "One writes not to express but to move beyond. You can't. / I think of the birds that sing not to be heard but to continue."[23] Storytelling is my song. I write the story, so that I may continue, so that I may live. But I am not sure I will ever move beyond. In fact, I am not sure I want to move beyond. I am, after all, quite attached to my suffering. It follows me, and I it, like a ghost. Such a pain. Such a pleasure.

* * *

I am discussing Claudia Rankine's *Citizen* with my students. We have just finished looking at the chapter named for Trayvon Martin. In that chapter, Rankine includes John Lucas's alteration

---

22 Ibid., 175.
23 Savich, *Diving Makes the Water Deep,* 178.

of a public lynching, the Black bodies removed from the photograph and a white man in the foreground pointing upwards to
an empty tree branch. We talk about the simultaneous hypervis-
ibility and invisibility of the Black body, the public spectacle of
lynching, and the ways in which the murder of Trayvon Martin
can be thought as a modern-day lynching. Next, we turn to the
cover of the book: a hood, torn from a sweatshirt, no body to fill
it. A student says, "we are looking at Trayvon Martin's ghost."
He goes on to describe how the absence of the Black body is a
reminder of the trauma that remains after the body is deceased;
"despite everything, the body remains."[24] The deaths of Trayvon
Martin and all his ancestors and all who come after haunt us in
the stillness of those photographs. The trauma of anti-Blackness
haunts us as racism endures.

Nathan Snaza writes of how haunting and "rememory" are
ways of "attuning to the always already collective materiality
of the past and its violences, and the ways that those historical violences are present and ongoing. [...] slavery and settler
colonial violence haunt every situation in the United States."[25]
In other words, the ghost has a real presence. It has been demanding its due and our attention for centuries. David Naguib
Pellow writes, "racism is a toxic behavior and ideology that has
a negative impact on us all, but especially those who are its direct targets."[26] Claudia Rankine writes, "you are not sick, you are
injured—you ache for the rest of your life."[27] She moves so deftly
between different invocations of "you" that we can never be fully
certain exactly which you she is talking to or about. I think of
the collective pain that results from the harms of racism, even
while so many people benefit from racism's effects. I imagine
the different yous who make up those collectives. I think of
how recent popular discourse on the affective energies of col-

---

24 Rankine, *Citizen,* 69.
25 Nathan Snaza, *Animate Literacies: Literature, Affect, and the Politics of
    Humanism* (Durham: Duke University Press, 2019), 20.
26 David Naguib Pellow, *Resisting Global Toxics: Transnational Movements for
    Environmental Justice* (Cambridge: MIT Press, 2007), 46.
27 Rankine, *Citizen,* 143.

lective and individual traumas have led us to the conception of a "pain body," whose energetic damage we all move in, with, and through. What would it be to imagine different collectives of we who suffer in the systemic damages of racism, ableism, sexism, heterosexism, and cissexism and all those collective hauntings?

We are not sick; we are injured. Sometimes we are both sick and injured. We are all in some sort of pain. There is always greater pain and suffering in the world. Racism is an injury that will cause all of us to ache for life, those whom it is directed towards more than others, but in different ways, we all suffer from it. I do not know the pain of racism directed toward me; my whiteness affords me that privilege. I am differently pained by how racism hurts so many and so many whom I love so dearly. How might the pain in my body awaken me to those abominations and violences in the world? How might I grow closer to the depths of those pains of the outside world that reverberate on a loop? If your pain is different from mine, how can it ever be *ours*?

Reflecting on Toni Morrison's *Beloved,* Avery Gordon urges white readers to understand the novel as a ghost story of the history of trauma and inheritance of slavery. Listen carefully, Gordon urges, "we will hear not only 'their' story, the old story of the past, but how we are in this story, even now, even if we do not want to be."[28] To see Trayvon Martin's ghost in the empty hooded sweatshirt is to "listen to the image" even in its silences and stillnesses, to hear the story, to be in the story, to make contact with his ghost and all the ghosts of continued systemic injustice.[29] To feel the pain, to be transformed by it. To throw time out of joint—recurring, ending, repeating, enduring. I want to take stock of the collective negative impacts of racism, but I cannot shake the image of the white man with swollen pockets laughing all the way to the bank as he steps over the bodies of all those who suffer for his successes. I'm pretty sure he does not

---

28 Gordon, *Ghostly Matters,* 190.
29 To "listen to the image" is a nod to Tina M. Campt, *Listening to Images* (Durham: Duke University Press, 2017).

want to be in this story. But he is. To which collective we does he belong?

In 2013 Ta-Nehisi Coates wrote an op-ed for *The New York Times*, "In Defense of a Loaded Word." The central argument of the piece saw a reprise in 2017 in a video that went viral on social media. In the video, Coates responds to a white student's question about who has the right to use the "n-word." First, he reminds us that words do not have meaning without context. "I'm sorry," Coates says, "I'm going to say the word." He says the word and draws analogies to other words that gain meaning in context, words he also enunciates: "bitch," "faggot," "white trash."[30] I hear the echo of my mother's somewhat proud refrain, frequently pronounced after a day of heavy drinking: "I may be white trash, but at least I ain't no n-----." I struggle to write the word. I am not sure if I should write the word, even if it has its context. I want you, reader, to be clear on the words my mother uttered, how violent they are, but my body resists its writing, aches down to the marrow. Certainly, I cannot say the word. I will not say the word. It is a matter, again, of failing to write what cannot be spoken, of letting the crude gaps gape the wound, of meeting the ghosts. I must make contact. I must write of the violence, of the pain that is otherwise so unutterable and unlanguagable. Still, some things I cannot write.

My father, with similar frequency and under similar conditions, would rant about "all the fucking faggots." He was not talking about me—I don't think he was, at least not at the time— but I have been called a "fucking faggot," a "dyke," a "queer," a "goddamn tranny" enough times. I can say the words. I can write the words with ease. I embody the words. Some words are mine to take back, others are not. Every word does not belong to everyone. There is no singular collective *we*.

---

30 Random House, "Ta-Nehisi Coates on Words that Don't Belong to Everyone | 'We Were Eight Years in Power' Book Tour," *YouTube,* November 7, 2017, https://www.youtube.com/watch?v=QO15S3WC9pg; Ta-Nehisi Coates, "In Defense of a Loaded Word," *The New York Times,* November 23, 2013, https://www.nytimes.com/2013/11/24/opinion/sunday/coates-in-defense-of-a-loaded-word.html.

The ghosts live in language, conjured sometimes through speech, sometimes through text. Traumas haunt us differently, silence us in different ways. The words come and go. The sting of their pain lingers on and in the body. Think again of the photographs. The stillness. The body removed, remains in its absence. The body haunts. The trauma haunts the body through pain. Sometimes we simply cannot feel another's actual pain, even if we feel pain for their pain. It haunts us all, but differently, some more vulnerable to the pains of those hauntings than others. *You. I. We. Not-we.*

I have been angry lately about what I think of as an injustice done to me, a case of potential discrimination in my workplace. But I do not see it as an injustice done only to me. I know I am but a blip in the longer history of injustices and discriminatory behavior enacted by this person. I consult a mentor-friend about the situation, a woman of color who is no stranger to discrimination and injustice. Someone must stop this guy, I say. Maybe I will be the one to speak up. She says, "so what? This guy discriminated against you. This happens all the time. Everywhere. You can't let it get to you. You can't let it haunt you. You just have to let it go." But it does haunt me. Why do we have to let it go, I want to know. I say again: but it is unjust, why not agitate? "There are more and greater injustices in the world," she says. "I'm done talking about this. The list of injustices I'm fighting is too long, and I've given you my advice." There are always more and greater injustices in the world. There is always greater pain and greater suffering. Each moment of injustice and suffering reveals one deeper, as it reveals itself.

So what if one white guy in a position of power discriminated against me? There are guys like him everywhere doing this stuff to so many more people. How can I change anything? What can any one of us do? How much can these smaller trespasses reveal of all the greater systemic suffering that haunts our collective bodies? I wonder what it means to unlock empathy, to attempt to share what has been deemed unsharable, to be in and with one another's pain and suffering. Savich suggests the movement toward empathy, either for another person in pain or sought from the other while we are in pain, refigures the self by expanding it—suffering is simultaneously a self-absorption and an incitement to empathy. Or, as Leslie Jamison reminds us, empathy demands a porousness.[31] We must expand ourselves, open ourselves to the other. Our own suffering both absorbs us in our own ego and requires a porous opening to the suffering of others. Which is to say, our suffering must have a collective bearing. We must be able to travel into and through one another's stories. We, collectively and individually, endure in guttural moans and heavy silences. *We. Not-we. We.* We need a communal endurance and survivability, so we can live together amongst all these ghosts.

* * *

For years, I have been managing chronic pain in its ebbs and flows in the spaces where tendon, ligament, and cartilage meet bone throughout my body. In addition to joint pain, I have experienced debilitating pain in my sternum, each flare-up sending me into a panicked worry. What if this time it really is a heart attack? A flare feels like this: a dull ache in my chest begins subtly, creeping up in intensity over a day or two. Then, suddenly, the ache erupts into a wind-sucking, immobilizing throbbing. In one particularly bad bout, a partner returned home to find me supine on the floor, silent tears coursing my cheeks. She admonished me for not calling her and insisted on taking me to the emergency room. It will pass, I say. We're going, she says. So we do. I discover if you show up to a hospital emergency room complaining of chest pain, you will be fast-tracked for an EKG, where, even if the test returns normal, you are still ahead of the queue to see the doctor. The doctor tells me the EKG is normal, but I have a chronic inflammation of the costal cartilage that connects my sternum to my rib cage. Deal with it, or opt for steroid injections into the sternum, he says. And work on your

---

31 Savich, *Diving Makes the Water Deep,* 58; Leslie Jamison, *The Empathy Exams: Essays* (Minneapolis: Graywolf Press, 2014), 6.

posture. My shoulders hunched, I leave the ER feeling helpless. For years, this is the explanation I waited for. Chronic, he said. This is your life. Deal with it.

Chronic. According to the *Oxford English Dictionary,* chronic means "of or relating to time"—pain of the chronic sort is necessarily temporal; of disease, chronic means "lasting a long time," "lingering." It can also mean "continuous," "constant," or "recurring."[32] Chronic pain may last or it may be repeated. It is not once and for all or finally and forever, but it lasts forever, in a sense. Or, as Johanna Hedva notes, the word "chronic" is etymologically rooted in the Latin chronos, meaning "'of time' and specifically, 'a lifetime'. [...] So a chronic illness is an illness that lasts a lifetime. In other words, it does not get better. There is no cure."[33] It does not get better, but something might happen. The illness endures. The pain endures. The suffering endures. There is always more and greater pain and suffering in the world.

Leigh Gilmore writes, "chronic pain lasts too long, it is untimely, and when it erupts or disappears, it leaves skid marks across one's life plans."[34] My pain is not constant, but it recurs and sometimes it lingers. When I have a particularly bad flareup, I am left breathless, unable to do much else but lie on my back until the pain passes. I am halted as time presses on all around me. I am on pause while the world continues to happen. I think of Berkowitz again, when she writes, "when the onset of this pain follows a traumatic event (as it often does), it's hard not to understand that trauma as a certain kind of key."[35] To turn the key, Berkowitz turns to Peter A. Levine's book, *In an Unspoken Voice,* in which he makes the connection between trauma and various bodily health concerns. Levine is trying to suss out a "biology of trauma" with the understanding that trauma, even when there is no physical trauma to bodily tissue, manifests in

---

32 *Oxford English Dictionary,* s.v. "chronic," https://www.oed.com/view/Entry /32570?redirectedFrom=chronic#eid.

33 Johanna Hedva, "Sick Woman Theory," *Mask Magazine,* January 2016, n.p.

34 Leigh Gilmore, "Agency Without Mastery: Chronic Pain and Posthuman Life Writing," *Biography* 35, no. 1 (Winter 2012): 95.

35 Amy Berkowitz, *Tender Points* (Oakland: Timeless, Infinite Light, 2015), 15.

the body through illness and pain, as well as through the usual somatic responses to PTSD we have come to expect and understand.[36]

The chronic pain in my sternum is linked to a diminutive and diminishing posture, a bodily manifestation of my desire to make myself small as I turn the traumas in my chest inward, a concave suffering. I cannot pinpoint which trauma pushed me into this curl. Was it the shrinking away from the abuses of my childhood, flinching at my father's raised palm and belt-snap? Or was it, instead, a desire to fold my shoulders around my growing breasts in order to make them appear less protrusive? Or was it my various attempts to flatten my chest with tight undergarments that sunk pain into my breastbone? It is arguably a combination of all of the above that collapsed my frame, but when I sought a diagnosis of "gender identity disorder," now referred to as "gender dysphoria," I told my therapist I needed to remove my breasts because I was always trying to hide them so people would read me as a man. If I am honest, it was not only my desire to move my body toward some approximate manhood that finally brought me to the removal of my breast tissue. I thought, also, that without breasts, I would be able to open my chest again, to release some of the chronic pain and perhaps some of the trauma lodged there.

We hold onto the traumas and the traumas hold onto us, making pain in our bodies. Levine suggests traumatized people are "repeatedly frightened and restrained—by his or her own persistent physiological reactions and by fear of those reactions and emotions."[37] In a way, Freud's "repetition compulsion," long understood to be locked in the psyche is actually manifest in the body, and the physiological reactions persist as well. To heal and release oneself from this restraint, Levine recommends somatic work that actively allows the body to move physically and re-

---

36   Peter A. Levine, *In an Unspoken Voice: How the Body Releases Trauma and Restores Goodness* (Berkeley: North Atlantic Books, 2010).

37   Ibid., 66.

lease the energy of trauma.[38] I was curling into a cage of myself. I needed to release the energy of trauma not by simply moving or activating movement in my body but by releasing, or removing, an actual part of my body.

In the many years following my top surgery, my posture has indeed straightened out a bit. My pain has improved, my flare-ups are fewer and farther between, and sometimes, people even think I am a man. I cannot be sure if the amount of healing in my body can be attributed to the physical adjustment I made in the flattening of my chest or in the emotional healing that came with it, but I know that I cannot separate the emotional healing from the physical procedure. To be clear, I am not entirely without pain. Pain still rises in my chest from time to time. It also moves through my wrists, the cartilage torn and thinning and in need of surgical repair; around my elbows where bending and bearing weight is painful at times; into my knees where I am greeted by an unpredictable sharpness with either bending or straightening the leg. The injury in the forest that day simply mapped new pain onto already delicate and inflamed joints. The onset of new illness simply mapped new pain onto more bodily tissue. The pain migrates. It lingers. It is constant. It multiplies, a gathering of wolves. A wolfpack. It is untimely. It is of time. Which is to say, it has a history that precedes my birth. It lasts too long. We do not last so long. The body does not last, but it remains.

* * *

There are many ways to feel, to be with, to become ghosts. Ghosts have a real presence. They demand our attention. "Haunting," Avery Gordon writes, "is not the same as being exploited, traumatized, or oppressed, although it usually involves these experiences, or is produced by them." In other words, the ghosts are born out of the traumas, exploitations, and oppressions we endure. Importantly, their haunting "alters the experience of be-

---

38 Ibid.

ing in time, the way we separate the past, the present, and the future."[39] The past follows us into our presents and futures. We return to our pasts. We repeat. They repeat. Gordon imagines haunting as shorthand for "singular yet repetitive instances."[40] Notably, Freud distinguishes "remembering" from "repeating": while remembering is relegated to the psyche, abstracted as "an experiment carried out in the laboratory," Freud insists that repeating necessitates "conjuring up a piece of real life."[41] Repeating is remembering made tangible.

Even more notably, then, is Freud's invocation of conjuring as part of the process of repetition, a conjuration that demands "real life" and thus demands a body. Repetition is a conjuring, a haunting. For Freud, the compulsion to repeat replaces the impulsion to remember. Trauma is thus reproduced "not as a memory but as an action," and, of course, we repeat without even consciously knowing we are repeating.[42] Even if we forget, the body remembers. Eve Tuck and C. Ree describe haunting as "relentless remembering and reminding" and as "both acute and general; individuals are haunted, but so are societies."[43] Settler colonialism and its attendant racism continue to haunt us all. The snake in the flooded basement, as Tuck and Ree describe it, continually rears its head. The wolves emerge from between the trees. Haunting is not the same as being traumatized, but we might think of it as an effect of being traumatized, whether individually or collectively. It is a conjuring, a remembering, a repeating of trauma's ghosts. Never the last time. The time is relentlessly out of joint.

39 Gordon, *Ghostly Matters*, xvi.

40 Ibid.

41 Sigmund Freud, "Remembering, Repeating, and Working-Through," in *The Standard Edition of the Complete Psychological Works of Sigmund Freud*, Vol. 12: *The Case of Schreber, Papers on Technique and Other Works (1911–1913)*, ed. and trans. James Strachey with Anna Freud (London: Hogarth Press, 1958), 152.

42 Ibid., 150.

43 Eve Tuck and C. Ree, "A Glossary of Haunting," in *Handbook of Autoethnography*, eds. Tony E. Adams, Stacy Holman Jones, and Carolyn Ellis (Walnut Creek: Left Coast Press, 2013), 642.

The temporality of trauma is a chronic force: the trauma returns, the pain returns, the healing comes again and again. Time is nonlinear, the body moves backward and forward; the body is vertical, the body is horizontal, the body is prostrate in pain, psychic or somatic. Queerness, according to José Esteban Muñoz, is horizontal. Queerness has been, has never been, is, but is not quite yet. And it is ecstatic, let us not forget. Muñoz writes, "knowing ecstasy is having a sense of timeliness's motion, comprehending a temporal unity, which includes the past (having been), the future (the not-yet) and the present (the making-present);" it is a call to a "then and there, a not yet here."[44] Ecstatic time always allows us the space and possibility of the not-yet, to reshape the past in the yet-to-come. Ecstasy might give us an order to the untimely. To make of hope a timeliness. Nothing is forever. Nothing is once and for all.

In pain or illness, I cling to the hope that this body does not have to be once and for all, but in a way, the body is forever. Even after death, we must take care of the remains. The physical matter decomposes but never leaves. This is simply the law of conservation of mass. What then is ever really lost from a body? I cannot help but wonder how trauma, queerness, and pain continue to circulate around one another, pushing me forward in time to the person I wish to become and backward to the child I was, seeking out answers for how and why and who I am, and how and why and toward what or whom I desire. Remember that wounds, when healed, can always be reopened. The past matters not only to discover what was lost but also what might be recovered or reclaimed. The past matters because it is always here now. Such is the chronicity of pain, and such is the chronicity of hope.

"Dream" has many valences: hope, wish, fantasy, nightmare, haunting. Freud describes the role of dreams for those who suffer from "traumatic neuroses" as leading people back to the instances in which trauma occurred. These dreams, unlike many

---

44 José Esteban Muñoz, *Cruising Utopia: The Then and There of Queer Futurity* (New York: New York University Press, 2009), 186–87.

he discusses in *Interpretation of Dreams*, do not function as wish-fulfilments. Rather, the dreams of traumatic neuroses arise "in obedience to the compulsion to repeat, [...] to conjure up what has been forgotten and repressed."[45] Dreaming is perhaps another way in which the body remembers, bringing fantasy, nightmare, and haunting into the sleeping body and its psyche. Something we cannot help but repeat, an obedient compulsion, an unconscious addiction.

In the past year, I have been waking with some frequency in the small hours of the morning with my heart racing and my body in a cold sweat, from dreams, nightmares really, in which I am in the throes of illness again or my body has reversed the surgery I had, sealing me up, making the damage permanent and unfixable. In these dreams, I return with frequency to the physical tissue trauma in my body and to the mental and emotional trauma that accompany it. The time of trauma is one of repetition, a return, a reapparition of the trauma itself or, relatedly, the gap in which the trauma was produced. The pinch of skin between the sutures, the spaces where our wounds gape open.

The dream produced of traumatic neurosis is also a conjuring, a reapparition of ghosts. This is why we call it a nightmare. It haunts us. Far from a wish fulfillment, the traumatic nightmare is a flashback, a recollection of the latent but consciously unknown, what Cathy Caruth calls our "unclaimed experience."[46] The nightmare is quite simply a replay, a return. Trauma returns. Pain returns. In treating pain and illness, we must therefore attend to the symptom, Freud insists, "not as an event of the past, but as a present-day force [...] which consists in a large measure in tracing it back to the past."[47] Pain's repetition demands an evaluation of our own compulsions, addictions, and the ghosts

---

45 Sigmund Freud, *Beyond the Pleasure Principle*, trans. James Strachey (New York: W.W. Norton, 1961), 37.

46 Cathy Caruth, *Unclaimed Experience: Trauma, Narrative, and History* (Baltimore: Johns Hopkins University Press, 1996).

47 Freud, "Remembering, Repeating, and Working-Through," 151–52.

they conjure. Looking back is how we find ourselves here. Looking back, to recall Berkowitz, is what we need to do to get better.

* * *

I have begun seeing a trauma therapist who focuses on somatic experiencing, pushing me to get in touch with the places where emotion lives in my body and where feelings may be attached to my pain and suffering. In a recent session, I tell her I just want to rehearse the story I am currently suffering. I need to externalize it. I have become addicted to its telling, feeling as though another person sharing in the incredulity of events and recognizing my suffering gives me a pleasurable hit of something, something I'm not quite sure how to name, but it is something I crave. In my likely false syllogisms, I imagine that it is chronic pain's refusal to stop that forecloses pleasure's possibility, even while other pains, with their terminus within sight, arouse pleasure. I revisit this question anew: how might the pain resulting from chronic illness, or any pain of the chronic sort arouse pleasure? I suspect it has something to do with its sharability, in being able to share the enduring story of the suffering or in simply enduring one's own suffering through the other's pleasure, in bearing the unbearable. Which is maybe just another way of saying, "misery loves company."

I want to divulge all the details and fold her into the narration. I want her to bear witness to the story. I want to put her in the story even if she does not want to be in it. Instead, she wants to bear witness to my feelings and to the deep wounds of trauma where the story sediments in my bones, blood, and tissue. In that session, she refuses to let my brain rehearse the story. She asks me instead to ground my feet, to track the emotion through my body, and to let my emotions take space and shape and color and movement. In this process, I learn a new way to share suffering through affect and through the body, the ways in which it conjures shapes and colors outside the realm of the languageable.

As I write this, I am approaching the one-year mark since I became ill and experienced medical complications that have led to a new chronic pain and extended physical, emotional, and psychological suffering. When I was ill, my body feverish and aching and the infection creeping through my blood and threatening my organs, my partner at the time, *L,* first told me that she could not understand why I was making such a big deal about what was happening to my body, that if it happened to her, she wouldn't think it was a big deal at all. She then reminded me, repeatedly, for months in the ongoingness of my pain and illness and suffering, that this was not the worst thing that could happen to me or my body, that she has seen worse things happen to other people's bodies, that at least I wasn't dying of cancer like her father had. There is always more and greater suffering in the world. *L* could not separate her own traumas from mine. She could not help but be self-absorbed in her own suffering. I could not help but be self-absorbed in mine.

In that first session with my therapist, I learn something important about these questions I have been asking about the sharability of pain and suffering. About the limits of empathy and the impacts of empathy. As I ground my feet and visualize roots planting into the dirt, steadying my quavering and wrecked body, I imagine my limbs unfolding and opening upward, my heart and throat growing open to the world, finding fullness in a cavity that had been feeling empty and drained of life. In that moment, I blurt out, "I just wanted her to care." I am talking about *L.* I do not doubt that she actually did care. What I learn is that there is a difference between knowing someone cares and feeling that they care; though feeling, to be certain, is another way of knowing, a knowing deep in the body. When I say, "I just wanted her to care," what I mean is that I wanted her to show she cared in a way I could recognize. Feeling cared for is exactly what I am craving in the rehearsal of the story. I am searching for enough care to fill the void that formed where the care I needed was not given.

Our relationship could not survive my illness, our pain, and our suffering. Our relationship could not survive sadness's sei-

zure and *L*'s and perhaps my own refusal of the kind of porousness that empathy demands. I wanted and needed *L* to share
in my suffering, not by suffering with me but by listening to its
telling and by recognizing that all of it *is* a big deal for me. I
don't have to know what your pain feels like to care. I don't have
to suffer in the same way to care. *L* struggled to show her care,
which resulted in what felt like a constant dismissal of my suffering, and that is what haunts me and takes shape as another
wolf that stalks me, or that I stalk, through the woods. How do I
get the wolf to stop gnashing her teeth? How do I recognize that
the wolf is not a monster, that *L* perhaps had her own ways of
showing care that I could not make sense of, and that she, too, is
suffering? How do we suffer and tend to suffering collectively?
How do we demonstrate care and hold people in their inarticu-
lable but utterable, guttural pain even while we suffer? Come,
reader, let us take care of one another.

* * *

Johanna Hedva's "sick woman theory" accounts for the sensitivi-
ties of the body and mind to regimes of oppression. She writes,
"it is that all of our bodies and minds carry the historical trauma
of this, that it is *the world itself* that is making and keeping us
sick."[48] If we are not sick, we are injured. The world itself is keeping us in pain. The world itself is the story in which we suffer.
Alyson Patsavas calls for a cripistemology of pain that recognizes the political urgency that comes from knowing how precarious the lives of people affected by barriers to healthcare and
pain treatment are.[49] Those living with pain, illness, disability,
and in relation to the ongoingness of racism, settler colonialism, transphobia, sexism, homophobia, and abuse, live in a time
of precarity or a precarious temporality. "The ghost cannot be

---

48 Hedva, "Sick Woman Theory," n.p.
49 Alyson Patsavas, "Recovering a Cripistemology of Pain: Leaky Bodies,
Connective Tissue, and Feeling Discourse," *Journal of Literary & Cultural
Disability Studies* 8, no. 2 (2014): 203–18.

simply tracked back to an individual loss or trauma."[50] Those lives most haunted by the traumas and pains of the pasts, past-presents, and present-pasts are living in chronic precarity—a lifetime covered in skid marks. Conjured ghosts. Relentless. Demanding their due.

Suffering is exceptional for some, ordinary for others, but, as a phenomenon, it is so ordinarily of this world, regularly affecting ordinary people. Even when it amounts to such an atrocity that we might wish it were an irregular occurrence. Lisa Blackman makes the case for a politics of ordinary suffering that necessitates an account of suffering as "not an exceptional phenomenon, but rather part and parcel of the costs of neoliberalism(s)."[51] I cannot help but draw a parallel to Ann Cvetkovich's conceptualization of insidious trauma, that is, the trauma endured in everyday life under capitalism.[52] In neoliberal-capitalist-settler society, suffering and trauma have become so typical, so ordinary. I think back to Patrick Wall's declaration that no ordinary person experiences pain without unpleasantness.[53] How extraordinary, exceptional even, might a pleasantness in pain then seem. That to live a life of pleasure can be a radical refusal to pay the fee.

* * *

Let us return to where we started. As I write this, with ice packs wrapped around my wrists, I want to cry. I cry not for the pain itself, but for the suffering, because I know it will recur and persist. I know writing will continue to be painful. I know I have again entered the time of pain. I know I never really left it. And with the onset of new illness and new pain, I come to terms with

---

50 Gordon, *Ghostly Matters,* 183.

51 Lisa Blackman, "Affective Politics, Debility, and Hearing Voices: Towards a Feminist Politics of Ordinary Suffering," *Feminist Review* 111, no.1 (2015): 26.

52 Ann Cvetkovich, *An Archive of Feelings: Trauma, Sexuality, and Lesbian Public Cultures* (Durham: Duke University Press, 2003).

53 Wall, *Pain,* 29.

a new entry point into pain's chronicity across the landscape of the body, in the nerves and in the joints. It endures. I am enduring. I am haunted. "Haunting lies precisely in its refusal to stop," write Tuck and Ree.[54] Chronic pain refuses to stop once and for all. The body refuses to stop. It remains. It haunts as it is haunted.

So many nights I startle awake, throat closed, the scream refusing to erupt. I continue to dream in monsters, in the nightmares of wolves. I think back to the forest, my eyes focused down the path, watching the dog who wants to be rewilded like his wolf cousin as he crashes toward me through the verdure of wildwood and brush. I think back to the delay as the pain explodes anew in my body. I sat there in that forest waking up to the pain again, but quietly, as quiet as hair, remembering and repeating my relentless search for the wolves, wondering how they haunt not only my own body but also the body politic.

I have walked us through a literal wood. But I think again of Berkowitz's walk through the metaphorical woods, where the wolves emerge from the trees, where "you need to walk alone into a forest. You need to walk until you meet a wolf."[55] Sometimes we need to be alone, to be lonely, to be lonely and alone with the wolves as we let time collapse on us. Everything is out of sequence. I return to the solitude of the forest, two years before my feverish time with L. I return to make sense of all the events that followed. Trayvon Martin was murdered over eight years ago; Black boys are still being killed today. Black children. Black men. Black women. Indigenous people. People of color. Disabled people. Poor people. All subjected time and time again to the violences of a white supremacist colonial nation-state. Hunted and haunted. The foundation of the United States is built on so many broken backs, rivers of blood paved over. So little changes. Time marches on. Time marches back.

In *Hunger: A Memoir of (My) Body,* Roxane Gay writes at the intersection of her own personal traumas—rape, assault, and

---

54 Tuck and Ree, "A Glossary of Haunting," 642.
55 Amy Berkowitz, *Tender Points* (Oakland: Timeless, Infinite Light, 2015), 17.

harassment—and how her embodiment as a fat Black queer woman is always already subject to the traumas of institutionalized racism, body shaming, sexism, misogyny, and homophobia. She writes, "even the happiest moments of my life are overshadowed by my body and how it doesn't fit anywhere. This is no way to live, but this is how I live."[56] This is how we live. We endure. I think also of Yanyi, who writes, "It must not be life, what I've been doing. It can't be life, to not want to live."[57] Yet in not wanting to live, we live anyway. We are living in the time of not wanting to live. We are living in the time of ghosts.

The wolves are also ghosts. They cannot be separated from their spectrality. They peek around a tree stump, eyes keen, ears attuned. The trauma rears its head again and again. In pain, we cannot walk. We must sit with it, lie with it, curl up with it, hobble as we carry on. That day in the forest, I literally met a dog, who brought on physical pain. The dog is not a wolf, but the wolves emerged from the trees to meet their cousin. I was never really alone in the forest. But feeling alone, lonely even, in my pain, I become more attuned to the many wolves peering from between the trees, asking me to remember the traumas that haunt, that inform the pain radiating through my body and through the body politic. If the confrontation with ghosts is a meeting of change and transformation of both the self and social relations, then, living in those silences, in the stillness of the forest or the photograph or the text, I also feel a spark of hope for what might happen.

---

56 Roxane Gay, *Hunger: A Memoir of (My) Body* (New York: HarperCollins, 2017), 205.

57 Yanyi, *The Year of Blue Water* (New Haven: Yale University Press, 2019), 19.

4

"An Awful Transform": Conjuring Addiction

In this act of magical transformation
I recognize myself again.
> — Susan Stryker, "My Words to Victor Frankenstein
> above the Village of Chamounix"[1]

A hurt is at the center of all addictive behaviors.
> — Gabor Maté, *In the Realm of Hungry Ghosts*[2]

Every Tuesday, I go to the hospital. I walk through the sliding glass doors alongside people carrying assorted flower bouquets, teddy bears, heavy shoulders, and sleep-weary eyes. I sometimes feel compelled to carry my own body through the doors as if I am bearing the fear of impending death and the anticipation of loss, as if someone I love is slowly drifting away from me, day by day, in a scrubbed white room on the fifth floor. Not because I actually want to go through such an ordeal — I have, and there

---

1   Susan Stryker, "My Words to Victor Frankenstein above the Village of Chamounix: Performing Transgender Rage," in *The Transgender Studies Reader,* eds. Susan Stryker and Stephen Whittle (New York: Routledge. 2006), 251.

2   Gabor Maté, *In the Realm of Hungry Ghosts: Close Encounters with Addiction* (Berkeley: North Atlantic Books, 2010), 38.

is nothing romantic about it — but because I want my hunched shoulders, my furrowed brow, and the solemnity of my pursed lips to communicate my porousness to my hospital companions. The English word "empathy," as it was invented in the field of psychology, is a translation of the German word *Einfühlung,* which translates directly as "feeling-in." "Empathy" draws on the Greek *empatheia, em* (in) and *pathos* (feeling) to arrive at that literal translation of the German, "feeling-in."[3] When empathy was first coined by two psychologists in 1908, this concept of "feeling in" referred not to a shared experience of emotion but to the projection of one's own feelings into an object or other; in other words, it meant nearly the opposite of what we mean when we demand empathy today.[4] Nevertheless, Leslie Jamison riffs on the concept of empathy as a "feeling into" or a way of feeling the other. She describes it as a penetration, a kind of travel — you enter into another person's pain.[5] Or, maybe you penetrate them with your own. Either way, we pierce and are pierced. We travel through one another. At the hospital, I want to enter their pain. I want them to enter mine. I want to move through them and with them. Perhaps because I want us all to feel a sense of belonging together.

While most visitors ride up the elevator, I ride down to the subbasement level, the dregs of this hospital tower, as low as you can go, to dig deeper into my own pain. I think of how Jeannie Vanasco describes the basement as the perfect metaphor, a Freudian one. "The id lives in the basement, right?"[6] The id, the *base* self (no wonder it would make a home in the basement), all instinct and want, wild. How unruly. How uncanny. But what does it mean to travel below the basement? Who lives there?

3   Susan Lanzoni, "A Short History of Empathy," *The Atlantic,* October 15, 2015, https://www.theatlantic.com/health/archive/2015/10/a-short-history-of-empathy/409912/.

4   Ibid.

5   Leslie Jamison, *The Empathy Exams: Essays* (Minneapolis: Graywolf Press, 2014), 6.

6   Jeannie Vanasco, *Things We Didn't Talk About When I Was a Girl: A Memoir* (Portland: Tin House Books, 2019), 240.

In the subbasement of this hospital, there are two cold meeting rooms alongside a bland cafeteria that serves bland food. I assume the food is bland because I watched the orderlies and nurses douse their plates with salt before digging in, but I have never actually eaten there. I sat in the cafeteria once during my first visit to this hospital. I sat there staring out the window cut into the San Francisco hillside where I could just barely catch a peek of the street above and the feet of passersby on the sidewalk. I tapped my foot nervously, trying to muster the courage to walk through the doors of the adjacent meeting room. I considered getting back on the elevator, walking out the doors, around the corner, and down the hill. I imagined myself giving a quick glance at the cafeteria windows as I walked by, as if I hadn't just been sitting in there a bundle of nerves, as if I didn't even know there were people sitting down there looking up at my feet running past. I did eventually push myself out of the hard, plastic chair in the cafeteria. Shaking, I glanced back toward the elevators, that escape route, as I turned and walked, instead, into my fear, into the meeting room. And now here I am: a person with a weekly routine, a twelve-stepper, someone who goes to a support group, a person in recovery.

* * *

As I embark on my own journey through a recovery program, I pick up Leslie Jamison's book on addiction and recovery. She begins the book by expressing her worries about "trotting out the tired tropes of the addictive spiral," noting how people's eyes glazed over every time she told them she was writing a book about addiction and recovery.[7] How boring; the story we've all heard dozens of times now. A person battling addiction triumphs against all odds but remains haunted by the constant battles against their own addictive wants that possess them like demons, like claws. Jamison notes that she wanted to tell those

---

7   Leslie Jamison, *The Recovering: Intoxication and Its Aftermath* (New York: Little, Brown and Company, 2018), 9.

people with the glazed eyes that her book is different. It's "*about* that glazed look in their eyes," about how hard it is to tell stories of addiction because they seem to be on a repetition loop.[8]

I think about her goals with the book as my own eyes glaze over. I want so badly to follow Jamison through her story of addiction and recovery, but I get stuck where her question lands hard. How do we write about addiction and recovery without trotting out the tired tropes? The thing is, I know I don't really want to write about recovery because I am still figuring out what recovery means and what it looks like. I do not believe I have crossed into the realm of the recovered. I am not even sure I am really on any path to recovery. I wonder if the tired tropes are found in writing about recovery rather than about addiction itself. But surely there are tired tropes in writing about addiction too. Maybe what I want to do instead is let the story be the addiction rather than about the addiction. I want to write the addictions, in all their forms, in all my endless want, in all their endless wanting.

* * *

In anticipation of the release of issues 7 and 8 of Edie Fake's *Gaylord Phoenix* following a seven-year hiatus, I decide to re-read the compilation of issues that was released in 2010. In my rereading, I become fixated on an image that recurs throughout the book, a crystal claw gouging the thigh of our anti-hero, Gaylord Phoenix, a queer creature who embarks on a journey of transformation in a fantasy world full of other unfamiliar creatures, mazes, caverns, forests, and strange geometries. The book begins with the Gaylord exploring a secret grotto — a cavern, a cave, an enclave, a subterranean cavern, even a sub-basement, perhaps — "deep in the night" where a crystal claw awaits "poised in shadow."[9] Under the cover of darkness, the claw enters the thigh of the Gaylord. After some struggle, the

---

8   Ibid.
9   Edie Fake, *Gaylord Phoenix* (Jackson Heights: Secret Acres, 2010), 9–11.

Gaylord finds himself irrevocably changed by the crystal claw. His body transforms, transmogrifies, as he develops a new tube-like proboscis to match his newly visible genitalia, which also takes the shape of a tube, capable of both penetrating and being penetrated.

In this regard, he embodies a kind of hybridity or mixity. Drawing on Foucault, Hil Malatino writes of monstrosity as "mixity" — the common thread between every figure of the monster is the idea of mixture and combination. And Foucault describes the monster variably as "the mixture of two individuals," "the mixture of two sexes," and "a mixture of life and death" — the space where living is done. Both penetrating and penetrated. *Einfühlung. Empatheia.* Empathy. This idea of mixture and mixity is what allows Malatino to reclaim the intersex subject as monstrous. Malatino insists on a "right to monstrosity" and a "right to transgression" as constituent of a right to determine selfhood and to exist in difference, to refuse to become fixed or corrected into conformity of a supposed "natural" or "normal" order. Malatino writes, "monstrous bodies are wondrous precisely because they confound the order of things."[10] Wondrous or wonderful: from wonder, etymologically rooted in astonishment or marvel or the miraculous.

Malatino claims the intersex body, then, is a "monstrous wonder" and suggests also that such a figuration has implications for how we might imagine intersex, trans, and genderqueer subjectivities alongside perhaps even disabled subjectivity into a "coalition of monsters — those beings that embrace corporeal nonnormativity, hybridity, and mixity as a source of strength and resilience capable of challenging understandings of extraordinary bodies as pathological, aberrant, and undesirable."[11] A collective suffering. A collective pleasure. Yes, again, how extraordinary, how irregular. How marvelous. How wondrous. How wonderful. How awesome. How awful?

---

10 Hil Malatino, *Queer Embodiment: Monstrosity, Medical Violence, and Intersex Experience* (Lincoln: University of Nebraska Press, 2019), 48.

11 Ibid., 64.

With his new appendages, the Gaylord soon catches the attention of a person who possesses similar genitalia. After several lustful scenes in which they variously penetrate each other, the Gaylord has another sudden encounter with a shadowy form of the crystal claw which injects him with bloodlust. As the shadowy crystal figure pierces his thigh, his nose functions as a kind of projector, displaying his thoughts for all to see. In this scene, the projection reads "I have crystal bloodlust." There is a caption that accompanies the scene, "An Awful Transform."[12]

With this "awful transform," the Gaylord becomes even more monstrous, as his nose and genitals both temporarily become pointy cone-like structures and his teeth are bared sharp like a wolf's. In this moment, he is described as being "possessed by the claw" with the notation, "Blood Drops."[13] We will see many more stabbings of the thigh throughout this first collection, but there are several questions that pull me back again and again to this stabbing scene: Why the bloodlust? What does it want? How does it transform? I want to know exactly what is being done here, in these instants that drip and drop, thick with blood.

* * *

In an interview with Graham Kolbeins of *Rad Queers,* Edie Fake describes drawing the scenes of thigh-stabbing as a representation of his experience learning to take testosterone via injection.[14] Once over breakfast with Fake, he told me how he tried to get through the injections by imagining his thigh to be a pot roast, ready to be plumped with the thick fluid, the testosterone injection a kind of basting. I think back to Cris Mazza, playing "Cris" in her fictional memoir film. She imagines her thigh as a ham, casting her own judgment that it's "not a very good one."[15]

---

12 Fake, *Gaylord Phoenix,* 30–31.

13 Ibid., 34.

14 Graham Kolbeins, "Rad Queers: Edie Fake," *The Comics Journal,* February 5, 2014, http://www.tcj.com/rad-queers-edie-fake/.

15 Frank Vitale, dir., *Anorgasmia: Faking It in a Sexualized World,* produced, written, and and performed by Cris Mazza, 2015.

I think of the ways in which we divide our bodies into cuts of meat, described with the names we use for flesh meant for consumption, "ham" or "roast." I think of how a preoccupation with gender brings us to the meatiness of our bodies, to the hunks of flesh we pierce and cut open. I think of how we make these cuts of flesh significant in their rendering of femininity or masculinity. Here, too soft the flesh; here, too dimply and round; here, too curvy and plump; here, too flat or flaccid; here, too smooth; here, too hairy; here, too sinewy.

I think of my own thigh, the way I slap and pinch at the muscle to loosen it up before an injection, the way I imagine the needle piercing through each layer of epidermis, dermis, and subcutaneous fat before it slides into the muscle fibers. I watch the drop of blood rise out from the needle wound. I dab it away. I lust after it, the sting of the needle, the rise of blood, the transformation of my body. I wonder how the testosterone takes hold of my body or how my body takes hold of testosterone, each possessing the other. This is how I break my own body into pieces and parts to be stabbed and sliced through in this tiny opening of the flesh. This opening reminds me of my porosity, how easily an object can enter my body, how easily a molecule can be pushed into my organism, left to flit about.

* * *

According to Malatino, the physicians who coined the term "hormone" imagined it as a kind of chemical messenger akin to a "carrier pigeon in the bloodstream, flitting between organs, delivering bits of information that work to elicit corporeal transformation."[16] The hormone molecules are taken up by my body, drawn in and utilized in the production of cells, in the reshaping of flesh, texture, and voice. Do I possess the hormone in my body? Does it become mine? Or does it possess me? It enters me; I enter it. I remember the psychic who told me the testoster-

---

16   Hil Malatino, "Biohacking Gender," *Angelaki: Journal of the Theoretical Humanities* 22, no. 2 (2017): 188.

one is like medicine for my body. I think she is right about this, but there is such a fine line between medicine and drug, cure and abuse. Testosterone is a regulated substance. I use it legally and access it through a prescription. It is also possible to obtain and use testosterone illegally. And even drugs that are obtained legally can be abused. One can become addicted to regulated or unregulated substances. One can always become addicted. One can always become possessed.

In the subbasement of the hospital, we read as a group from the "Big Red Book," our anonymous "bible" that holds the secrets of our names and our histories. The book tells us we must be honest about our use of mood-altering chemicals. We must realize that our "addiction to drugs, work, sex, or food is a symptom of being raised in an abusive or neglectful family." We must understand these things. I must understand these things about myself. My own addictions to pain, to substance, to injection, to mood-altering chemicals, to physique-altering chemicals all have their roots. These meetings have forced me to think quite a bit about my alcohol use and my unwillingness to give it up even as I beat myself up over whether or not I drink too much sometimes and if that means I am just like my father. But I'm not really talking about alcoholism right now, or I am but in a different way. I don't want to trot out those tired tropes.

What I am really wondering is if it is possible to be addicted to testosterone itself, the regulation of which may lead one to believe so. I think again of how Paul Preciado distinguishes testosterone as a drug that is both medication to be prescribed and substance to be abused, depending on one's diagnosis or lack thereof. Preciado marks the parallels between the state's regulation of hormones and narcotics, noting how sex hormones are politically controlled by the state, resulting in restrictions on and management of their use that is arguably comparable to the state control and regulation of narcotics.[17] Testosterone is

---

17 Paul Preciado, *Testo Junkie: Sex, Drugs, and Biopolitics in the Pharmaco-pornographic Era,* trans. Bruce Benderson (New York: The Feminist Press, 2013).

not a narcotic, but I ingest it into my organism via intravenous injection. I am impatient for my next fix. I am not addicted. I am diagnosed and treated. But if I weren't diagnosed and treated, then I would have to obtain testosterone illegally. If I use a regulated substance that has not been prescribed to me, I am technically abusing a drug, whether or not I am addicted. Preciado has to choose between two psychoses, one of diagnosis or one of addiction. But it is also possible to become addicted to substances prescribed to treat a diagnosis. Maybe diagnosis and addiction need not be mutually exclusive. Opioids are a simple case in point. Addiction often begins with prescription. But opioids are narcotics. Can we also become addicted to nonnarcotic substances that alter us in ways we cannot fully track or comprehend?

I wonder to what extent I am self-medicating and to what extent I am being medicated for a disorder, a symptom, a glitch.[18] The testosterone is both medicine and addictive substance. I am both a medicated subject and an addict. But I am still unsure what exactly it is I am addicted to: the substance, the process, the changes that come along the way, or the pain and soreness that linger at the site of injection? What would it mean to be addicted, not necessarily to the substance but to the process, to the needle, to the wound, or to the act of wounding and transforming? In the comic, Gaylord Phoenix opens the wound in his thigh over and over again; a repetition, a reapparition, an addiction, a compulsion. If we follow Freud, most every repetition has its roots in trauma. If addiction is repetition, then in trauma we find the hurt that lies at the center of all addictive behaviors. "You have to open the wound! Get your history back!," Fake declares in an interview with *Mildred Pierce* magazine.[19] *Get your history back.* Each opening is a return, each repetition another first time, a fresh encounter with history repeated.

18 By using the word "glitch" here, I am nodding to Jenny Sundén, "On Trans-, Glitch, and Gender as Machinery of Failure," *First Monday* 20, no. 4 (2015).

19 Megan Milks, "Edie Fake's Radical Bloodlust," *Mildred Pierce Zine* 4 (2011): 6–10.

We must realize that our addictions are the symptom of a history of abuse. I must realize this about myself. I have become part of this particular *we*. The people in the room in the sub-basement of the hospital tell stories that are uncannily familiar and that awaken buried somatic memories. My body shakes and my eyes weep as I listen. Healing cannot be done alone: "now is the time to call on webs too thick to be broken. To travel the paths made by pouring ourselves into others," Edie Fake writes.[20] I think of Leslie Jamison in recovery, and I think again of her writing about empathy: "Trauma bleeds. Out of wounds and across boundaries. […] Empathy demands another kind of porousness in response."[21] We are porous. Now is the time to pour ourselves into one another. I travel deep, way under, into the lowest part of the hospital building, into the darkest parts of myself.

When it comes to my three minutes of share time, I talk about the sting of my father's palm against my flesh accompanied by the sting of his words in my ears. I talk about the sting of *R*'s words and the uncanniness of the pain; how at home I feel in the bite, how much I want it even though I hate it, how I worry I might have become addicted to *R* because her love feels like the love of my father, backhanded, bittersweet. I talk about the sting as the needle pierces my thigh. I talk about all the pain and all the wanting. "Move through each other," Fake writes, "I know us best when our borders fly open."[22] I invite the people in that recovery group to move through me as I move through them. We come apart for each other. We piece each other back together. We know each other best. We become addicted to one another.

The "Big Red Book" tells us we are the "walking wounded." There is a hurt at the center of our addictions. I am addicted to the hurt. I lust for it, and it is, perhaps, a kind of bloodlust — addicted to the drug, addicted to *R,* addicted to the want of a fa-

20 Edie Fake, *Gaylord Phoenix* #8 (Brooklyn: Pegacorn Press, 2017).

21 Jamison, *The Empathy Exams*, 5–6.

22 Edie Fake, *Gaylord Phoenix* #7 (Chicago: Perfectly Acceptable Press, 2017).

ther, addicted to the meetings, addicted to the pain. They all run together. I am not sure I know the difference any more.

* * *

Brian Cremins imagines *Gaylord Phoenix* as a superhero comic that, following in the vein of American superhero comics, "document[s] a desire to reshape/reimagine the body as an expression of grief or as a means of mastering traumatic situations."[23] The hero allows us to imagine the body otherwise, to heal the trauma by living otherwise, to be rescued and reshaped by the one holding the superpowers. Cremins elaborates, "the wound is the site of revelation, a mark of experience, a reminder of the past."[24] A mark of experience. A mark. Cris Mazza, in her teenage interaction with a boy named Mark who coerced her into performing sex acts she didn't want to perform and who scolded her when she refused, writes, "I was marked."[25] Mark marked her. Jeannie Vanasco, writing on how to choose a pseudonym for her best friend in her youth, the boy who raped her, lands on the name Mark. The word mark, she notes, is mainly defined as a boundary. "And that's what this is about: boundaries."[26] Boundaries: the lines we draw and mark that when crossed and broken, mark us.

In collectively reading the "Big Red Book" in the subbasement, I learn how to think of psychological abuse as leaving its own kind of mark: "the abuse left no visible marks, but it is stored in our bodies just the same as slapping and hitting leave marks on the body." So many ways to be marked. The hitting, the crossing, the breaking, and the bruising all injure the body in different ways. Cremins continues in his analysis of *Gay-*

---

23 Brian Cremins, "Bodies, Transfigurations, and Bloodlust in Edie Fake's Graphic Novel 'Gaylord Phoenix,'" *Journal of Medical Humanities* 34 (2013): 302.

24 Ibid., 309.

25 Cris Mazza, *Something Wrong With Her: A Real-Time Memoir* (Los Angeles: Jaded Ibis Press, 2013), 61.

26 Vanasco, *Things We Didn't Talk About,* 8.

lord Phoenix: "a wound which has healed, however, conceals these memories, sentences them to oblivion."[27] That is, until, as Cremins notes, one of the Gaylord's lovers reminds us that all history will return. When the wound is sutured or bandaged shut, treated and healed, the cut becomes a scar, which is its own mark. The mark conceals the memory. But all history, all memory will inevitably return.

After a series of spells — deep, deep magic, dread magic, dark magic, more than magic — the Gaylord's lover who has been severed and sutured together in all their misadventures, kneels before Gaylord Phoenix, a dagger at his side, his finger to the wound. He declares, "all memorie will return."[28] In the next scene, the Gaylord asks the lover for help, but, with this request, the lover moves his hand to his own scar on his neck, where his head was stitched back onto his body. From the scar arises a bombardment of his own memories of wounding at the hands of the Gaylord. In that haunted memory, he turns away from the Gaylord, drops the dagger and exclaims, "help yrself" as he floats away. The Gaylord then plunges the dagger, like a needle, into his thigh. The wound bursts open and releases an assortment of shapes and color. "This realm rolls back," we learn, as the wound takes him back in time through memory and strange terrain along with the plea to refuse to let the structures hold him.[29]

Trauma — personal, collective, and institutional — bleeds out of the wound. Although wounds may conceal, they leave a mark. They can always be reopened. Without discrete edges, we bleed into one another and into the histories of our dark pasts. Wounds hold ghosts. Ghosts hold the story. The wounds hold our return. Throughout the comic series, Gaylord Phoenix journeys with a slashed thigh, variously open and reopened with each stabbing, whether self-inflicted or conjured by the crystal. He becomes a monster haunted by his own ghosts. And in the

27 Cremins, "Bodies, Transfigurations, and Bloodlust," 309.

28 Fake, *Gaylord Phoenix*, 161.

29 Ibid., 162–67.

act of magical transformation, he seems to recognize himself again.

The crystal and the dagger serve as a stand in for the needle. What does the needle conjure? Which wounds does it open up? Which histories does it return? Which memories and dark pasts does it invoke? The needle delivers the drug testosterone into my system, each injection a wound, inevitably caught up in the violent racist colonial legacies that brought this drug to me. Each injection a wound that awakens the fears and anxieties of sounding like and being like my father or of becoming a "Mark," a man who crosses the mark and marks another in the process. Even as I reshape and reimagine my body, I cannot find the superhero here. Only a series of wishes, a drug, a frightened anti-hero, the child curled into a corner, hiding from all the things that have marked him. Will I ever recognize myself again?

* * *

I am struck again and again by how closely aligned the monster comes to the animal. Both so wondrous; both so terrifying, often hiding in the shadows. Connecting Malatino's rendering of the intersex body as a monstrous wonder in a coalition of genderqueer monsters, I think of the way the Gaylord's transness is presented as a kind of monstrous mixity in coalition with intersexuality. I think of the way Aaron Apps overlays the intersex body with animality, writing of how the body is made into an object, made abject, and made into the animal other — poked, prodded, objectified, feared, and even hunted and haunted. Writing of eating animals, shitting animals, and becoming animal, Apps arrives in and as animal at the end of his memoir: "I was made animal. I am animal. I say here is my animal self."[30] Here is my animal self. Here also, is my monstrous self.

I am monster animal. I think back to the wolf, also a monster animal. The essay collection, *Arts of Living on a Damaged Planet* is divided into two complementary halves, "Monsters" and

---

30 Aaron Apps, *Intersex: A Memoir* (Grafton: Tarpaulin Sky Press, 2015), 62.

"Ghosts." As I have been writing, I have found those categories more and more difficult to distinguish. Ghosts and monsters chase me even as I chase them. I become monster; I become ghost. The monster and the ghost blend into one another. The boundaries dissolve. A father. A hole. A multiplicity.[31] The wolf becomes monster becomes ghost.

Carla Freccero writes of how the wolf grew into a monster in the settler imagination, to be feared and hunted before one could be hunted by it. But wolves are rarely seen. Instead, they leave remnants and signs of their presence, such as in the destruction of a flock of sheep, the killings taking place under the cover of darkness, to be discovered in the bloody aftermath illuminated in the light of day.[32] In the invisible wolf-hunt, I think there is a closeness, also, to haunting. Jon T. Coleman describes wolves as having a "ghostly presence": "settlers heard howls, but they rarely spotted their serenaders. The fearsome beasts avoided humans. People frightened them, and colonists knew this [...]. Humans and wolves scared one another, and their mutual unease kept the species apart."[33] In fact, in this separation wrought of mutual fear, humans and wolves coexisted for eons. But settler colonialism shifted that relationship when agrarian societies marked a new livelihood in the settler landscape. Livestock became a valued property and wolves, among other wild creatures, became a threat to property and thus to livelihood and thus to human life.[34] The wolf easily became the monster lurking in the shadows, the murderous ghost haunting the dead of night. The settlers, as we well know, were quite adept at in-

---

31 Gilles Deleuze and Félix Guattari, *A Thousand Plateaus: Capitalism and Schizophrenia,* trans. Brian Massumi. (Minneapolis: University of Minnesota Press, 1987), 38.

32 Carla Freccero, "Wolf, or Homo Homini Lupus," in *Arts of Living on a Damaged Planet: Ghosts and Monsters of the Anthropocene,* eds. Anna Lowenhaupt Tsing et al. (Minneapolis: University of Minnesota Press, 2017), M91–M105.

33 Jon T. Coleman, *Vicious: Wolves and Men in America* (New Haven: Yale University Press, 2004), 9.

34 Ibid.

venting the enemies they wanted to kill, making animals out of men, making monsters out of animals.

Let us talk about how the wolves were chased down and killed, which is a different kind of bloodlust, yet fueled in a way by testosterone spread in the bodies of men, in the spread of man through settler-colonial expansion. "The last wolves did not die brokenhearted, longing for open fields and meaty prey. They died afraid, biting at steel contraptions or vomiting strychnine."[35] Strychnine is a chemical derived from the seeds of the trees *Strychnos nux-vomica* — a tree that produces "vomiting nuts" — or *Strychnos ignatii Bergius* — a tree that produces Saint Ignatius beans. Though it is mostly used as a poison today, it has a long history of experimentation dating back to the sixteenth century. According to Jeffrey S. Cannon and Larry E. Overman, pure strychnine was first isolated from the Saint Ignatius bean in 1818 and was touted for its supposed benefits in increasing appetite and memory, toning skeletal musculature, and working as an anti-venom to treat snakebites. Before its neurotoxic effects were fully understood, it was even used as a performance-enhancing drug for athletes. It has now come to be understood as a severe neurotoxin which overexcites the nerves, causing muscular convulsions that result in an inability to control respiration, leading to asphyxiation. In other words, its ingestion causes one to choke to death on one's own vomit or to suffocate in a convulsive state. Strychnine has become such a phenomenon in the molecular sciences that it still presents challenges for researchers to develop more efficient synthetic processing techniques. There are currently seventeen total synthesizing techniques that have been developed, yet scientists continue to work on more, seeking to minimize the steps to an ever more effective synthesis.[36] To what end, I am not entirely sure — to more expediently manufacture an instrument of chemical death?

35 Ibid., 213.

36 Jeffrey S. Cannon and Larry E. Overman, "Is There No End to the Total Synthesis of Strychnine? Lessons Learned in Strategy and Tactics in Total Synthesis," *Angewandte Chemie International Edition* 51, no. 18 (2012): 4288–311.

Because of its powerful toxic effects, strychnine became an easy solution to the invented wolf problem. With the domestication of stock, the slaughter of wolves on the plains and prairies reached its peak from 1875 to 1895. David L. Mech and Barry Holstun Lopez, among other historians, recount how men took advantage of the fact that wolves sometimes scavenge carrion and will even devour rotted and soured meat. Strychnine was purchased in huge quantities and used to lace chunks of meat or to dose small animal carcasses that were then strewn about the ranges where wolves were known to roam. As Lopez puts it, "ranch dogs died. Children died. Everything that ate meat died."[37] The campaign against an imagined and mostly unknown monster was ruthless and relentless, with no regard for the casualties left in its wake. And though strychnine and other forms of poison population control were outlawed in the United States in 1972, the method is still used on a limited basis in parts of Canada, particularly Alberta.[38] We have not stopped fighting the wolves with our toxic technologies and our wily traps and tricks.

But strychnine was never reserved for only wolves. In addition to its many experimental uses I name above, it has also notably been used to treat queerness. In 1899, a medical doctor by the name of Denslow Lewis speculated that lesbians suffered from "sexual hyperesthesia," or "excessive sensitivity to stimuli." According to Timothy F. Murphy, Lewis considered sexual hyperesthesia to be the result of girls who had too luxurious an upbringing. In other words, spoiled girls grew up to be lesbians. Lewis tried many cures for these sexual-hyperesthetic women, including cocaine solutions, clitoral surgeries, and, Murphy

---

37 Barry Holstun Lopez, *Of Wolves and Men* (New York: Charles Scribner's Sons, 1978), 180.

38 David L. Mech, *The Wolf: The Ecology and Behavior of an Endangered Species* (Garden City: The Natural History Press, 1970), 311; Bob Weber, "Alberta's Use of Poison as Wolf Control Criticized, Feds Asked to Review," *Global News*, December 18, 2020, https://globalnews.ca/news/7530444/alberta-wolf-control-strychnine-poison/.

writes, the administration of strychnine by hypodermic.[39] In *Madness,* sam sax writes of his grandfather's scouring of history in order to understand how to fix his grandson's queerness. sax lists the many attempts at cure: "hypnosis : group talk : cocaine : bladder washing : electroconvulsive/shock therapy : strychnine [...].''[40] Strychnine, a deadly poison masquerading as cure.

Same problem, same solution, it seems. Drug. Poison. Cure. Coleman writes, "they poison wolves with strychnine [...]. They set wolves on fire, kill them with dogs, and capture them alive only to release them with their mouths, or perhaps, their penises, wired shut."[41] sam sax continues, "strychnine : chemical & nonchemical castration."[42] Castration. An anecdote to the over stimulated and hyperaroused lesbian, strychnine functioned as a form of chemical castration. Wolves' penises were wired shut, arguably a type of castration. sax doesn't mention burning, but, like wolves and witches, queers have been burned. Queers and wolves have been poisoned, castrated, and killed. I think of killing wolves and curing queers with the same poison. I think of my regular administration by hypodermic of another substance, testosterone.

Testosterone, too, carries its own dirty colonial history. Rebecca M. Jordan-Young and Katrina Karkazis detail the history of endocrinology that would eventually lead to synthetic testosterone development. They describe the history of hormone discovery and later extraction through the self-experimentations of physiologist and neurologist Charles-Édouard Brown-Séquard who injected testicular extracts of guinea pigs and dogs, though not wolves, into his person. Later came laboratory manipulations of nonhuman animals such as roosters, bulls, and rats as well as experimentation on incarcerated men at San Quentin Prison in the Bay Area of Northern California. They trace the "science" behind those experiments to eugenicist and rac-

---

39 Timothy F. Murphy, "Brief History of a Recurring Nightmare," *The Gay & Lesbian Review,* January 1, 2008, https://glreview.org/article/article-42/.

40 sam sax, *Madness* (New York: Penguin Books, 2017), 57.

41 Coleman, *Vicious,* 3.

42 sax, *Madness,* 57.

ist ideologies that touted whiteness as superior in its models of exemplary hormonal balance, derivative of and contributive to the ongoing mythologies and racist fantasies of the violent Black man and the persistent dehumanization of people of color and incarcerated persons.[43] Like strychnine, testosterone has also been used as a performance-enhancing drug with a promise of beast-like strength. The history of testosterone is also a history of racism and colonial violence, making animals out of men, inventing monsters.

* * *

Back to the basement below the basement and the "Big Red Book": "at times of trauma where does a child run toward? Home. But where do you run when the trauma is within the home?" I recall a recent session with my therapist in which she impels me to feel through the details of a particular memory that marked me and schematized a core belief into the blueprint of my body. I am a child and my father is yelling at me, reminding me of what an "idiot" I am. What does it feel like in that memory, my therapist wants to know. I garner a mental image of one of the houses we lived in during my childhood, but it is hazy. The room is filled with cigarette smoke, and the lighting is a dimmed yellow-orange through the smog. I describe it as reminiscent of a "bad exposure" in a photograph. Still, it pricks. The murk and darkness are closing in on me, suffocating me. But this is home. So frightening, so uncanny. I want to run from the room. But instead of running from the monsters and ghosts, I stay to confront the trauma, to open the wounds, and to conjure the history in and through my body and my wounding. What would it mean to face my father in that memory?

My father, it should be obvious by now, is one of the many wolves in this story. We do not need to invite him to the table;

---

43 Rebecca M. Jordan-Young and Katrina Karkazis, *Testosterone: An Unauthorized Biography* (Cambridge: Harvard University Press, 2019).

he has already demanded his seat.[44] The wolf and the father have become interchangeable in Western European narrative. Writing of *The Woodsman,* an adaptation of perhaps one of the most famous folkloric stories involving a wolf, *Little Red Riding Hood,* Carla Freccero writes, "the father is already there in the place of the wolf, the wolf is already inside."[45] My father, the wolf, is already inside this story. He has been for years.

Additionally, alcohol and the wolf are not metaphorical strangers. Kaveh Akbar poetically paints the many portraits of the alcoholic in *Calling a Wolf a Wolf,* hoping to dull its fangs through naming.[46] But he does not succeed in dulling its fangs, and he is not actually calling a wolf a wolf. He is deploying, again, the wolf as metaphor and metonymy for the thing he cannot name directly. He calls it so many names, except for the one it is: addiction. Addiction to substance, to alcohol. Alcohol, a toxin that must be metabolized out of the body, largely by the liver, one of the body's most effective detoxifying organs. Too much alcohol over time can lead to liver failure, as well as a host of other health problems. Too much alcohol in one sitting can lead to alcohol poisoning. Alcohol is essentially a poison, relatively safe in small doses but otherwise deadly. Akbar's wolf-as-alcohol-addiction is an apt metaphor considering it was poison that predominantly destroyed the wolf population in the Americas. The wolves were killed because it was not so simple to merely dull their fangs. Their fangs instead became sharper and sharper in our figurative imagination.

There through the haze, my father bares his fangs, the acrid stench of alcohol on his tongue and in the hiss of his breath. There through the haze lands the sting of his words and the sting of his hand. There through the haze, the needle pierces, a singular fang gouging my thigh. There through the haze, I am be-

---

44 I am riffing here on Augusten Burroughs's account of life with his abusive, alcoholic father in his memoir *A Wolf at the Table: A Memoir of My Father* (New York: Picador, 2008).

45 Freccero, "Wolf, or Homo Homini Lupus," M99.

46 Kaveh Akbar, *Calling a Wolf a Wolf* (Farmington: Alice James Books, 2017).

coming everything I fear. There through the haze, I swallow and choke, I vomit and convulse. So much pain. So much anger. Susan Stryker writes how, like the monster, she harbors rage, "rage colors me as it presses in through the pores of my skin, soaking in until it becomes the blood that courses through my beating heart."[47] Blood. A broiling. Blood roils with anger. It spills and soaks. *Bloodlust*. I am monster. I am monster animal. My heart beating a pulse of sadness, anger, grief, rage. Back. Forth. Mourn. Rage. Yowl. Howl. Like a wolf.

* * *

I am angry that so many wolves are dead. I am angry that the wolves died in fear in the throes of strychnine poisoning and that lesbians were dosed with strychnine to try to poison the queer out of them. I am angry that nonhuman animals and certain humans — people of color, the incarcerated, queers, the disabled — have been deemed subjects of experimentation for centuries to develop drugs and poisons and an array of other products. With each injection of substance, that history returns. All history returns and in its return memory. All trauma returns and in its return pain. With each memory, more pain. With more pain, more want. Endless want.

Let us not forget, wolves tend to move in packs. The figure of the lone wolf is a fantasy, a mythic legend of monstrous proportions. Which is another way of saying that the ghosts are many. I imagine there is a ghost, or several, in every wound. I wonder then if a ghost is also at the center of our addictions, right along with the hurt. Imagine the wound as a slice or cut, each cut a ritual conjuration, where *ritual* is defined in part by its repetition as convention, as habit, as practice. The conjuration calls forth what appears to be otherwise absent. The weekly injection is a ceremonial piercing of flesh. The weekly meetings are a routine of reading and crying into a group of kin. A ritual of addic-

---

47 Stryker, "My Words to Victor Frankenstein above the Village of Chamounix", 249.

tion. An awful transform. A necessary transform. Cremins imagines Gaylord's transformation as a kind of transmogrification,
following Nikki Sullivan's description of transmogrification
as a "strange or grotesque transformation: [...] characterized
by distortion, exaggeration, extravagance, and, [...] unnatural
combinations."[48] In the grotesque, I am immediately drawn into
the gaped open mouth, its own kind of psychoanalytic wound. I
imagine the disembodied mouth Samuel Beckett cast to scream,
"not I, not I" into the darkness of the theater, the gaping mouth
never really the "I" of the self. Only, the mouth never actually
shouts, "not I." The mouth merely screams, "aaaaahh!," "what?
Who? No! She! [...] What? Who? No! He!"[49] She? He? Who? I?
Not I. Not I. Not I.

There is nothing but a mouth, a grotesque opening, a fanged
fissure. Here, here it gapes. Mikhail Bakhtin wrote that the
mouth was the most important of all the human features for
shaping the grotesque. "The grotesque face is actually reduced
to the gaping mouth; the other features are only a frame en-
casing this wide-open bodily abyss. [...] Moreover, the body
swallows the world and is itself swallowed by the world."[50] The
mouth a hole in the whole of the body, an abyss wrapped in flesh
and bone. Lips pursed. Lips parted. Gaping, swallowing, being
swallowed, the pulse of the throat — how awful; how monstrous.
What monsters am I? I. Not I. What monsters have I been?[51] I.
Not I. What monsters am I becoming?

I think of Susan Stryker's declaration, "I want to lay claim
to the dark power of my monstrous identity without using it as
a weapon against others or being wounded by it myself."[52] But
I think sometimes we cannot help but be wounded, and per-

48 Cremins, "Bodies, Transfigurations, and Bloodlust," 306.

49 Samuel Beckett, *Not I* (London: Faber, 1973).

50 Mikhail Bakhtin, *Rabelais and His World,* trans. Helene Iswolsky (Cam-
    bridge: MIT Press, 1968), 317.

51 The question, "What monsters have I been?," is a nod to Kenji C. Liu,
    Monsters I Have Been (Farmington: Alice James Books, 2019).

52 Stryker, "My Words to Victor Frankenstein above the Village of Chamou-
    nix," 246.

haps wound, in order to lay those claims, in order to get those histories back and to transform and rebuild our bodies. Some have considered these types of inflictions on the self an affliction marked by self-mutilation, rather than an act of transformation. Sullivan explains that self-mutilation is often thought by psychologists to be symptomatic of a history of abuse that results in mental health problems or self-loathing. Sullivan notes that self-mutilating practices are also associated with drug addiction and other types of general criminality.[53] Reflecting on the slide between, in both description and prescription/treatment of, addiction, queerness, and crime, I spin the popular rallying cry, "be gay, do crime" into "do trans, be crime."

Criminal. Addict. Monster. Animal. Human. The borders between those terms are fictive and porous. Categories without discrete edges. They bleed into one another in the collective imagination. Importantly, Sullivan reminds us that most people think about their bodily modifications as ways to adjust the body into a more livable, survivable home. Hardly a mutilation. Sullivan even wants to break down the dichotomy between "good" and "bad" body modification. But I wonder if it ever is really good or bad. Maybe it just is. Suffering. Changing. Surviving. So what if I am mutilating my body, as I transform my gender and sex? So what if I make myself monstrous? And what if my mutilation is rooted in a history of abuse? Trauma leaves many types of marks on the body, sometimes we must reopen those wounds ourselves in order to move forward.

Cut open the sutures. Let us gape in all our monstrosity. To be monstrous is to be both extraordinary and evil. To be both hideous and beautiful. Stryker, again, "you are as constructed as me […]. I call upon you to investigate your nature as I have been compelled to confront mine. I challenge you to risk abjection and flourish as well as have I. Heed my words, and you

---

53 Nikki Sullivan, "Transmogrification: (Un)Becoming Other(s)," in *The Transgender Studies Reader*, eds. Susan Stryker and Stephen Whittle (New York: Routledge. 2006), 552–64.

may well discover the seams and sutures in yourself."[54] This is another way of saying that we are all pieced together. The human form is one of mixity. As Scott F. Gilbert writes, noting that roughly only half of the cells in the human body contain a human genome, we are holobionts by birth, or, "we are not *anatomically* individual at all."[55] We are a composition of microorganisms — mixed and monstrous molecules pieced together to create the illusion of a whole. We are all constructed. We hurt because we are wounded. We both ache and inflict pain on ourselves and others. We all have our marks. We all have our addictions. We are seams and sutures. We are the walking wounded. We are monsters, all. But some of us are imagined to be more monstrous, made into monsters to be hunted, poisoned and burned, chased down by monsters too cowardly to confront their own monstrosity or their own bloodlust. We are monsters, all. But monsters, too, are as variable as the people inside them. Investigate that nature. Discover your own seams and sutures.

----

54 Stryker, "My Words to Victor Frankenstein above the Village of Chamounix," 247.
55 Scott F. Gilbert, "Holobiont by Birth: Multilineage Individuals as the Concretion of Cooperative Processes," in *Arts of Living on a Damaged Planet,* eds. Lowenhaupt Tsing et al., M75.

5

What Testosterone Can Do

Is it even possible to separate out what T can do from what people want it to do?

— Rebecca M. Jordan-Young and Katrina Karkazis, *Testosterone: An Unauthorized Biography*[1]

As you practice building a home in yourself, you become more and more beautiful.

— Thich Nhat Hanh, *How to Love*[2]

Testosterone is slow. Suspended in cottonseed or sometimes sesame oil, it is viscous, thick and slow-moving. Before drawing the drug into the needle, one must warm the bottle in the hands to loosen up the molecules for a more rapid uptake and injection. Then the draw must be done with a larger gauge needle that can handle its viscosity. The needle is then swapped for a thinner needle in order to reduce pain as the needle punctures the skin and enters the muscle tissue. With the syringe jutting out of my thigh, I depress the plunger, and slowly the thick liquid makes its way through into my muscle, each cc a small, slow trickle into my body. Once the hormone enters my body, it will move into

---

1   Rebecca M. Jordan-Young and Katrina Karkazis, *Testosterone: An Unauthorized Biography* (Cambridge: Harvard University Press, 2019), 5.
2   Thich Nhat Hanh, *How to Love* (Berkeley: Parallax Press, 2014), 23.

my bloodstream and and flit about my organs. My body will receive the chemical messages of the hormone. With this chemical information, my cells will grow and change slowly over time, reassembling themselves and reassembling me.

But one day, I will look down at my body or glimpse my face in a mirror, and it will all feel so sudden. I will have hair where once there was none. The cut of my jawline will seem so abrupt. In reality, those follicles had been forming little by little with each drip of testosterone into my endocrine system, and the muscles and bone structure of my face shift microscopically day-by-day. This is what testosterone can do. This is what testosterone does in the home of my body. As Jules Gill-Peterson asserts, the testosterone molecule can do so much, and it has many homes: in the flesh of the human body, in the healthcare system as a regulated medicine, and in our waterways where it has entered through our sewage system and where it becomes an environmental toxin that will accumulate in plants, nonhuman animals, and humans alike.[3] With each puncture of my flesh and each slow plunge of the needle, I become the artisan as I slowly reshape the home of my body. I willingly participate in the medical regulatory system. I no doubt flush traces of the hormone — the bits my body does not synthesize and rather expels — into the environment where it will enter and accumulate in other bodies. I take and destroy. I am taken and destroyed.

* * *

In the opening to their "unauthorized" biography of testosterone, Rebecca M. Jordan-Young and Katrina Karkazis write about an episode of *This American Life* in which host Ira Glass and producer Alex Blumberg, along with several other people in the NPR office, talk about testosterone's socio-cultural significance and what the levels of T in their bodies might mean.

---

3   Jules Gill-Peterson, "The Technical Capacities of the Body: Assembling Race, Technology, and Transgender," *Transgender Studies Quarterly* 1, no. 3 (2014): 403.

As I read Jordan-Young and Karkazis's analysis of the social mystique of testosterone via this episode, I get stuck on a quote they highlight from Blumberg: "my testosterone, and how it affects me, and how I react to it, I think about on a daily basis all the time."[4] I am of course a bit surprised to learn of a cisgender man's preoccupation with the testosterone his body produces and his worry, as he elaborates further in the episode, about heeding its call toward a toxic masculinity. But I am more fixated on the first two words he utters, "my testosterone." That possessive pronoun, laying claim to the testosterone in his body as his is what strikes me. He possesses his testosterone, but to what extent does it also possess him?

My body also produces some of its own testosterone, and I supplement that production with weekly injections. In all my worry and talk and writing about testosterone, I've never once thought to call the testosterone that courses through my body, produced or injected, my testosterone. What might it mean to feel so entitled to testosterone, so connected to it that it becomes mine? Why does it still retain, in my psyche, the place of a foreign object that I am introducing into my body, not mine, even as my body synthesizes it and responds to it, taking it up into my bloodstream and cellular structure? Will testosterone ever become mine?

Even in my hesitancy to lay claim to the testosterone that takes up space in my body, making its home there as I simultaneously utilize it to (re)build my own home, I am reminded of how medical technologies have become the tools and materials of this craft that is the building of a home in my body, piecing together the fractures of the whole, which remove and accumulate, make and break. Testosterone can do a lot of things; not all of them are things I want it to do. We do not get to pick and choose the side effects of a drug. I do more than put the substance into my body and wait for various kinds of growth. I also remove parts of my body, have flesh cut away and cast off. I also add to my body prosthetics that phantasmatically become of my

---

4 Jordan-Young and Karkazis, *Testosterone,* 2.

flesh. Building can also require taking away. I am building this home in pieces of flesh removed here or there, added here or there — a body, a home of myself. Always becoming more and more. Beautiful.

* * *

A rather general and plain observation is that we are always losing pieces of our body. Does this mean we are also losing pieces of our selves? Remember the hair left at the bus station or in our lovers' beds. Recall Claudia Rankine: "and despite everything the body remains."[5] The "body remains" becomes the body's remains, the pieces left behind with our leaving and with our becoming. On a molecular level, we are always losing pieces of our bodies as we exhale or drip or shed fluids, skin cells, nails, and hair into the world and onto/into each other. But there are many different ways to come apart. "Let's face it. We're undone by each other," Judith Butler writes in *Undoing Gender*, "and if we're not, we're missing something. [...] One does not always stay intact. It may be that one wants to, or does, but it may also be that despite one's best efforts, one is undone, in the face of the other, by the touch, by the scent, by the feel, by the prospect of the touch, by the memory of the feel."[6] Butler is writing of the ways in which our relations with each other undo us, moving gender and sexuality away from things we possess into ways we are dispossessed in our being for another. We might notice this most in moments of desire but also in moments of grief. Sometimes I cannot tell the difference between the two. A heart swells and the same heart breaks. We are always undoing each other, which is another way of saying that maybe we were always in pieces.

We lose pieces of ourselves, psychic and physical, in tears and wails, in laughter and song, and in the shedding of hair or skin cells. What do we lose when we remove pieces of the body,

---

5   Claudia Rankine, *Citizen: An American Lyric* (Minneapolis: Graywolf Press, 2014), 69.

6   Judith Butler, *Undoing Gender* (New York: Routledge, 2004), 19.

and what more might we gain? In *The Wounded Body,* Dennis Patrick Slattery recounts an evening before he is to undergo hip replacement surgery. A nun comes to pray with him and over him. She asks him if he wants to speak to the bones in his hip that will be removed during the surgery. With some coaxing, he begins to speak to his bones and soon finds himself weeping at the anticipated loss of them. He notes the longstanding traditions across religions to pray over bones. He ponders this practice and speculates on the soul's connection to the body, "perhaps something of our own soul is permanently in our body, in each of its parts. To lose something of ourselves is to lose something of psyche, even of a memory that is embedded deep in every organ."[7] As I read, I press my hand to my chest. Beneath my shirt are those two arcing scars where my breasts used to be.

Several years ago, I received a diagnosis of "Gender Identity Disorder," now reclassified as "Gender Dysphoria," so I could access the surgery that would involve the removal of my breast tissue and the reconstruction of my nipples to more closely reflect a typical "male" chest. Having never had a major surgery before, I was filled with fear and anxiety the night before the surgery. There was no one to pray with me or over my body, but I sent some little prayers of my own into the heavens, small wishes that I would wake after the procedure free of complications, free of breasts, free of regrets. When all was said and done, I did not for a moment mourn the loss of my breast tissue. Never did I grieve it or even think to weep over the tissue to be excised from my chest.

Audre Lorde, who wrote in her journals of the loss of her breast due to the growth of cancer, had a very different relationship with her breasts than I had with mine. And breast cancer came to threaten her life in a way I do not know firsthand. But the way she writes of loss still gives me pause: "any amputation is a physical and psychic reality that must be integrated into a new sense of self. The absence of my breast is a recurrent sad-

---

7   Dennis Patrick Slattery, *The Wounded Body: Remembering the Markings of the Flesh* (Albany: State University of New York Press, 2000), 5

ness, but certainly not one that dominates my life."[8] After years
of fantasizing about cutting my own flesh and pulling away the
tissue, I was eager to finally have my own breasts gone. And it
is true that this loss brought about a new physical and psychic
reality for me, one that I am still learning to integrate into my
sense of self, a learning process that sometimes feels like it does
dominate my life. I have not since experienced the absence of
my breasts as a sadness, though it is undoubtedly colored by a
melancholic tinge. If I am mourning, I no longer recall what the
object of mourning is exactly. And I wonder now which other
parts of myself were carried away that morning on the operating
table. Which bits of my being were stored in the tissue that were
subsequently packed into a biohazard container and sent off to a
pathology lab before they were disposed of as hazardous waste?
Where have those bits of me gone? Still, even in raising these
questions, I refuse to linger on the loss. On the contrary, I had
always thought where I lost flesh, I gained much more in those
wounds. I gained a new sense of self.

So many elements of gender transition are imagined in the
valence of loss. Whether physical or social, there is much discussion of what is lost in transition — flesh, family, community, lovers, friends, or social privilege. No doubt, some of these
things lost can also be imagined as things gained: new chosen
family, newfound community and friends, and, perhaps even
some privilege if one's transition moves toward social legibility
as a man. And if transition entails growth of new tissue, that
might also be considered a gain of flesh. But when flesh is removed from the body, the preoccupation is often with loss.

In August 2006, *The New York Times* published a feature story on transgender men, following the ways in which transition
abrades the ideals and sensibilities of lesbianism, such that for
these men, their relationships are the cost of their transition.
In giving up their breasts, they also lost their relationships with
their lesbian partners. With so much lost, it is unclear what, if

---

8   Audre Lorde, *The Cancer Journals* (San Francisco: Aunt Lute Books, 1980),
     16.

anything, is gained. The article is also accompanied by a few photos, one of them is of Shane Caya, standing shirtless, smiling slightly as he looks somewhere outside the frame of the camera. The caption to the photo reads, "Shane Caya displays his mastectomy scars."[9]

Gayle Salamon is critical of what she perceives to be a preoccupation with loss in the article. Analyzing the photo and its caption, Salamon writes against the fixation on Shane's scars. Instead of highlighting his masculinity, Salamon argues that the caption focuses on "a violence done to femininity in order to achieve that masculinity. The caption sees missing breasts, rather than a male chest."[10] It seems Salamon would prefer a caption that reads, "Shane Caya displays his chest." For Salamon, the scars can only convey loss and absence, the missing breasts that stand in for the loss of femininity, violently traded for masculinity. Furthermore, Salamon writes, "insisting that this is a picture of Shane's *scars* rather than Shane's pecs offers his chest as 'the horror of nothing to see.'"[11] Such logic requires us to think of scars as nothing but the signifier of the lost breasts. But there is plenty more to see here in the scars.

I must pause here in order to note the ways in which the display of Shane's scars might also echo the body on display in the freak show, where the body is made a spectacle to consume in curiosity. Shane displays his scars for the curious, cisgender viewer who consumes the otherness of the marked and scarred trans/formed body. (Transmogrified? How monstrous those scars, still a horror.) But what would it mean to reclaim the marks and scars of transformation and transition in this moment? We do, in fact, see the scar in the photograph. It is more than a mere "tell" of gender. Scars mark the seal of the wound and all that lies beneath it and within it. They hold so

---

9 Paul Vitello, "The Trouble When Jane Becomes Jack," *The New York Times,* August 20, 2006, https://www.nytimes.com/2006/08/20/fashion/20gender. html.

10 Gayle Salamon, *Assuming a Body: Transgender and the Rhetorics of Materiality* (New York: Columbia University Press, 2010), 111.

11 Ibid., 12.

much — a violence sometimes, yes, but also healing and change and growth. Or, as Sara Ahmed writes, it is time we "rethink our relation to scars," where "a good scar is one that sticks out, [...] a good scar allows healing, it even covers over, *but the covering always exposes the injury, reminding us of how it shapes the body.*"[12] I want to reach out and touch Shane's scars, as if to unite a pulse between us. As if, like in my dream as I fall asleep with Ely Shipley's poetry, I might press our scars together, a way to share in a particular kind of becoming through the wound, a reminder of the shape of a body. Again, my hand slides beneath my shirt to my own chest where I feel the lightly raised ridges of tissue, a real presence on my body, definitely something, hardly nothing — not a reminder of an absence or a loss but a touchpoint of a body remade and in the making.

* * *

Other trans studies scholars have also considered the mark of the cut or the cut itself to be one full of presence and possibility rather than a loss or record of absence. In their movement between the embodiment and enfleshment of the amputee and the transsexual, Nikki Sullivan and Susan Stryker imagine a phenomenological and ontological inversion of what has come to be thought of as an act of negation or disablement, such as amputation or castration, into an opening up of spaces of possibility. Similarly, in her meditations between the starfish and the transsexual body, Eva Hayward explores how the cut might be generative and may function in healing. For Hayward, whose speculations are mostly focused on the cut of the penis in the formation of the transsexual body, the cut is "not necessarily about castration, but an attempt to recast the self through the cut body."[13] Hayward imagines the cut, or in this case the

---

12 Sara Ahmed, *The Cultural Politics of Emotion* (New York: Routledge, 2004), 201–2, emphasis in original.

13 Susan Stryker and Nikki Sullivan, "King's Member, Queen's Body: Transsexual Surgery, Self-Demand Amputation and the Somatechnics of Sovereign Power," in *Somatechnics: Queering the Technologisation of Bodies,* eds.

scar, not as something that is curative or as that which makes us whole, but as something that offers up a more complex, layered experience of living in a body folded and scarred. If there is not necessarily a regeneration from the cut, like the arm of the starfish that grows back when severed, something is still generated from the cut and its scarring. And it is in that very scarring that I search for the generation of the beautiful, the love story; not in reshaping the body toward some imagined ideal but in the growing into and becoming of body, always marked and wounded, always in the process of making and remaking, and always pieced together.

A psychoanalytic detour, an appendage:

Sometimes the cut is about castration. Castration as desire. Castration as punishment. Castration as violence. Castration as craft. Who is doing the cutting and why? That matters. The body matters. I have a memory of reading Judith Butler's Bodies That Matter when I was a graduate student. In my memory, Butler suggests in the chapter on the "lesbian phallus" that the prosthetic, in other words, the dildo, becomes a part of the lesbian body through a process of phantasmatic identification. The dildo stands in for the penis, which stands in for the phallus, to have and to be, to have and to lose.

I revisit Butler, and I trace the genealogy of their thinking to Freud's introduction to narcissism. Freud describes the capability of any body part to send "sexually exciting stimuli to the mind" as "erotogenicity," which thus suggests that other body

Nikki Sullivan and Samantha Murray (London: Routledge, 2016), 55–67; Eva Hayward, "More Lessons from a Starfish: Prefixial Flesh and Transspeciated Selves," *Women's Studies Quarterly* 36, nos. 3–4 (Fall/Winter 2008), 71–72.

parts might stand in for the genitals and function as eroto-genic zones, or genital analogs. He then declares that such erotogenic potential might be considered a "general charac-teristic of all organs."[14] Butler takes up Freud's theory of the potential erotogenicity of all organs and concludes that "to be a property of all organs is to be a property necessary to no organ, a property defined by its very *plasticity, transferability,* and *expropriability*."[15] If any organ can more or less be an ero-togenic zone, then erotogenic sensation is not necessarily an inherent property of any organ; the erotogenic moves through the body. It is plastic—or silicone—and transferable.

Moving from Freud to Lacan, Butler builds from the Lacanian mirror phase: "if the body is 'in pieces' before the mirror, it follows that the mirroring works as a kind of synechdochal extrapolation by which those pieces or parts come to stand (in and by the mirror) for the whole; or, put differently, the part substitutes for the whole and thereby becomes a token for the whole."[16] Put another way, our pieces or our parts be-come symbolic representatives of our wholes and our holes. Though those we leave our parts with may never again ex-perience our wholeness, they may hold onto the symbol of the possibility of our wholeness. The phallus is not the penis, though the penis often symbolically stands in for the phallus. But the erotogenic is movable, transferable, plastic, and dis-placeable. The phallus, too, is displaceable, which means that its symbolic referent exceeds or is other than the penis. Butler writes, "consider that 'having' the phallus can be symbolized by an arm, a tongue, a hand (or two), a knee, a thigh, a pel-

14 Sigmund Freud, "On Narcissism," in *The Standard Edition of the Complete Psychological Works of Sigmund Freud,* Vol. 14: *On the History of the Psycho-Analytic Movement, Papers on Meta-psychology and Other Works (1914–1916),* trans. James Strachey with Anna Freud (London: Hogarth Press, 1964), 84.

15 Judith Butler, *Bodies That Matter: On the Discursive Limits of Sex* (New York: Routledge, 1993), 61.

16 Ibid., 80.

vic bone, an array of purposefully instrumentalized body-like things."[17] I think of other body-like things—a prosthetic limb, a titanium joint, a silicone cock—they all have their instrumental purpose.

I have pieced my body together through the use of silicone prosthetics, purposefully instrumentalized to be body-like, to be my body. I have a soft packer that I sometimes wear, and I have an array of silicone dicks for fucking. I had one favorite cock, of the strapless variety, in a peachy color that approximates my skin tone as closely as such a thing can. This particular design has a bulbous end that I insert into myself and hold in place with my pelvic floor muscles, as the phallic, penis-shaped end extends from my body, its closeness to my flesh allowing for that transferability, plasticity, and erotogenicity. This prosthetic piece comes to symbolize a kind of whole of my sex, filling my hole to create this wholeness. I have instrumentalized this body-like thing, taken it into and of my body, a phantasmatic identification.

Because I was traveling across the continent so frequently to be with L, I decided to leave this piece of me with her. Doing so spared me the potential embarrassment in the TSA line, and, at that point in time, I only really needed it when I was with her. After our relationship ended, L refused to return my cock, leaving my request for it unanswered in her ghosting. I consulted a couple friends about whether or not I should pursue the recovery of my cock or just let it go. One friend, appalled by L's behavior, insisted that in keeping my cock, especially after I asked for it back, L had broken every queer ethical code that any queer should know to abide by. It's simple queer ethics, my friend said. Another friend described what L did as a "potential act of transphobic violence." It feels like an unwilled castration. I do, in fact, feel violently cut.

---

17 Ibid., 88.

I tell another friend how I have started to imagine my cock out there doing things and, well, more likely, doing people, without me. I recall a movie I loved as a child, called *The Hand.* The film, featuring Michael Caine as Jon, tells the story of a man who loses his right hand in a car accident. He and his wife search everywhere for the amputated hand but cannot recover it at the scene. His hand later takes on a life of its own and exacts murderous revenge on various people throughout the film.

Notably, the car accident in which Jon loses his hand follows the movie's opening scene when his young daughter prods a severed lizard tail with a stick. As she moves the stick closer to the tail, the tail twitches. She asks her father how the tail, without being attached to a body with a head and a brain, "knows" of her approaching stick. He responds by telling her the twitch is just a reflex of the nervous system, but she insists that the tail knows. Uncannily, when Jon's daughter later asks him what happened to his hand after the accident, he tells her it ran away, granting the hand an agency not too unlike the epistemological agency his daughter granted the lizard's tail.

The horror of the film is that his hand does seem to be out there committing murderous atrocities without him, as his psyche spirals further and further into darkness and paranoia. Or is it? The hand knows. Or does it? The film ends with Jon strapped to an exam chair while an analyst tries to get him to take responsibility for the actions he has pinned on the hand. He tries to warn her that the hand is near her neck and wants to kill her. She of course doesn't believe him, and we then watch the disembodied hand strangle her to death. But the analyst had earlier released the straps around Jon's right arm, the one that is missing a hand. After her death, he laughs as he releases his other arm and stands. We are left to wonder whether we have just glimpsed Jon's imagination of yet another murder he has actually committed or if we have witnessed the actual murder carried out by the disembodied hand.[18]

Freud writes in his essay on the uncanny of how dismembered limbs or body parts—he particularly names "a hand cut off at the wrist"—have something "peculiarly uncanny about them" especially when "they prove able to move of themselves."[19] We are drawn to the uncanny because it evokes the familiar, sometimes long repressed. It is both the thing we fear and the thing we know so well, it feels like home. The uncanny is exactly what horror writers play on. I don't remember what my specific attachments were to this film as a child, but I remember wanting to believe in Jon's innocence and in the possibility that the loose and wandering hand was the actual culprit. As I recall the film now, I am unsettled at the thought of my own phantom appendage living on and fucking and haunting me in all its exploits. How terribly and peculiarly uncanny, in a true Freudian sense.

How terribly and easily we take each other apart. We take each other in parts. How easily we undo each other. I found myself recently repeating this idea to myself—that we undo each other—as I thought of the ways in which I have felt literally undone, or pulled into pieces, by L's kidnapping of my cock. What a horrific sadness the things we are capable of doing to those we love and stop loving, hearts and bodies rent, into parts and pieces. What a violence to keep a piece of someone they didn't want to give away. What a violence to keep us broken and fragmented and dreaming of a fantasy of a wholeness that will never be. And too, what a felicitous reminder of the pieces we always already are.

---

18 Oliver Stone, dir., *The Hand* (Warner Bros., 1981).

19 Sigmund Freud, "The 'Uncanny,'" in *The Standard Edition of the Complete Psychological Works of Sigmund Freud,* Vol. 17: *An Infantile Neurosis and Other Works (1917–1919),* ed. James Strachey with Anna Freud (London: Hogarth Press, 1955), 244.

Clarice Lispector's character G.H. declares that while writing and speaking, at least at first, she has to pretend someone is holding her hand, even though she cannot see beyond the hand to the body to the face with eyes and a mouth. Yet, she insists the amputated hand does not scare her. It is not a horror. Instead, she imagines that her invention of the hand arises from love. She cannot envisage the body to which it should be attached because, she thinks, she cannot love enough. "I cannot imagine a whole person because I am not a whole person."[20] She knows she is always already in pieces. She describes holding someone's hand as joy, imagining the embrace as a comfort lulling her into the unknown of sleep.

There is a comfort in holding onto the pieces. We must hold onto the pieces because we will never be or have the whole—not too unlike Lacan's positioning of the phallus. I wonder if, despite the violence of L's holding onto my appendage, there might be for her a comfort in grasping at the pieces or if I, too, might find comfort in that grasp. "I am so afraid that I can only accept that I got lost if I imagine someone is holding my hand," Lispector writes as G.H.[21] I am so afraid that I can only accept being incomplete if I imagine someone else is always taking me apart.

Let us return to the pieces that come together, a sutured whole, even if full of holes. If, for Hil Malatino, it is mixity, which may sometimes entail a suturing or piecing together, that makes the body monstrous, I also want to suggest that there is a beauty in those marks of monstrosity and in the stories that the scars hold.[22] Though, I also recognize that finding beauty in a cut

---

20 Clarice Lispector, *The Passion According to G.H.*, ed. Benjamin Moser, trans. Idra Novey (New York: New Directions Books, 2012), 10.

21 Ibid., 9.

22 Hil Malatino, *Queer Embodiment: Monstrosity, Medical Violence, and Intersex Experience* (Lincoln: University of Nebraska Press, 2019).

can be a privilege afforded when scarring is not the result and reminder of a nonconsensual surgery. Sometimes the work of finding beauty in a scar is also the work of finding life in and through trauma. And sometimes it is simply about being able to tell the story, a move toward healing. Hayward suggests that we create our embodiment by "taking up a fold in our bodies, by folding (or cutting) ourselves, and creating a transformative scar of ourselves."[23] My scars have transformed me, but I have also transformed them, making a scar of myself. The cut is generative as well as regenerative. The scars mark the places where my flesh was rent apart and sutured back together, a reminder of where one piece ends and another begins, a whole that is always composed of distinct parts. I think again of how Ely Shipley describes the two incisions on his chest as "each a naked stem, flaring with thorns."[24] I see the shape of these thorny stems in the scars on my own chest. From the stem grows new life in and on my body. I grow into my body. Where a lover touches tentatively, I describe the scar as the place where fear and absolution meet.

Tracing the new thin red line that runs down the side of his leg after his hip replacement surgery, Dennis Patrick Slattery writes, "the wound is the trace of the memory, what I have left of the experience; it also marks the place of what I would call deep memory, an indelible recollection that one feels always at the edge of the field of consciousness."[25] Indelible. Unremovable. Unforgettable. Permanent. The wound always remains. A storehouse. Deep memory returns. I cannot overlook Slattery's choice to call the new scar on his body a "wound." There is such a thin line between the scar (a presumed wound sutured and healed) and the wound (festering still, in need of suturing). My scars are what I have left of the experience. The experience of having once had breasts and of having had them removed.

23 Hayward, "More Lessons from a Starfish," 73.
24 Ely Shipley, *Boy with Flowers* (New York: Barrow Street Press, 2008), 9.
25 Slattery, *The Wounded Body*, 6.

To say that the scars are what we have left of an experience is to say that they have presence and substance. A scar is *something* present, *something* to have, and *something* to see. It demands its due. The scar is also a new experience, a new piece of the landscape of the body. Before I went for my top surgery, I was so nervous about the procedure and the uncertainty of what my body would look like and what shape and coloration the scars might take. I fretted over the accusations that such a procedure, what some have even deemed an "elective" surgery, is a kind of damage being done to an otherwise "healthy" and unscarred body. Was I marring my own body in my choice to remove "healthy" breast tissue and to house two new scars where there had previously been unmarked, intact flesh?

I remember sitting with *M* on a beautiful fall day on our campus as graduate students, and he listened patiently as I unloaded all these worries and got them off my chest, so to speak. I remember how he looked at me, his eyes always so full, as if his overflowing compassion would bring tears at any moment. He relayed how he shared some of those worries and at times had fixated on the imperfection of his chest, the way the flesh had puckered here or the way the scar extended there. And with that, he lifted his shirt and said, "but look, I have grown to love my scars, and I can show them to you here with that love. They have become a part of the landscape of my body." In all these efforts I have been detailing to reclaim my body, a part of that process has been in learning to love the scars that have become a part of me as they take shape on and through my body. My scars are reminders not only of the choices I have made for myself but also of what I have survived. Or as Ahmed puts it, a "good scar reminds us that recovering from injustice cannot be about covering over the injuries," and we need scars to serve as "signs of an unjust contact between our bodies and others."[26] There is no such thing, I have come to believe, as a body unmarked and seamlessly, naturally whole. All bodies are marked by contact.

---

26 Ahmed, *The Cultural Politics of Emotion,* 202.

They are landscapes pocked by indentations, holes, dimples, puckers, and ridges.

* * *

Susan Stryker writes of the trans body as "an unnatural body," "flesh torn apart and sewn together again in a shape other than that in which it was born."[27] Flesh torn apart. Flesh sewn together — sites where incisions become scars, where the body takes on new shape. This rending and rendering of the body, what Stryker calls a "monstrous benediction," is a blessing too, a kind of prayer.[28] As a monstrous one, it can be just as extraordinary as it may be frightening.

I imagine a monstrous benediction as a particular blessing on the trans body made of violence or violently made. Wounded and built of scar tissue, all the abject horror of what we see in the wounds and scars is a body built, a body becoming more and more beautiful. In Alice Notley's *Benediction,* every poem is a meditation on leaving the body and being in the body, a prayer toward flesh. "I now don't live in the body they know and approve," she writes.[29] I have whispered so many quiet prayers for the body met with disapproval, the troubling body, the body threatened by violence for being unknowable. In public restrooms, at rest stops, at the doctor's office, at the grocery store, on the street, in the park, and on the airplane, I am always reminded of my incongruence and how I don't live in the body they know and approve. "Incongruence," Lisa Jean Moore writes, "occurs when what others expect about the progressive logic of someone's body conflicts with the anticipated biography."[30] I no

---

27 Susan Stryker, "My Words to Victor Frankenstein above the Village of Chamounix: Performing Transgender Rage," in *The Transgender Studies Reader,* eds. Susan Stryker and Stephen Whittle (New York: Routledge. 2006), 245.

28 Ibid., 254.

29 Alice Notley, *Benediction* (Tucson: Letter Machine Editions, 2015), 186.

30 Lisa Jean Moore, "Incongruent Bodies: Teaching While Leaking," *Feminist Teacher* 17, no. 2 (2007): 96.

longer know how to anticipate my own biography or what others anticipate in me. My body has become so unexpected.

In the incongruence, in the monstrous benediction, I return to the place where fear and absolution meet. The scars hold the memory of fear if not fear itself; that is, the fear of becoming, of cutting, of being, of always becoming, and of never simply being. My prayers are love letters to my body that seek forgiveness and are always forgiving. Forgiving the touch of a lover, tentative or painful, as the touch of a lover forgives the body. This is the body that opens toward another, toward the self, and toward beauty. Slattery proclaims, "to be wounded is to be opened to the world; it is to be pushed off the straight, fixed, and predictable path of certainty and thrown into ambiguity, or onto the circuitous path, and into the unseen and unforeseen. One begins to wobble, to wander, and perhaps even to wonder not only about one's present condition but also about one's origins."[31] I think it is no accident that Slattery marks the wound as pushing us off the *straight* path. I think of queerness in relation to wounding: wounded, no longer straight but crooked, wobbly. Sara Ahmed describes queerness as that which is "off line" or "oblique"; queer bodies are those that make things seem "out of line," and queer orientations are "those that don't line up" and see the world "slantwise," like slanted scars with jagged edges.[32] An unforeseen path with each step of transition: Who am I? What am I becoming? Who will I be? Who was I?

To ask about my destination requires me to ask about my origin. Every departure is a new risk, always uncertain and wobbly, veering off, carving new paths, and opening again and again to the world. Ahmed elaborates, "even when orientations seem to be about which way we are facing in the present, they also point us toward the future. The hope of changing directions is that we don't always know where some paths may take us: risking departure from the straight and narrow makes new futures

---

31 Slattery, *The Wounded Body*, 13.
32 Sara Ahmed, *Queer Phenomenology: Orientations, Objects, Others* (Durham: Duke University Press, 2006).

possible, which might involve going astray, getting lost, or even becoming queer."[33] Or being wounded. Becoming scarred. Does becoming queer — veering from the straight path — necessitate some kind of wounding?

If we revise the scar as a presence or a mark of queerness rather than an absence, nothingness, or site of loss, then we must account for the ways in which scars mark our bodies as visibly wounded, or even invisibly wounded — let us not forget psychic scarring in the marks of trauma and its residual ghosts. Slattery writes, "our wounds name us and give the trajectory of our destiny. They identify and mark us. Our name, along with our wound, records us in the world. [...] If we can be recognized, then we can be wounded."[34] I once heard someone declare that naming is always a violence. To be named is to be recorded in the world is to be recognized is to be made available for wounding, subjectified and subjectivated. But I also wonder how misrecognition wounds. How the refusal or inability to see the scar or the refusal or inability to name and identify proper gender or to use one's correct name creates new scars and opens old wounds.

* * *

I recall sitting in a room full of colleagues discussing gender in transition. In this group of about fifteen people, about a third of us fall somewhere under what might be described as the transgender umbrella, and the rest are cisgender people of various queer and non-queer proclivities. Somebody mentions hormones, and one person in the group points to two transgender men in the room and invites all of us to scrutinize their bodies. "Look," this person says, "at what testosterone can do to a body." I am rage and sadness. I am compassion and pain. I am disturbed by the invitation to pick apart the flesh of these two people, to decipher what makes their bodies trans or what makes

---

33 Ibid., 21.
34 Slattery, *The Wounded Body*, 15.

their bodies the bodies of men. I feel like I am being invited into a home without the permission of the home's occupants. I look away. I look down at my own body, a collection of muscle and tissue, bone and blood, scars and wounds, and skin rent and stitched. I am simultaneously pained and relieved at the misrecognition of my own body, a body that I have been pumping low doses of testosterone into for two years. I am angry and saddened that my body is not recognizable as one that visibilizes what testosterone can do to a body. But I am also relieved not to be held up to that scrutiny and not to have the doors to my home blasted open.

Let's face it, in that moment, I am not quite sure if I am undone or redone. But I do know the moment feels like a violation. The etymological root of violation can be traced to the Latin *violationem,* which is a stem of *violāre,* meaning to treat with violence, outrage, or dishonor.[35] I am outraged at the violation, the breaching of the homes of the bodies of my peers, the misrecognition of my own body. Because this moment feels like a violation, it also feels violent. Jenny Sundén writes, "it seems to take a fair amount of violence to make materially specific bodies coincide with a particular gender."[36] I think Sundén means to account both for the cutting and stitching and folding of the body as a kind of violent reworking of the flesh and also for the psychic violence that occurs in the undoing of the body through gendering. If we can be recognized, we can be misrecognized. I think we can be wounded either way.

There can be violence in naming and misnaming. There is violence in seeing or not seeing the body for what it is. There is violence in technologizing the body, removing tissue, reshaping flesh and bone. There is violence in racialized medical histories, in the colonization of bodies picked apart and reshaped to advance medical technologies. There is violence in piecing the

---

35 *Online Etymology Dictionary,* s.v. "violation," https://www.etymonline.com/word/violation.

36 Jenny Sundén, "On Trans-, Glitch, and Gender as Machinery of Failure," *First Monday* 20, no. 4 (2015).

body together. Jasbir K. Puar refers to trans(normative) piecing as "a recruitment into neoliberal forms of fragmentation of the body for capitalist profit."[37] For Puar, the trans body that "pieces" represents "the commodification not of wholeness or of rehabilitation but of plasticity, crafting parts from wholes, bodies without and with new organs."[38] These pieces of medical technologies have become so marketable, each piece of the body a purchase, a piece taken from another whole. The body becomes a collection of holes and wholes, but never whole.

To be clear, piecing, for Puar, relies on an assumption that the trans body wants to be or ought to be transgressive. And it relies on an assumption that the trans subject depends upon legal and medical institutions to "realize themselves as trans in the first place," the very presumption I have been undoing in this writing of my own undoing.[39] "In the first place" is a beginning. Realization, both a start and an end, is to understand oneself as trans in the first place and to make real the body as a trans body in the last place. This is a unidirectional move from start to finish. Even as I do rely upon legal and medical institutions for access to surgery and hormones, they do not help me realize anything about or for myself. They lead me only into more questioning of who and what I am being and becoming as I meet with the difficulty or impossibility, even, of uttering the words, "I am trans." As if trans is a thing I ought *to be*. I just want to be me, I have said. I have never said, "I am trans." It is easier to declare, "I am a monster," it seems. I have yet to realize myself as trans in any sense. I am only realizing myself as a body wounded and sutured, being and becoming.

Ultimately, Puar reveals the trans body as hardly transgressive but as normatively embroiled in neoliberal market economies wherein the so-called transnormative subject "views the body as endlessly available for hormonal and surgical manipula-

---

37 Jasbir K. Puar, *The Right to Maim: Debility, Capacity, Disability* (Durham: Duke University, 2017), 36.

38 Ibid., 46.

39 Ibid., 36.

tion and becoming."[40] But my hormonal and surgical manipulation did nothing to move me into the transnormative category constructed by my colleague that day. I would be remiss if I did not note the ways in which the construction of transnormativity depends also upon presumptive whiteness in the medico-juridical constructions of the transgender body, the very structures that ostensibly make it possible for the trans subject to properly realize themselves as trans in the first place. Toby Beauchamp also notes the ways medical science normatively codes gender through race and class privilege, suggesting that even people of marginalized genders can approximate the norm by "clinging to ideals of whiteness and class status."[41] Another way to think about this is to mark the insidious ways settler colonial structures and ideologies persist in our internalizations of dominant cultural formations. Eve Tuck and C. Ree describe the endurance of settler colonialism as a haunted structure, a structure that is "an ongoing horror made invisible by its persistence — the snake in the flooded basement."[42] This is to say that idealized, white-settler masculinity, by which even the chemical synthesis of testosterone was historically measured, continues to haunt us in its own serpentine monstrosity.

A friend once told me about a seminar she attended in which the category of the "white man" in its ideal form was described as an aspirational one that nobody can actually attain. Idealized masculinity, then, is always already coded through a particular idealization of whiteness, and can only ever be approximated. Knowing this, I grapple with the particular racial dynamics in the room that day as a Black trans scholar invited us to scrutinize testosterone's impacts on the bodies of one Black subject and one white subject. What testosterone could do to a body seemed, for that moment, to be suspended in a deracialized ap-

---

40 Ibid., 42.

41 Toby Beauchamp, *Going Stealth: Transgender Politics and U.S. Surveillance Practices* (Durham: Duke University Press, 2019), 32.

42 Eve Tuck and C. Ree, "A Glossary of Haunting," in *Handbook of Autoethnography,* eds. Tony E. Adams, Stacy Holman Jones, and Carolyn Ellis (Walnut Creek: Left Coast Press, 2013), 642.

proximation of manhood. But the whiteness of that masculinity slithered beneath the surface of the skin. My colleague was looking for the ways in which testosterone could bring about an aspirational, transnormative masculinity that is already inherently encoded through whiteness. My colleague was asking us to look for a particular presentation of masculinity on those bodies that we had all already been ideologically inculcated and conditioned to look for. It was no longer a question of what I wanted from testosterone but what we wanted from it, in that chasm between what the molecule actually is and what we imagine it capable of doing. Gaping. Invisible. Pernicious. *Sssssss.*

Ultimately, within this internalized dominant framing, the hormonally and surgically manipulated pieces of the bodies of my two peers were held up for scrutiny while the pieces of my body went unnoticed, pieces that then were rendered into a whole perceptibly without need for rehabilitation, a body presumably fixed rather than plastic. At the same time, the pieces of my body are actually constantly transgressing normative categorization, even when I do not intend or desire to be transgressive. I am trying only to make my body habitable. I have never imagined that trans becoming necessitates an endpoint or an arrival at finally *being* trans. My colleagues became and *were* trans in that room that day in a way I did not and was not. Which is to say, trans piecing has always already been trans becoming, often without telos and often without recognition of what or who one is or might be.[43]

---

43 My insistence on conceptualizing "trans becoming" as always already a refusal of unidirectional teleology is a direct response to Puar's assertion that "trans becoming masquerades as a teleological movement, as if one could actually become trans," even as she suggests her concept of "becoming trans" opposes "trans becoming" by highlighting the impossibility of a linear telos, of permanence, or of an endpoint (Puar, *The Right to Maim,* 56). Not only does this inversion actually fail grammatically, but, as I write above, to imagine trans becoming as teleological is to rest transness already on normative assumptions about what it means to "realize oneself as trans in the first place" and what that means for a directionality of transition.

There is no promise of a definitive futurity in which to land once and for all. Nothing is ever finished, really. And the trans body is not exceptional in this unraveling of time's forward march to a promised arrival. In perhaps an oversimplification of Hegel's dialectic, I would venture to suggest that *all being is becoming*. Or, as Deleuze and Guattari suggest, *becoming* passes between past and future; it is a "block of coexistence," "outside any fixed order or determined sequence," like the machine, they say.[44] To follow Erin Manning's tracking of Daniel Stern's psychoanalytic theory of relation development, Manning imagines the skin as an endless porous topology: "there is no stable identity that emerges once and for all. Becoming-human is expressed singularly and repeatedly throughout a life."[45] The body's endless availability for endless becoming seems to be simply part of the human condition.

For, isn't it the case that any body is made endlessly available for surgical and hormonal manipulation? Hasn't the body always been plastic? As Sullivan writes, "all bodies mark and are marked; [...] entwined in (un)becoming rather than [...] simply mired in being."[46] Or, as Stryker and Sullivan compellingly argue together, all embodiment is conditioned by material integration, or in other words, "the integrity of the body — that is, the ability of the body *to be integrated* — is thus, paradoxically, dependent on its enfleshment as always already torn, rent, incomplete, and unwhole."[47] Aren't we all pieces integral to the semblance of a collective wholeness? Aren't we all normatively embroiled in neoliberal market economies and the violences of biocapital, some of us variably complicit, some of us persecuted

---

44 Georg W.F. Hegel, *The Phenomenology of Spirit,* trans. Terry Pinkard (Cambridge: Cambridge University Press, 2017); Gilles Deleuze and Félix Guattari, *A Thousand Plateaus: Capitalism and Schizophrenia,* trans. Brian Massumi (Minneapolis: University of Minnesota Press, 1987), 292, 347.

45 Erin Manning, "What If It Didn't All Begin and End with Containment? Toward a Leaky Sense of Self," *Body & Society* 15, no. 3 (2009): 36.

46 Nikki Sullivan, "Transmogrification: (Un)Becoming Other(s)," in *The Transgender Studies Reader,* ed. Stryker and Whittle, 561.

47 Stryker and Sullivan, "King's Member, Queen's Body," 64.

by those very machinations? Even at the atomic level, we are a sutured patchwork of pieces. "Materiality," Karen Barad writes, "in its entangled psychic and physical manifestations is always already a patchwork, a suturing of disparate parts."[48] We are all pieced together, a network of sutures and scars. And in this piecing, aren't we all always undone? Aren't we all topologies and topographies? Aren't we all geometries and geologies? Aren't we all mountains and valleys? Aren't we all becoming into and away from our own being?

* * *

To be sure, the bioavailability of *any* body in various systems of piecing is not meant to let my own complicity in the medical-industrial complex off the hook. Of course, I must face the complex ways in which my testosterone use — my literal incorporation of the fruits of history's violence — implicates me in systems of racism, and colonialism. Recall testosterone's history of animal and human experimentation.[49] With each dose of testosterone, Paul Preciado confesses he is killing the blue whale, the bull, and the prisoner sentenced to death in his desires for some shape of masculinity in its administration: "I draft a contract whereby my desire is fed by — and retroactively feeds — global channels that transform living cells into capital."[50] There is money in the making of men. Masculinity is something I both fear and desire. Despite my fear, I invest my desires in hormone injections and surgical interventions. I transform my living cells. I entangle myself in this business of making and becoming men and monsters.

---

48 Karen Barad, "Transmaterialities: Trans*/Matter/Realities and Queer Political Imaginings," GLQ: A Journal of Gay and Lesbian Studies 21, nos. 2–3 (2015): 393.

49 See Jordan-Young and Karkazis, *Testosterone*; and Paul Preciado, *Testo Junkie: Sex, Drugs, and Biopolitics in the Pharmacopornographic Era,* trans. Bruce Benderson (New York: The Feminist Press, 2013).

50 Preciado, *Testo Junkie,* 163.

These gruesome histories and technological developments make possible the small vials of testosterone I purchase every few months. Jaime Shearn Coan writes of "extending / thin metal into thigh" as a way to let the "divine slide in."[51] In the poetics statement that accompanies the poem, Coan welcomes the "presence of our ghosts (including our former selves); to call attention to how they blend and bend our bodies in new directions."[52] I read Coan's promise of the divine as that invitation to our ghosts. Eli Clare thinks of testosterone as "honey and light, the smell of sugar pine, infusing [him]."[53] Clare recognizes the metaphor as his attempt to escape the medical-industrial complex as he comes to terms with the incongruence of sweet honey and the reality of the drug: "I wasn't injecting honey and light into me but rather a chemical compound, contributing to the profits of Sun Pharmaceutical Industries. I was stepping through the door held open by the promises of cure."[54] The drug does promise a cure of sorts, a response to a diagnosis of gender dysphoria, a way to reshape a body into a more habitable home. But this is not a home of pure divine light where birds flit and honey drips. It is haunted. There is a cost and a profit gained in a body gained for bodies and pieces lost.

I hold the vial up to the light. The yellow substance is not honey but is largely composed of cottonseed oil. Cotton. So many bodies were enslaved and broken in the history of cotton cultivation and harvest, and so many were killed in the domestication of land and agriculture. I draw that history from the vial into the syringe, and I welcome the presence of ghosts. As I look at the yellow liquid, I see the abuse and violence, but I also see the so-called "promise of cure" in this chemical substance that elicits a transformation from my body, that blends with and

---

51 Jaime Shearn Coan, "forcing the hand," in *Troubling the Line,* eds. TC Tolbert and Trace Peterson (Brooklyn: Nightboat Books, 2013), 262.

52 Jaime Shearn Coan, "Poetics Statement," in *Troubling the Line: Trans and Genderqueer Poetry and Poetics,* eds. Tolbert and Peterson, 265.

53 Eli Clare, *Brilliant Imperfection: Grappling with Cure* (Durham: Duke University Press, 2017), 179.

54 Ibid.

bends my body in new directions, that makes my former self into a ghost. I see all that testosterone can do. My muscles take in all that is cruel and all that is divine. The wounds of history enter through a small prick in the skin, a tiny wound that expels just one drop of blood, a whole world in that globule. As I dab the red away, I pray. I ask for forgiveness in how and what I am becoming.

* * *

Prayers for forgiveness but also prayers of gratitude. I am grateful that testosterone is available to me and that I have the privilege to access it legally and to inject it into my body myself, to become my own artisan. But next to those vials of testosterone in my drawer are also bottles of pills that I must take to manage physical illness. These pills similarly implicate me in the pharmaceutical industrial complex, and they make me complicit in the medical economies that have exchanged flesh and life for technology and cure. These industries that harm also help us keep our bodies from falling to pieces entirely. I do not know much about the manufacture of the pills I take, and I do not know what specific violences they bind me to each time I swallow them. But I know that I need them, and that the promise of treatment they offer may not be a cure, but they are life giving, even as they traffic in histories of pain and suffering. That suffering has every bearing on my living on.

From the violence, sometimes one finds life. The needle prick generates change in my body that makes life livable. To cut away flesh gives a new shape to my chest, one that pulls me upright in a way that makes it feel easier to keep breathing life into my lungs. Yes, the cutting and wounding can indeed be generative and healing. But so many wounds do not heal, and so many wounds are easily reopened. So many wounds continue to gape. I recall my phantasmatic identification with my cock and its subsequent castration. A line from an early Ani DiFranco song comes to mind: "my cunt is built like a wound that won't heal."[55] I used to hear this line and imagine the cunt as a wounded pleasure spot, impossible to heal in its relentless reopening, in all its constant fucking. It was a line that always brought a fantastic pleasure to my budding feminist consciousness, but it was never one I could fully relate to in my frequent periods of celibacy and asexuality.

But now, I do think of my cunt as a wound that won't heal, cut where my cock, taken from me, used to be. I think of how my mother was given an episiotomy during my birth, a cut through her vagina and perineum. How I came into the world through a literal cut and how I myself continue to be cut. My cunt, too, has actually been cut open by a surgeon. Testosterone causes the vaginal tissue to become hypoestrogenic. Without enough estrogen, it is rare but possible for the vagina to seal itself. There were other complicating factors, but this is partly what testosterone did to my body, or what my body did with testosterone.

It was through this process that I learned terms like "lysis," which essentially means "a destruction." My surgical order read, "lysis of adhesions." With a scalpel and cauterizer, my surgeon destroyed the adhesions that had formed in my body that bound together tissue where it should not be bound. I learned the difference between a procedure that ends in "ectomy" in which tissue or organs are surgically removed and one that ends in "otomy," which entails a mere cut without necessarily removing anything. In my procedure, the cut both removed or destroyed something (an adhesion) and created something (an opening). The surgeon's cut was a restorative one, but it has also actually made my cunt into a wound that won't heal, producing a new site of chronic pain for the rest of my life. The cunt, usually a metaphorical wound, has become a literal gash. I think of Julietta Singh when she writes, "the vagina remains, almost

---

55 Ani DiFranco, "Out of Habit," on *Ani DiFranco* (Righteous Babe Records, 2019, remastered).

ubiquitously, a place of experienced or anticipated trauma."[56] It would seem, in a way, that anyone born with a vagina is born already wounded.

* * *

I imagine there is a ghost in every wound. We might conjure loss as much as we conjure presence. I lost something in the figurative cut and taking of my cock, but I gained something in the scars that give new shape to my chest. In my most recent procedure, I lost the adhesions that were threatening my life, but I gained scar tissue that will pain me for life. When I stick a needle into my thigh muscle, I am not certain exactly what I am gaining and what I am losing. I have not realized myself as trans in the first place or in the last place. I am not sure which doors I am stepping through or blasting open. I am not sure what I am becoming. I am not sure what kind of body I am piecing together. I am not sure who I am praying to or what I am praying for. I am not sure what I am conjuring and calling to presence — manhood, the appearance of manhood, the ghosts of the abuse I have known at the hands of men, the ghosts of the men and animals who were subject to medical experimentation in order to have the hormone extracted from their bodies so it could be synthesized for entry into mine. All I know is that my body is transforming and will continue to transform. "Conjuring," Avery Gordon writes, "is a particular form of calling up and calling out the forces that make things what they are in order to fix and transform a troubling situation."[57] I do not imagine testosterone as a fix to a troubling situation of my body. Rather, the drug, a promised cure to a troubled body, seems to make my body all the more troubling.

---

56 Julietta Singh, *No Archive Will Restore You* (Earth: punctum books, 2018), 68.

57 Avery Gordon, *Ghostly Matters: Haunting and the Sociological Imagination* (Minneapolis: University of Minnesota Press, 2008), 22.

Look. Just look at what testosterone can do. In my inability to grieve what I cannot imagine losing, I have begun to mourn, as well as celebrate, what I am gaining. Instead of running from the ghosts, I run toward, open the wounds, conjure forth the violence in and of my body, and remake my body in pieces. Conjuring has become a kind of prayer that reaches toward flesh with each injection and with each graze of a fingertip over the rigid lines that cross my chest. My prayers take the form of love letters to all the ghosts I carry and conjure. My body is a practice and a practice in building, in becoming more and more. Monstrous. Extraordinary. Beautiful.

6

Love Leaks and Strange(r) Intimacies

it was no longer a matter of sex.

this new molecular relationship made distance and intimacy
words
that tangled.
or to say it another way.
we were all close.
beyond close.

— Alexis Pauline Gumbs, *M Archive*[1]

I wonder what it must be like to trust a stranger with your
undoing.
— Hanif Abdurraqib, *They Can't Kill Us Until They Kill Us*[2]

The week of Thanksgiving, just about one month after my
breakup with *R*, my friend *B* comes to town and we commiser-
ate over each of our recent breakups and offer each other the
small comforts that come when two broken hearts try to fit their
pieces together. *B* tells me he thinks he might be a sex addict.

1   Alexis Pauline Gumbs, *M Archive: After the End of the World* (Durham:
    Duke University Press, 2018), 17.

2   Hanif Abdurraqib, *They Can't Kill Us Until They Kill Us* (Columbus: Two
    Dollar Radio, 2017), 45.

He largely deals with his heartbreak by having noncommittal sex with strangers. I tend to deal with my heartbreak by withdrawing into quiet solitude. "Dealing with" might not be the accurate way to describe what we are doing, but maybe it is. Avoiding, drowning out, ignoring, stuffing down are all ways of dealing, of feeling outside and around the heart pains. Drinking is another way. The night after Thanksgiving, B and I decide to go out drinking. If anything, it feels good for me to get out. At the bar, B decides he will be my wingman. He says I need to find someone, even if just for tonight. He is sleeping on my couch, so he has no intention of taking anyone home that night. I consider if I would even want to take someone home. I had never done that before, that is, I have never trusted a stranger enough to go home with them or to bring them home with me, to be done and undone by them.

We go to the bar where, just over a year ago I met R for our third date, went home with her, and fell into her bed for the first time. I am now considering the possibility of falling into someone else's bed or finding someone else to fall into mine. B and I are a few drinks in when we meet D. She lives in New York, but she is in San Francisco visiting family for the holiday. Tonight is her night out with old friends before she heads back tomorrow afternoon. One of her friends tells us that D would be into either me or B or both of us. It becomes apparent D is into me when she leans over and asks me if she has a place to sleep in San Francisco that night or if she needs to catch the last BART train back to the East Bay.

When D comes home with me, the first thing we do is talk. She asks me about testosterone. She asks me about my kinks and wants and desires. She tells me about her experiments in bondage and submission and non-monogamy. She tells me she has recently embraced identifying as a slut. I tell her how I have been told by more than one person that I am an emotional slut and that I want to write a book about it called "The Tender-Hearted Slut." We laugh, we kiss, and then I ask her if she wouldn't mind cuddling in lieu of sex. I have been feeling like I want to be held by someone, but no one I know within proximity feels like the right person for the job. I wonder what it will be like to touch, to hold, and be held by a stranger.

She agrees to a cuddle sleepover, and we embrace and talk through the night and into the morning. *D* asks me about my work on nonsexual pleasures. As I caress her arms and back, I tell her about how I think we need to appreciate the pleasure of touch simply for being the touch that it is, rather than imagining it on the way to some perceived greater pleasure. She reminds me that kink is all about pleasure for pleasure's sake. She is right, I agree. BDSM and kink help remind us of the pains and pleasures we can experience whether or not they bear a relation to an orgasmic endpoint. What a way to be with one another, in touch and in dialogue, in pain and in pleasure, wanting it all in its fullness and wanting nothing more. This night with *D* is my first one-night stand, an asexual one-night stand.

* * *

At a live show by The Weeknd in Seattle, Hanif Abdurraqib takes note of the bodies in the space of the theater and how they touch or avoid touch. The Weeknd begins his set by asking if he can make the audience cum. He sings about sex for an hour with pornography projected on the screen behind him, yet, Abdurraqib notices, the people in the audience are barely touching. In fact, they are "performing distance" in a setting that usually draws bodies together as the music flows through them. Abdurraqib speculates that the lack of touch amongst the audience is derivative of The Weeknd's dismissal of love in his songs about sex; he is chasing a feeling rather than a person; there is no love driving the pursuit of physical intimacy.[3]

I think of another song by The Weeknd, "Tell Your Friends," in which he sings about his own sexual recklessness while observing that all around him, everyone else seems just as reckless: "everybody fucking, everybody fucking." All this fucking leads

---

3   Abdurraqib, *They Can't Kill Us Until They Kill Us,* 40–44.

to what I might describe as the song's apothegm: "they told me not to fall in love, that shit is pointless."[4] I can't help but think of the iconic queer pop band, Pansy Division, who similarly testify that "real love don't stand a chance" because when people talk about love, it sounds like "blah blah blah blah blah 'cause they really mean sex sex sex sex. People just want to connect."[5] Love, that shit is pointless. If so, and if we just want to connect, then sex is what we're left with. There is no love driving the pursuit of intimacy. Everybody fucking. Except when they're not.

As The Weeknd's Seattle show comes to an end and the curtain lowers, Abdurraqib notes the closing lyrics of his song about one-night stands, "Wicked Games," finally ask for some kind of love: "so tell me you love me / only for tonight, only for tonight / even though you don't love me / just tell me you love me." He asks for someone to tell him they love him, just for tonight, even if they don't. After wondering what it might be like to heed The Weeknd's call and trust a stranger with his undoing, Abdurraqib quips, "I suppose the lesson is that the one-night stand takes as many forms as the desires of the people inside of it."[6] I think of how Samuel Delany writes, "there are as many different styles, intensities, and timbres to sex as there are people."[7] There is a very fine line between what we call "sex" and what we call "intimacy," "pleasure," "desire," "sensuality," or "connection." There are infinite forms for desire, intimacy, and love to take. There is, after all, sometimes a difference between intimacy and fucking. Sometimes they fade into one another. And sometimes, we just need to learn the difference. There are so many ways to spread our love out in time and in space. What a way to be with one another — what a pleasure — inside that desire of simply touching, of speaking a love to one another, and

---

4   The Weeknd, "Tell Your Friends," on *Beauty Behind the Madness* (Republic Records, 2015).

5   Pansy Division, "Luv Luv Luv," on *Absurd Pop Song Romance* (Lookout! Records, 1998).

6   Abdurraqib, *They Can't Kill Us Until They Kill Us*, 45.

7   Samuel R. Delany, *Times Square Red, Times Square Blue* (New York: New York University Press, 1999), 45.

of asking for one kind of love among so many kinds of falling and loving and being together, if even just for one night.

I like Abdurraqib's lesson. I want to take it to heart and allow the one-night stand the possibility of taking any shape or form in relation to the desires inside it. I especially want to hold space to imagine an intimacy between bodies engaged in a one-night stand that elides sex altogether. I want to imagine such an intimacy as a type of love that is just as "real" a way to connect. In creating this promise of possibility for the one-night stand, I return to the song that inspired Abdurraqib. In "Wicked Games," this particular set of lyrics always rattles me: "bring your love, baby, I could bring my shame / bring the drugs, baby, I could bring my pain / oh, I got my heart right here / oh, I got my scars right here."[8] The Weeknd is not simply asking for love for love's sake in the span of an evening. He is asking for love to his shame, the numb of drugs to his pain. He is asking from the one-night stand a salve to the broken and scarred heart. He is not asking for sexual healing but rather for love's balm, an unctuous slip between fucking and loving. Love, here, a kind of suture. A butterfly stitch across a pulsing burst.

* * *

I don't think I wanted *D* to love me that night. But I wanted a touch that felt like care, a bond that might forge a temporary seam across a rift in my heart. I wanted an intimacy with a stranger that was touching but not fucking. I just wanted to connect. I wanted contact.

In tracing the history and loss of sex theatres in New York City's Times Square, Samuel Delany writes of the importance of "contact" as a crucial element of city life that fosters cross-class interactions, the very thing gentrification seeks to eliminate. Importantly, contact is a kind of intimacy with strangers that is built into the fabric of urban life.[9] I want to call such encounters

---

8   The Weeknd, "Wicked Games," on House of Balloons (XO, 2011).

9   Delany, *Times Square,* 123.

"strange(r) intimacies" to mark the moments of deep possibility in which we might exchange love, touch, thoughts, or words with someone we barely know or do not know at all within the course of a night or in the space of a breath, tiny bursts of togetherness that might also feel a bit strange.

Thinking through this notion of "strange(r) intimacies" led me to Nayan Shah's book, *Stranger Intimacy,* in which he traces the governance of bodies of migrant workers of color in North America who forge interracial relations in order to push back against American imperialism. He uncovers a history of intimacy that challenges the status quo and governmentality. He debunks the idea that permanence means stability, the expectation that households must be arranged around the nuclear family, that sexuality can be clearly defined as either homosexual or heterosexual, and that gender is binary. Shah's stranger intimacies buck these norms in their resilient kinship organizations as ways to survive the violences of colonialism and imperialism, blurring the boundaries between erotic desire and "abiding affection and care."[10]

I am also invested in making space for intimacies that bring bodies together across difference, in queerness, against the regulation of the state, and in opposition to normative ideologies, which thus dissolve the clear distinctions between erotic desire and caring affection, sexual and nonsexual intimacies. I am interested in the "strangeness" of asexual encounters in particular both because they can be *with strangers* and because they can *make strange* or *be strange* in challenging us to think against a sex normative progress narrative that positions the sexual encounter as the narrative climax in the story of two or more bodies coming together. My want from strange(r) intimacies is a reorganization of the desires inside and between bodies, where when we say love, we don't always have to mean sex. And contact is not always sexual.

---

10 Nayan Shah, *Stranger Intimacy: Contesting Race, Sexuality, and the Law in the North American West* (Berkeley: University of California Press, 2012).

Contact is intercourse though, both "physical and conversational," both sex and not sex.[11] Different shapes of intimacy, sometimes so fleeting, the bumps and blips register as mere residue, the everyday film of life we rinse away in the shower, dropped down the drain and forgotten.[12] Delany describes contact variably as the conversations had in line at the grocery store, banter shared between neighbors who have stepped out onto their stoop at the same moment, or the chit-chat struck up with the person who plops down on the bar stool next to you at the local pub. Beyond these niceties, contact can also entail casual sex, or public sex, that ultimately leads to what Delany describes as "nonsexual friendships and/or acquaintances lasting for decades or a lifetime."[13] Sex leads to lifelong nonsexual intimacy. In this framework, sexual and nonsexual intimacy/contact cannot be disentangled.

It would seem that nonsexual encounters most usually occur because of the possibility of sexual encounters that continue to fuel desire and pleasure for and with each other. First, we desire sex, then we desire love or nonsexual lifelong intimacy. But I want intimacy to take many forms. I want to imagine lifelong nonsexual intimacies that pre-exist sex or do not necessitate the sexual encounter. I want to linger in the possibilities present in nonsexual desires for contact, nonsexual desires for nonsexual pleasures, and the nonsexual intimacies that permeate our lives. A moment of fleeting touch. A moment of passing intimacy. A momentary stitch across a rift. A moment of strangeness with a stranger.

* * *

---

11 Delany, *Times Square,* 123.

12 Lauren Berlant writes of intimacy as a way to name "the enigma of [a] range of attachments," some institutionalized and/or formative, some that "rarely register as anything but residue." Lauren Berlant, "Intimacy: A Special Issue," *Critical Inquiry* 24, no. 2 (1998): 283.

13 Delany, *Times Square,* 123.

I am sitting in a coffee shop in Oakland, writing about contact. I watch as a man moves through the shop, hat turned up in his hands, asking for money. He eventually buys a coffee and sits at the table by the window. Through the window, he makes eye contact with a young woman sitting at the table on the other side of the glass. He waves and points at her frequently, and she politely smiles, nods, and waves back at him. When he finishes his coffee, he moves outside and offers her a fist-bump. She obliges. He then sits at the table across from her, and gives her three more fist-bumps before he rises and walks away. I cannot help but watch with a smile and revel in this moment of contact I am witnessing. Shortly after he walks away, she leaves. He soon returns to sit at the table and continues offering fist-bumps to more passersby. I am delighted. Ross Gay, in an entry about one of his daily delights titled, "The High-Five from Strangers, Etc.," details an array of pleasant and delightful moments of physical contact with strangers — a hand on the shoulder, a smack on his impressive bicep, or a high five, which is not too unlike the fist-bump. "I love, I delight in," he writes, "unequivocally pleasant public physical interactions with strangers."[14] When he writes physical, he does not mean sexual. Still, there is so much delight, so much pleasure, so much intimacy.

What does it mean to exchange intimacy in nonsexual ways with a stranger? How can we understand these intimacies as being important in ways we haven't yet thought because we so often create a pipeline from intimacy to deep and long-term emotional knowing and/or romantic/sexual relationships? What might we make of these fleeting encounters and how we may still carry them with us beyond the point of contact, refusing to let them be rinsed down the drain? The high-five or fist-bump from a stranger, the chat on the escalator, two pairs of eyes meeting across a subway car. What traces, what ghostings are these? What can they tell us about the permeability of bodies, about the collectivity of pleasure and delight? Delany writes, "cities are attractive to people because of the pleasures the city

---

14 Ross Gay, *The Book of Delights* (Chapel Hill: Algonquin Books, 2019), 28.

holds."[15] What pleasures hide in the cracks in the sidewalk, in the whoosh of subway cars, in the shuffle of bodies in crosswalks? What pleasures hide in the places we often forget to look?

I know someone for whom the city pulses with sex, where every moment of eye contact with a stranger is a glimpse of bedroom eyes. Each passing flirtation a flit of raw, carnal desire. Each brush of the shoulder pulses with the electric hum of sex sex sex. Each moment of contact the promise of a possible fuck. The metropolitan landscape buzzes with an erotic charge that vibrates through her body and throbs in her cunt as she weaves through bodies on the sidewalk and huddles with strangers in densely peopled subway cars. Life in the city is a perpetual hard-on. For her, fucking and intimacy do not have discrete edges. They are always bleeding into one another. There is no difference. Fucking is an invitation toward intimacy, intimacy always an invitation to fuck.

Comparatively, I have always thought of myself as moving through the city with a bit more caginess. I tend to avoid the touch of strangers and usually find nothing erotic or sexual in the glance across a subway car or in the graze of another body against mine. But recently, I have begun to imagine a way to move through the city tuned into a different erotic, one that oozes nonsexual, intimate possibility and jovial connection or plays of pleasure and power. The city's underlying throb of sex rarely makes its way into my own loins. Instead, the momentary locking of eyes, the spark in the static skim of a stranger's elbow, all these moments of fleeting metropolitan intimacies hum with the promise of a different kind of contact, inspiring stranger notions of pleasurable encounters in my heart, mind, and soul. A hunger to be with one another outside the possibility of sex.

In larger cities, I often find myself uncomfortably pressed against the bodies of strangers on crowded metro trains. At first, my mild claustrophobia made it nearly impossible to even step onto these trains, and I had not always been too keen on being intimately pressed into the smells and tastes of people I don't

---

15 Delany, *Times Square*, 169.

know. But as I have been reflecting more on the moments of intimate possibilities in strange(r) physical encounters, I have started leaning into those strangers, experiencing their smell and touch. It is admittedly uncomfortable at times, but it is also sometimes oddly pleasurable, always strangely intimate, my own little secret. To be clear, I am not forcing myself onto anyone. No one should ever be harassed into unwanted intimacies. Rather, I am paying attention to the ways in which we are already close. I am simply leaning into the boundary between self and other, with restraint, and often eager to pull back myself. I wonder if the man I lean my back into also presses his back into mine in a moment of subtle, shared pleasurable contact. I wonder if the people around me take in my smell as I take in theirs. These small points of contact we consent to by our very nature of being embodied and being in physical proximity to one another. I wonder how we are choosing these exchanges, even as so much of what we exchange is beyond our control.

* * *

We are always already intimate with one another. Mel Y. Chen writes about how porous our bodies are, that we are always breathing each other in, though sometimes with unfortunately violent toxic effects. Chen writes, "when physically copresent with others, I ingest them. There is nothing fanciful about this. I am ingesting their exhaled air, their sloughed skin, and the skin of the tables, chairs, and carpet of our shared room."[16] We literally inhale and swallow each other and the objects around us in microscopic pieces. We are always inside one another, pieces of our bodies entering the bodies of others. All things and beings slough, spill, and leak into and onto one another — a quantum entanglement, of sorts, to invoke Karen Barad.[17] This

---

16 Mel Y. Chen, *Animacies: Biopolitics, Racial Mattering, and Queer Affect* (Durham: Duke University Press, 2012), 209.

17 Karen Barad, "Quantum Entanglements and Hauntological Relations of Inheritance: Dis/continuities, SpaceTime Enfoldings, and Justice-to-Come," *Derrida Today* 3, no. 2 (2010): 240–68.

spilling and leaking is a spacetimemattering across the planes of the sub-atomic and the physical, the pieces of matter and the matter itself, mattering in time and space and with each other. The quantum disrupts continuity as it leaps and queerly undoes the distinctions between here and there, you and me. Reflecting on quantum entanglement, poet Zaina Alsous writes, "You can disrupt my matter even when you are not in the room," which may be another way of saying, we leave our marks on one another.[18] Pieces of our selves not only remain when we leave a room, but may also enter rooms we have never been in — our sloughed skin, our hair, our scent, and our breath. Travelling. Leaping. Erupting and disrupting.

A viral interruption, an eruption:

Notably, I cannot ignore that I am writing of this atomic intimacy in the midst of a global pandemic, in which the coronavirus, SARS-CoV-2, depends precisely on our porosity to pass through membranes and into our bodies, a potentially lethal microscopic invasion. To protect ourselves and each other, we are given a prescription of physical distancing, an elimination of the very contact I have learned to crave and want to practice. But its abstinence is a temporary necessity, lest we disrupt one another into a persistent deathpile.

My contact with strangers and loved ones alike has taken an ominous turn, tinged with fear and uncertainty. I hold my breath when someone passes too closely at the grocery store. I cross the street when someone is approaching me on the sidewalk. I dodge. I retreat. Anything to create distance between us. Anything to keep from breathing someone else into

18 Zaina Alsous, *A Theory of Birds* (Fayetteville: The University of Arkansas Press, 2019), 22.

my cells. We have all (again) been made familiar with our porous vulnerabilities. On a molecular level we are close, beyond close.

In charting our molecular intimacies, Chen also collapses the distinctions between living and non-living, between subject and object, and between human and animal. We can be just as intimate with a couch as we might a human lover. In Chen's moment of romance with a couch, we are given an intimacy that notably gestures toward the asexual. We are asked to imagine connections with objects being just as intimate as connections with lovers, regardless of the presence or absence of sexual activity. In these object relations, the world touches us as we touch it, or, as Chen puts it, "my skin is simultaneously the skin of the world."[19] The skin, the human body's largest organ, is also our opening to the world. It does not contain us. Instead, it pours us into all the ache and joy of the world and allows such to be poured back into us. Our edges, our perimeters become a fluid slurry.

Selfotherhumananimalsubjectobjectabject. Abject. Our very skin abjects us. Julia Kristeva describes the abject as that which does not respect borders. "There I am," Kristeva writes, "at the border of my condition as a living being."[20] Our condition as living beings is in the material stuff of the body, notably the stuff which revolts and disgusts us, reminds us of our own decay, rot, and movement toward death. Quoting Mary Douglas's account of the "marginal stuff" that spills forth from the body's orifices in the form of spittle, blood, milk, urine, feces, and tears, Kristeva characterizes abjection through the expulsions of the body,

---

19 Chen, *Animacies,* 202–3, 209.
20 Julia Kristeva, *Powers of Horror: An Essay on Abjection,* trans. Leon S. Roudiez (New York: Columbia University Press, 1982), 3.

describing such discharges and defilements as the "the body's inside [...] show[ing] up in order to compensate for the collapse of the border between inside and outside."[21] The skin that allegedly creates our outside border is permeable. We bleed into the world. The world bleeds into us.

Erin Manning similarly writes against the containment of the body, refusing to consider the skin as that which neatly bounds the body. The skin is instead porous, topologically folding with and through the world. Because of this endless permeability and malleability of skin, the body cannot be contained. It leaks. It spills. "It is a fold of immanent expressibility."[22] And this pervasive expressibility with the world is synesthetic and cross-modal: "a looking becomes a touching, a feeling becomes a hearing."[23] We smell and taste and hear as we are touched; our taste and smell and hearing are ways of touching. "Smell," Anna Lowenhaupt Tsing writes, "is the presence of another in ourselves."[24] Smell is an encounter, a permeation. Tsing also describes smell as "a sign of the presence of another, to which we are already responding," and in that response, "we are not quite ourselves anymore — or at least the selves we were, but rather ourselves in encounter with another."[25] The nose an orifice, a point of entry. Julietta Singh describes each orifice of the body as "an entry where we palpably open, where other bodies have been, and by leaving their traces in us have, in a molecular sense, become us."[26] We smell and are smelled. We touch and are touched. We move through one another. We are never only ourselves. We become one another. We pierce each other's skin.

---

21 Ibid., 53.

22 Erin Manning, "What If It Didn't All Begin and End with Containment? Toward a Leaky Sense of Self," *Body & Society* 15, no. 3 (2009): 35.

23 Ibid.

24 Anna Lowenhaupt Tsing, *The Mushroom at the End of the World: On the Possibility of Life in Capitalist Ruins* (Princeton: Princeton University Press, 2015), 45.

25 Ibid., 46.

26 Julietta Singh, *No Archive Will Restore You* (Earth: punctum books, 2018), 32.

Of another kind of skin, Kristeva writes, "when the eyes see or the lips touch that skin on the surface of milk — harmless, thin as a sheet of cigarette paper, pitiful as a nail paring — I experience a gagging sensation and, still farther down, spasms in the stomach, the belly; and all the organs shrivel up the body, provoke tears and bile, increase heartbeat, cause forehead and hands to perspire."[27] She cries, vomits, and sweats out her own disgust at the skin that is seemingly harmless but so abhorrent. All evoked from a look which is a touch which is a taste. The blood drips, thick and metallic. A roar in the ears. A tangy shock to the tongue. A ringing, synesthetic din.

* * *

A whole world in a drop of blood. A globular microcosm of cells and platelets and pathogens that condition our living. A whole making and unmaking of self, doing and being undone in the materiality of life, in its expulsions and spillages and expectorations. Kristeva writes how, among other bodily defilements and decay, the wound that pulses blood and oozes pus shows us, in its horrific materiality, what we otherwise continually "thrust aside in order to live."[28] "Freud had," Kristeva observes, "in enigmatic fashion, noted in connection with melancholy: 'wound,' 'internal hemorrhage,' 'a hole in the psyche.'"[29] Which is to say, the wound is melancholic, beyond mourning, the "here" of the gape, and the demand for sutures palpable. We must cover it up in order to live on.

The wound, the internal hemorrhage, the hole that drips blood and mucus and tissue brings me back again to a meditation on the vagina as wound. Margrit Shildrick argues that a feminist ethic must be attentive to embodiment, specifically to the embodiment of women, and such an attention especially de-

---

27 Kristeva, *Powers of Horror,* 2–3.

28 Ibid., 3.

29 Ibid., 55.

mands a foregrounding of leakiness.[30] The concept of the body as some discrete whole is a fabrication, especially when we account for all the holes through which we leak. As opposed to excrement and bodily expulsions that represent a kind of decay or threat to the ego from without, Kristeva characterizes menstrual blood as a "danger issuing from within the identity (social or sexual)."[31] Menstruation, an internal hemorrhage inherent to the female body, threatens our egos from within, undoing us on a regular cycle.

Rachel Frances Sharpe and Sophie Sexon created an experimental film essay drawing on Kristeva's notions of the abject and the exceptionalization of menstrual blood and breast milk, a life-giving fluid, as opposed to the abject expulsions of decay like shit, piss, and vomit.[32] Still, the milk can unsettle us. Lisa Jean Moore, writing after the birth of her child describes her breasts leaking in public, in the classroom while teaching. She takes stock of her incongruency, when the logics of containment of the body break down before the other: "when my body leaks, it creates and disrupts meanings."[33] We become unexpected before one another, disruptive in our abjection, unsettled by the monstrosity of the body. And the female body is made so much more visibly monstrous in its incubations and purges.

Sharpe's film, *Puncture,* is a meditation on the "monstrous feminine" in comparison to the crucifixion wounds on the body of Christ. The viewer is bombarded with flashes of festering flesh, dripping blood, leaking mouths and eyes, and a foaming admixture of blood and milk. The liquid slurry blurs the boundaries between fluids, between Christ and the monstrous

---

30 Margrit Shildrick, *Leaky Bodies and Boundaries: Feminism, Postmodernism, and (Bio)ethics* (New York: Routledge, 1997).

31 Kristeva, *Powers of Horror,* 71.

32 Rachel Frances Sharpe and Sophie Sexon, "Mother's Milk and Menstrual Blood in 'Puncture': The Monstrous Feminine in Contemporary Horror Films and Late Medieval Imagery," *Studies in the Maternal* 10, no. 1 (2018), https://www.mamsie.bbk.ac.uk/articles/10.16995/sim.256/.

33 Lisa Jean Moore, "Incongruent Bodies: Teaching While Leaking," *Feminist Teacher* 17, no. 2 (2007): 96.

feminine as divine, between child and mother. In dialogue with the film, Sexon writes, "the female body collapses the boundaries between self and other via reproduction. The reproductive capacity produces substances that bring the internal to the external; birthing, bleeding and breastfeeding. In socio-cultural terms, these traits cast the mother figure as an abject monster: that which dissolves the borders between the flesh and the world."[34] The female body, the mother, cannot help but be abject. The skin of the mother is the skin of the world. Leaking. Bleeding.

When I started testosterone, my doctor asked me if I would like to stop my period right away. She imagined the menstrual cycle as one that might cause another kind of disturbance or disruption to a self that is ostensibly undergoing a transition from womanhood to manhood. Though my period did not necessarily heighten my gender dysphoria, I did always find it a rather unpleasant experience, so I agreed to halt its future occurrences. With that, my doctor ordered me a shot of medroxyprogesterone acetate, commonly known by its brand name Depo Provera. The shot, which should be administered every three months until testosterone levels rise enough that the body shuts down the menses on its own, is meant to dose my body with enough progestin to suppress ovulation, thus bringing about a cessation to my menstrual cycle. The nurse administered the shot by hypodermic and plunged the needle into my ass cheek. Piece of cake.

Two weeks later, I bled. I bled nonstop for three months, my cunt a hemorrhaging wound. I learned this is one possible side effect of the drug: spotting or even excessive bleeding, rather than damming the spill. Alice Notley writes of bleeding from her vagina off her cycle and fears that it is a sign of cervical cancer. In the same instance, she writes of cutting onions and carrots, where a knife slips and blood blooms from her hand, into the soup. "There must be a moment when the wounds stop," she laments.[35] I must attend to my own embodiment. I become

---

34 Sharpe and Sexon, "Mother's Milk and Menstrual Blood," n.p.

35 Alice Notley, *Benediction* (Tucson: Letter Machine Editions, 2015), 242.

monstrous mixity. I bleed. I become incongruent. I bleed. I become abject. I bleed. I choose to imagine the endless leak as a kind of purging, all my womanhood pouring out of me. The wounds will never stop.

* * *

When the progestin molecule leaked into my body and flitted about, it caused me to spill blood for months. When the testosterone molecule leaks into my thigh muscle, the drug elicits changes in my body, or, there are changes my body elicits from the drug, such as hair growth, musculoskeletal reshaping, the ever-so-slight lowering of the voice, a spread of acne across my neck and jaw in the building of hair follicles — a beard yet to come.

When I was four years old, I crawled into my father's lap, my shins pressed to his thighs, my hands on each of his cheeks, as I rubbed the scruff of his face. I reached my face up to his, to feel the scratch of his jaw against my baby-smooth cheek. I pulled away and looked into my father's eyes. "I want to be a boy like you," I said. He laughed. Thirty years later, I chuckle at the memory. I rub my hand across my own cheeks and over my jawline, feeling the sandpaper rough of my facial hair poking through my beard of acne. But I don't want to be a man like him. I am not even sure I want to be a man. I am even a bit afraid of what a beard might signify and what it might make of my body for others in the world. And I am distraught by the acne, feeling abject in the pustular eruption across my face. I want to pull the sebum and puss out of me, to expel the filth and material decay of my body's oozing.

My acne gets so bad that even my doctor remarks on it. When I ask her about increasing my testosterone dose, the first thing she says is "your acne will get worse." A friend tells me he remembers his acne persisting for years after he started T. It will get worse before it gets better, he tells me regrettably. L tells me her ex was proud of his acne, viewing it as part of his process of entering into manhood, going through the puberty he felt he always should have had. She suggests I should likewise be proud of my acne. I try to accept that acne is just one of the many things testosterone does to my body, even if temporary and even if I am not, in fact, proud of it. But I also want to rebel against the transition narrative I feel L pushing on me in her attempt to make me like an other she has known intimately, trying to align each of our molecular intimacies with testosterone. I tell her I am not embarking on the same path toward manhood that her ex was. I remind her there are many ways to engage with testosterone. I am still allowed to hate my acne, the way it obsessively occupies my mental space and compels me to pick and fantasize about picking. I pull myself open. Hate oozing in a porous eruption.

* * *

Under the umbrella of what clinicians refer to as "body-focused repetitive behavior disorders," or BFRBDs, exists another umbrella category of "pathologic grooming," which includes trichotillomania (hair pulling), nail biting, and acne excoriée/neurotic excoriation/dermatillomania (pathologic or compulsive skin picking). BFRBDs typically have an early onset during puberty and young adulthood and are believed to be more common in young girls and women. In 1898, French doctor M.L. Brocq first described the habits of acne excoriation in young females, thus giving name to the condition as "l'acné excoriée des jeunes filles," which most directly translates to "excoriated acne of young girls." Though now the condition is often shortened simply to "acne excoriée" or generally lumped in with neurotic excoriations and obsessive compulsions, Florian Anzengruber, et al. note that in German and French speaking countries, the skin picking condition is today still referred to as AEJF, which stands for "acne excoriée des jeunes filles." Despite the passage of some one hundred twenty years since Brocq's classification of acne excoriée as a symptom of girlhood and despite evidence showing that the affliction does not affect only young girls, such an anachronism in naming suggests the habit is still largely considered to be an affliction of female adolescence.[36]

Norman Wrong, in 1954, reported that though the habit of picking at acne blemishes still seemed to develop predominantly in young girls, the condition ought to simply be called "excoriated acne of females," notably shifting from "young girls" to "females," as he found women up through the age of forty to also be afflicted with persistent and neurotic skin picking. It seems, however, that the presentation in adulthood could still largely be traced back to adolescent onset. In 2013, the fifth edition of the *Diagnostic and Statistical Manual of Mental Disorders* (DSM-5) began to include acne excoriée and excoriation (or skin-picking) under "Obsessive-Compulsive and Related Disorders." Excoriation's elevated status to a more specific disorder classification in the DSM distinguished it from its previous listing as a symptom of substance abuse, as a minor associated habit of trichotillomania, an impulse disorder not otherwise classified. Of the prevalence of excoriation disorder, it is noted that women tend to be affected at higher rates in adulthood, and boys more so in childhood, suggesting perhaps that we are dealing with what might best be referred to as acne excoriée of women and acne excoriée of young boys.[37]

Yet over the course of a lifetime, it seems that three-quarters or more of people presenting excoriation disorder are indeed female, which the DSM-5 notes may be indicative of gendered, cultural attitudes that emphasize in girls a greater preoccupation with appearance than in boys, resulting in a gender gap in terms of who actually seeks treatment for acne-related skin-

---

36 M.L. Brocq, "L'acné excoriée des jeunes filles," *Revue générale de clinique et de thérapique* 12 (1898): 139–97; Florian Anzengruber et al., "Wide Range of Age of Onset and Low Referral Rates to Psychiatry in a Large Cohort of Acne Excoriée at a Swiss Tertiary Hospital," *Journal of Dermatological Treatment* 29, no. 3 (2017): 277–80.

37 Norman M. Wrong, "Excoriated Acne of Young Females," *Archives of Dermatology and Syphilology* 70, no. 5 (1954): 576–82; *Diagnostic and Statistical Manual of Mental Disorders, Fifth Edition* (DSM-5) (Arlington: American Psychiatric Association, 2013), 254–57.

picking conditions.[38] Almost eighty years before the authors of the DSM-5 made this observation, Wrong had suggested that women and girls who practice excoriation can be divided into three groups: the first, the "slightly masculine type"; the second, the "vain type of girl" who focuses solely on her appearance; and the third, the "good-looking type of girl" who does not receive the attention she feels she is due from the opposite sex. This last category presupposes a heterosexual desire for attention and affection.[39] The latter two categories seem to be easily explained by dominant cultural attitudes about gender and beauty. It should be of no surprise that I am most fascinated by the first category of the "slightly masculine type." Wrong does not expound any further on this category, but it does make me wonder about a kind of "imperfect femininity," the masculine-type as a failed girl who is plagued by a neurosis of picking that makes her even "uglier" in her failed femininity. Or, maybe, another way to say it is that girls try to pick the ugly away while boys are generally not taught to worry about their appearance in the same way.

I am unsure how to chart these gender differentials onto my own body, my fantasy obsessions, and my picking compulsions. I did not experience acne in adolescence and thus did not develop any skin-picking habits. With my weekly dosage of testosterone, I am suddenly thrown into what many refer to as a "second puberty" that comes with an explosion of zits and pimples and other pore blockages in the follicular expansion across my face. Growing up, I was always told I had such a pretty face, if only I would smile more. The refrain so many unhappy girls are familiar with. As the acne spreads, I feel the ugly setting in. I imagine that everyone I encounter is fixated on my acne, a gape of horror in their eyes as they witness my own abjection in that carbuncular boil across my face.

I begin to fantasize about picking the lumps away into a smooth raw complexion. Nonhlanhla Khumalo, et.al describe the central symptom of excoriated acne as an uncontrolla-

---

38 DSM-5, 255.
39 Wrong, "Excoriated Acne of Young Females," 577.

ble urge to pick, which is "accompanied by a thought that the roughness of the skin can be fixed by picking, by a feeling of relief at the time of picking, and by a strong sense of subsequent regret, particularly if picking leads to tenderness or bleeding."[40] I develop these symptoms well into adulthood. Every time I pick, it is brought on by an urge to smooth the rough skin beneath my fingers. Every time I pick, I bring about pain and bleeding, a tenderness that leaves me full of shame and regret as my face grows uglier in the spurting and scarring. To channel Kristeva, "in the symptom, the abject permeates me, I become abject."[41] Here I bring my love; here I bring my shame; here then, too, I bring my pain. I got my scars right here.

* * *

Because of the link to acne as the originating impetus toward a picking compulsion, excoriation habits are typically focused on the face, though some people pick at the scalp or other areas of the body where blemishes are perceived. My acne occurs on my face and neck. It is there where I conduct my micro-surgeries. Some doctors suggest trimming the fingernails to limit picking habits, though others note that some people use tools to pick. I, being a nail biter, prefer a pair of needle-tip tweezers to pick and extract the sebum and puss from the skin of my face.

While the DSM-5 classifies excoriation under the umbrella of "Obsessive-Compulsive and Related Disorders," there are fine lines between diagnosable neurotic grooming habits and symptomatic habits that require some caution before diagnosis is bestowed. In particular, there exists a diagnostic category of "Other Specified Obsessive-Compulsive and Related Disorder," which functions to name the presentation of symptoms that are characteristic of OCD but don't meet the full criteria for such a

---

40 Nonhlanhla P. Khumalo et al., "Pathologic Grooming (Acne Excoriée, Trichotillomania, and Nail Biting) in Four Generations of a Single Family," *JAAD Case Reports* 2, no. 1 (2016): 52.

41 Kristeva, *Powers of Horror*, 11.

diagnosis. One of these "other specified" OCD-related categories is "Body-focused repetitive behavior disorder," which includes nail biting, lip biting, and cheek chewing that might cause clinically significant distress but cannot be better explained by other body-focused repetitive behavior disorders like hair-pulling or skin-picking.[42] Often, for the symptom to be considered a symptom, it must be marked by a kind of distress that involves multiple attempts to stop the picking or biting habit.

I chew my cheeks and lips, sometimes to the point of drawing blood. I think about it most when I have a dentist appointment. I am afraid the dentist will notice and remark on the raw and gnawed skin. No dentist has ever commented on my chewed cheeks, but one did warn me about the wear on my teeth due to nail-biting. I have bitten my nails for as long as I can remember. I have tried multiple times to quit biting my nails and have succeeded for very short spans of time before I suddenly, often unconsciously, resume the habit again. As I type this, my thumb nail pulses in pain where I have bitten it too far into the nail bed. It aches with each depression of the space bar. It's distressing. Pain, anxiety's cure. (The echo of my anxiety poem: nails to the quick bite — this is how I/he/you make me disappear).

Scott Herring imagines nail-biting to be a queer relationship to the body, linking it to other habits that arguably queer personhood and blur the boundaries of the self in our abject object relations. "We have only to mull over the richness of queer material relations to be found in bodily modification, keying cars, *biting nails,* collecting toothpaste, competitive eating, collecting twine, improper recycling, dumpster-hopping, and backyard-burning — not to mention old standbys like fetishism — to get a quick sense of the extraordinary object attachments in our present moment," Herring writes (my own emphasis added).[43]

---

42 DSM-5, 263–64.

43 Scott Herring, "Material Deviance: Theorizing Queer Objecthood," *Postmodern Culture* 21, no. 2 (January 2011). http://www.pomoculture. org/2013/09/03/material-deviance-theorizing-queer-objecthood/.

When I first read this entry, I resisted the idea that my nail-biting was somehow queer.

I once wrote, "perhaps 'queer' is not the best way to describe non-normative object hoarding and these other materialities. The majority of hoarders, nail-biters, dumpster-divers, and competitive eaters most likely have no reference point for living a 'queer' life on the sex and gender margins, and aside from their obsessions, bad habits, or odd quirks, may otherwise live heterosexual-, cisgender- privileged lives."[44] I wanted queerness to always be yoked in some way to gender and sexuality, to mark the violences and oppressions of what it means to live a queer life. But who is to say such object attachments are not somehow bucking the norms of our genders and sexualities in the intimacies they provoke? What Herring calls "aberrant material conduct," "motley activities," and "improper object usage" also elicit certain violences and oppressions on the margins of normative life.[45] Herring describes these marginal acts and ways of being as "something that approaches an enjoyable if fraught everyday praxis," or that which, as I might put it in Kristeva's words, approaches abjection.[46] Maybe my nail-biting has everything to do with my queerness, or maybe my queerness has everything to do with my nail-biting. Maybe I chew myself into pieces because it is the only way to live in the cuts.

The DSM-5, however, cautions the clinician, who may be cataloguing such motley, aberrant, material relations that a person may have with their own body, to recognize the difference between when a type of body dysmorphia that enables "Other Specified Obsessive-Compulsive and Related" habits arises from actual versus imagined flaws. The category, "Body Dysmorphic-Like Disorder with Actual Flaws" warns that if physical defects or flaws in physical appearance are more than slightly, that is, *clearly,* observable by others, the diagnosis is

---

44 KJ Cerankowski, "Illegible: Asexualities in Media, Literature, and Performance," PhD Thesis, Stanford University, 2014, 100.

45 Herring, "Material Deviance."

46 Ibid.

more in the distress caused by the preoccupation with these *clearly observable* flaws than in the psychotic obsession with perceived or imagined flaws. "Body Dysmorphic Disorder," on the other hand, presents as a preoccupation with bodily defects that are not clearly observable or are only slight in appearance, accompanied by repetitive behaviors of picking, grooming, as well as mentally comparing oneself to others or obsessively taking stock of one's appearance. These are preoccupations which cannot be "better explained by concerns with body fat or weight in an individual with an eating disorder" or do not classify as "muscle dysmorphia," which is "a form of body dysmorphic disorder that is characterized by the belief that one's body build is too small or is insufficiently muscular."[47]

These diagnostic criteria leave very little space between body dysmorphia and gendered body dysphoria. Of course I believe my body to be insufficiently muscular when one of the few things I want from testosterone is to grow into a bulk of swollen and striated presence. To build a protective castle of my body when I am uncertain of the violences that might be visited upon it in a world that hates monsters and those who live in-between. I cannot know if the acne that the testosterone coaxes forth on my face is clearly observable, slightly observable, or not at all observable when I fantasize and obsess over it, when I compulsively pick up the tweezers and dig an opening into my face from which I extract my own abjection. When I pick apart my face, I almost inevitably extricate, along with all the cellular gunk, a newly formed hair that was trapped beneath the surface of the globular pustule, the prescient promise of budding masculinity. When I develop this symptom of neurotic acne excoriation, I cannot be certain if it is the habit of the adolescent girl, the adult woman, or the adolescent boy that I am taking on. I cannot be certain if I am a boy or a girl, a man or a woman, bleeding and purging. A dysmorphic dysphoria.

I pick. I bite. I learn to trim and excise the parts of my body I wish to chew off.

---

47 DSM-5, 263, 242–43.

With the needle-tip tweezers, I dig beneath the surface of the skin, stretching the pore open against all the advice of dermatologists. With that spread comes satisfaction when the tweezers close their grip upon a solid chunk of tissue. I pull the white nodule from my skin and squeeze it between my fingers. Sometimes it bursts, all its "corporeal waste," in Kristeva's terms, spreading across the skin of my hands.[48] My own private (intimate) procedure. Yana Calou, writing of their own habits of scalp-picking, also describes the act as a procedure. A procedure which creates a physical manifestation of grief and pleasure, a procedure which marks a queer, grievous, pleasurable relationality to the landscape of the body. "My hands determine the terrain of my self," Calou writes, and "I am building kinship with my own body." [49] Kinship built through this strange, that is, non-normative and diagnosable, intimacy with one's own body.

Calou likens the terrain of their scalp to excavated earth: "I locate a piece of earth/self that I want to tear out. I work it up from the roots of my hair. Roots like those of desert junipers who live for thousands of years, cutting off water supply to parts of themselves during drought. They kill parts of themselves to save the rest of themselves."[50] The terrain of my own face has become one of mounds and craters, mountains and valleys. (Aren't we all topologies and topographies? Aren't we all geometries and geologies? Aren't we all mountains and valleys?) Returning to Wrong's 1954 study, I cannot help but ponder his own pondering: "it is doubtful whether the urge to pick represents anything more than a bad habit and not some obsessive compulsion from which they receive masochistic pleasure while excoriating themselves."[51] My bad habits have become my obsessions, spurred on by my compulsions. They are so pleasurable, even when they cause pain, even if I am left full of regret. I must be of an unmistakably masochistic character. My skin a loose

---

48 Kristeva, *Powers of Horror,* 70.
49 Yana Calou, "The Picking Diaries," *Hematopoiesis* 3 (2018): n.p.
50 Ibid.
51 Wrong, "Excoriated Acne of Young Females," 580.

earth, the skin of the world. I dig beneath the crust. I work the matter up and out. I kill a part of myself to save the rest. This is how I grieve. This is how I fill myself with shame. This is also my pleasure — corporeal, obsessive, compulsive, abject.

* * *

This is no innocuous pleasure. Let us not forget that excoriation is a diagnosable disorder. As with any disorder, excoriation, acne excoriée in particular, bears a complicated historical relationship to treatment and cure. In the early 1980s, two British doctors, Joan and Ian Sneddon, a psychiatrist and dermatologist respectively, studied eight adult women who had developed a habit of picking their faces over a period of at least twenty years, which means these women developed this habit in adolescence. The Sneddons describe how these women hate looking at themselves in the mirror because they feel ugly, yet they are compelled to look for new lesions they might pick. When no lesions are visible, the women describe the feeling of a throbbing beneath the skin, which they must scratch at until a lesion appears. They open themselves up in order to empty out the throbbing. When the opening becomes covered by a scab, the body's own cellular suture, they pick the scab, leaving themselves badly scarred and all the uglier, all the more abject.

Believing this habitual picking where there is no *clearly observable* physical lesion to be the result of some psychosis, the Sneddons experimented by treating these eight "neurotic" women with Stelazine, generically known as trifluoperazine.[52] Trifluoperazine is a drug that has largely been used to treat schizophrenia but has also been adapted as an anti-anxiety drug. In our current moment, trifluoperazine is no longer available under the brand name Stelazine, but the drug is still available generically and under other brand names. It continues to be used to treat schizophrenia. With low doses, it has also been

---

52 Joan Sneddon and Ian Sneddon, "Acne Excoriée: A Protective Device," *Clinical and Experimental Dermatology* 8, no. 1 (1983): 65–68.

used experimentally to treat Morgellons, a contentious disease that also results in obsessive skin picking and bodily lesions and that many medical professionals argue is purely psychological. Several experiments with the drug have also demonstrated its efficacy in inhibiting cancer cell invasion. It is multi-purpose, like most drugs.[53]

But in its treatment of anxiety, the drug has a specious past. Matthew H. Hersch has documented the history of Stelazine's US marketing by the drug company Smith Kline & French Laboratories since it first hit the market in 1958 as a treatment for schizophrenia. By the mid-1960s, the drug was also being marketed as an effective anti-anxiety drug for the everyday American office-worker or housewife. With a low dose, the drug promised to leave the otherwise anxiety-ridden Americans "calm, but alert," thus increasing productivity, unlike other tranquilizing anti-anxiety medications of the time that often left the user drowsy or a bit spaced out. The problem was that Stelazine had much more serious side effects, causing tremors, insomnia, and other neurological problems, such as tardive dyskinesia, which includes involuntary bodily movements like jerking and writhing as well as facial tics. And these side effects were known to occur in a significant percentage of the patients who took it, even in low doses and even when the patients were otherwise healthy. Still, Smith Kline & French Laboratories continued to market Stelazine as a low-dose, anti-anxiety solution through the 1970s.[54]

Given earlier associations of excoriation as a symptom of anxiety disorders, it must have made perfect sense to the Sneddons to utilize one of the more popular low-dose, anti-anxiety drugs of that era to treat acne excoriée in these eight women.

---

53 Bernice Y. Yan and Joseph L. Jorizzo, "Management of Morgellons Disease with Low-Dose Trifluoperazine," *JAMA Dermatology* 154, no. 2 (2018): 216–18; Ashleigh Pulkoski-Gross et al., "Repurposing the Antipsychotic Trifluoperazine as an Antimetastasis Agent," *Molecular Pharmacology* 87, no. 3 (March 2015): 501–12.

54 Matthew H. Hersch, "'Calm, But Still Alert': Marketing Stelazine to Disturbed America, 1958–1980," *Pharmacy in History* 50, no. 4 (2008): 140–48.

There is no follow-up study on whether or not the women experienced any of these neurotoxic side effects, but the Sneddons observed marked reductions in their skin-picking habits while they were dosed with the drug. I think again of the abjection of excoriation, the picking and smoothing away of the body's eruptions. I think of the abject picking as a queer kinship with the body, a motley activity, an aberrant material conduct. I think of the neurotoxicity of Stelazine and of the collapse between poison and cure. Recall, strychnine, too, is a neurotoxin used both to kill and to cure animals and queers. According to Kristeva, abjection sits at the crossroads of phobia, obsession, and perversion.[55] Yet again, perhaps out of fear, they have poisoned the perverse, the queers, the monstrous for their obsessions and compulsions. The poison works because we are molecules intimate with other molecules. Because we are hormones and blood and cells and skin. Because we are body. Because we are object. Because we are animal.

* * *

The animal and the abject are kin and kith. They each propel us between life and death. Shortly after describing herself as "ferociously alive," licking her snout "like a tiger who has just devoured a deer" (or like a wolf?), Clarice Lispector writes, "in my core I have the strange impression that I don't belong to the human species."[56] She is ferociously alive, but she does not belong. The boundaries are blurred. Abjection does not respect borders. How strange. How uncanny. How queer. Recall how Aaron Apps explores the movements from the abject to the animal to the abject animal. He begins his memoir, *Intersex,* with a scene of pleasurable indulgence of animal flesh, pig flesh, at a barbecue, followed by a scene of horrific public shitting, shit smearing under his thumbnail, the smell filling the air, his body

---

55 Kristeva, *Powers of Horror,* 45.

56 Clarice Lispector, *Água Viva,* ed. Benjamin Moser, trans. Stefan Tobler (New York: New Directions Books, 2012), 18, 22.

exploding all over the stall as he notices with horror that he is in the restroom that doesn't align to the gender made legible on his body. When he leaves the restroom, he quickly slips past the women standing in front of the mirror. He does not stop to wash his hands. He leaves covered in shit and stench and shame. Abject.

From there, Apps takes us on a journey through the endless abjections of the body, especially the intersex body, as it is made into an object, made abject, and made into the animal other — poked, prodded, objectified, and feared. He eats animals. He shits animals. He is made animal. "I say here is my animal self," he declares.[57] In the coalition of monsters, I find the kindred ontology and phenomenology between the "tranimality" and the "transspeciation" of the trans body and the monstrous mixity of the intersex body made animal. Making animals out of humans, making monsters out of animals. Or as Pansy Division put it, "we're all animals at the core."[58] Of intimacy, Berlant writes, "in practice the drive toward it is a kind of wild thing."[59] A wild thing, an animal thing. Ursula K. Le Guin suggests that we not only have to recognize ourselves as animals in a kinship relation to other animals but also as "creatures with other creatures, things with other things," our human selves becoming animal selves becoming creature selves becoming thing selves. The boundary between subject and object again becomes indistinguishable.[60] Our skin the skin of the world. Our skin the skin of the blue whale, the skin of the bull, the skin of the pig, the skin of the wolf, the skin of the buffalo. The skin of all we kill, all we ingest, and all we touch.

In Sarah Ciston's prose poem about place that is always noplace, being that is always not-being, she laments the "plains full of buffalo" sacrificed for "sprawling strip malls, parking lots that

---

57 Aaron Apps, *Intersex: A Memoir* (Grafton: Tarpaulin Sky Press, 2015), 62.

58 Pansy Division, "Luv Luv Luv."

59 Berlant, "Intimacy," 284.

60 Ursula K. Le Guin, "Deep in Admiration," in *Arts of Living on a Damaged Planet: Ghosts and Monsters of the Anthropocene*, eds. Anna Lowenhaupt Tsing et al. (Minneapolis: University of Minnesota Press, 2017), M15.

lead to more parking lots." "'Buffalo buffalo Buffalo buffalo buffalo buffalo Buffalo buffalo' is a complete sentence. Everything else seems incomplete," she writes.[61] I too lament the loss of the buffalo kin as I lament the loss of the wolves. The boundaries between buffalo, wolf, queer, monster, ghost, human, animal, poison, and cure have eroded. I write a poem inspired by a lover who imagines herself to be animal, who desires the lick of the snout, the fierceness of the thrashing maw. I write a poem inspired by Lispector and Apps and Ciston. A short poem:

> Animal animal Animal animal animal animal Animal
>   animal is not
>
> a grammatically correct sentence
> but it feels like one
> like mineral, element, like foliage we can name
> and classify and place each into adjective noun or verb
> leafrustle throatroar brookbabble
>
> never mind the grammar the body
> is its own sentence.

The body is its own sentence. It is a term, assignment, order, disorder, improper, incorrect, marked by the period, the bloody wound, the pustular point, the abject mark of the ugly. Melody Ellis synonymizes ugliness with, among other like words, "monstrous," "nightmarish," and "grotesque."[62] The wolf; the mouth; the gape. Ellis's synonyms lead from ugliness to disgust, a horror that "cannot be ignored or covered up," pushing us into the "realm of the abject, uncanny, weird and eerie, the Real, and the shameful."[63] Here, it gapes. Palpable. Here. Shame. Here. Pain.

---

61 Sarah Ciston, "TRAVELNET / 37°45'7.87"N, 122°25'12.50"W," *Poecology* 2 (2012), http://poecology.org/issue-2/sarah-ciston/.

62 Melody Ellis, "Writing Ugly," in *On the Politics of Ugliness*, eds. Sara Rodrigues and Ela Przybylo (London: Palgrave Macmillan, 2018), 293.

63 Ibid.

Here. Who covered it up? It cannot be covered up. It cannot be ignored. This festering wound, this leaking papule. It wants to be squeezed and sliced and cratered. Or, I want. I want to pick apart my own skin, becoming further unbound. An immanent psychosis. An imminent compulsion. What a horror. How uncanny. How ugly. How beautiful. How abject. How animal. How monstrous. What a way to be. What a way to be with and for each other, for oneself.

* * *

On another Thanksgiving Day, one far removed from that Thanksgiving encounter with D, I receive a text message from S. We are each spending this holiday alone, she in her new California apartment, unpacking the boxes that have just arrived for her, and me in a cabin in northern Appalachia trying to recover some pieces of myself in the silence and solitude of the oak and hemlock forests studded with sandstone caverns and rushing waterfalls. S recently moved across the world for a new job, still in a different time zone, but finally back in the same hemisphere as me. She is much closer physically but still feels so far away, as we have had little contact in the past year. The cabin I am renting is largely off the grid, but in the evenings I prop my phone in a window, where it occasionally picks up a light signal.

I am sitting on a stool at the kitchen countertop, when my phone jolts me with the sudden chime of its tone. When I rise to check it, I am surprised to see the message from S. She wanted to let me know she is thinking of me, and she wants to wish me a happy Thanksgiving, and she hopes I am held and feeling loved. I tell her I hope she didn't just think of me because she was remembering the Thanksgiving we spent together many years ago in San Francisco, during which I made her cry when I criticized her baking techniques. She tells me she always thinks of that Thanksgiving each year because, she reminds me, that day was also filled with so much joy. How easily I villainize myself in that memory. But she is also thinking of me because she is unpacking the boxes that had slowly been making their way around the world to her new home. "There's a lot of you in these boxes," she writes. I am immediately brought back into Hanif Abdurraqib's writing about intimacy and the pieces we make of ourselves and leave for the other in our leaving: "I think about how much of myself I've left behind for people to gradually find, heartbroken, over the course of several months."[64] I imagine S unpacking all the bits of myself I had left her to find. She collected pieces of me over the years, the remnants of never-to-be wholes. I feel heartbroken as I wish her a happy Thanksgiving.

After this exchange with S, I return to my reading of Audre Lorde's *The Cancer Journals,* and I am immediately struck by another type of intimacy made up of the molecular pieces of the body carrying over the airwaves. Writing of the days spent in the hospital after her unilateral mastectomy, Lorde tells of waking up one morning to the smell of her lover, Frances, outside her door. She couldn't see her because of the position of the bed rails blocking her view, but she could smell her and knew her presence. What intimacy to notice someone's smell. And from such a distance. A piece of another that we cannot box up and move with us around the world. A skim across the nose. A moment of entry. A fleeting touch. Just for tonight. Just for this moment. Just for this breath.

I want to return to where we began, to nonsexual touch and pleasure. To my one-night stand of cuddling and talking. The smell of D's hair clung to my bedsheets. The smell of her body wrapped into my clothing. We woke up to one another. We clung to one another in the aftermath of our leaving. Our intimacy took the shape of the desires of each of us inside it. Just for one night. But our molecular relationship lasted, bringing us beyond close.

I recently listened to a podcast in which Alain de Botton describes flirting as a nonsexual way in which two people "wake up to each other."[65] I am fixated on the multiple possibilities of

---

64 Abdurraqib, *They Can't Kill Us Until They Kill Us,* 46.

65 Krista Tippett and Alain de Botton, "The True Hard Work of Love and Relationships," in *On Being,* February 9, 2017, https://onbeing.org/programs/

what it can mean to wake up to another person, in the literal morning-after of an encounter and in the metaphorical coming alive to another, sparking or being sparked. When I tell a friend, a French scholar, about this podcast and my new obsession with the nonsexual possibilities of the flirtatious encounter, she tells me that the verb "to flirt" in older French is *fleureter* which comes from the French word *fleur,* or "flower." She talks of how for her fleur evokes both sex and beauty, the one doing the flirting is perhaps moved by beauty or by sex, the possibility of which underlies all our contact. I look up this etymology and find that *fleureter* in Old French means "to talk sweet nonsense" or "to touch a thing in passing," like "bees skimming from flower to flower."[66] So animal. So monstrous. So extraordinary. So beautiful. A caress. The brush of scopae. A corbicula overflowing. An asexual pollination.

What a way to be with one another. What pleasures in sweet nonsense and passing touches, some semblance of love in a skim. We cannot help but leak onto and into one another as we move from flower to flower. We cannot help but absorb and ingest one another in an intimacy full of love's infinite diffractions and neurotic exchanges. Maybe people just want to connect, but it is no longer a matter of sex. In some ways, we are always already connected, physical contact is but a passing reminder of our molecular intimacies. As many styles, intensities, and timbres as beings. "Irresistible attraction toward enfolding each other," Donna Haraway writes, "is the vital motor of living and dying on earth."[67] We live and die in the folds, in the seams, in the gaping gaps, in all that leaks. So creaturely. So strange. Aren't we, then, always trusting strangers with our undoing? Aren't we

---

alain-de-botton-the-true-hard-work-of-love-and-relationships-aug2018/.

66 *Online Etymology Dictionary,* s.v. "flirt," https://www.etymonline.com/ word/flirt.

67 Donna Haraway, "Symbiogenesis, Sympoiesis, and Art Science Activisms for Staying with the Trouble," in *Arts of Living on a Damaged Planet: Ghosts and Monsters of the Anthropocene,* eds. Anna Lowenhaupt Tsing et al. (Minneapolis: University of Minnesota Press, 2017), M25.

always undoing each other and ourselves? Aren't we always undone?

Move through each other; that is how we know each other best. The doors have long been blasted open. We are beyond close. Shit leaks. Piss leaks. Spit leaks. Pus leaks. Milk leaks. Blood leaks. Pain leaks. But so too does joy. So too does delight. So too does love. Which is another way of saying, I cannot contain myself.

Coda, or, The Sweet Hereafter

What happened surely changed me
and the hereafter is full of sadness that is raw and oh so sweet
— Tanya Davis, "Eulogy for You and Me"[1]

I want to write rage but all that comes is sadness.
— Audre Lorde, *The Cancer Journals*[2]

Writing in the aftermath of losing his mother to congestive heart failure, Saeed Jones reflects on the way grief returns in waves with each surge of memory, as if the grieving, due to the compulsion to repeat, will never end: "would it always be this way? Time cascading and crashing in on itself, each memory pushing me back toward the beginning of my grief. I didn't know if I could take it."[3] There have been times in the writing of this book that I didn't know if I could take it, all the callings on ghosts and remnants, tearing the sutures from the wounds, leaking the pain and loss into the words that fall onto these pages. To be frank, there were many times I was ready to give up and never imag-

---

1   Tanya Davis, "Eulogy for You and Me," on *Clocks and Hearts Keep Going* (Sandbar Music, 2010).

2   Audre Lorde, *The Cancer Journals* (San Francisco: Aunt Lute Books, 1980), 11.

3   Saeed Jones, *How We Fight for Our Lives: A Memoir* (New York: Simon & Schuster, 2019), 188.

ined making it this far. And as I finish writing these last pages, I am preoccupied with grief and what it wants of me and for me, even while I want also to access the rage and anger, to sneer back in the faces of all the growling wolves.

Over the last several days, I have spent hours walking through the woods, along rivers and creeks, and in between water-carved formations of Black Hand sandstone in the hills of southern Ohio. With every footfall, Max Porter's titular line, "grief is the thing with feathers" has become a sort of mantra rehearsed either in my head or quietly uttered out loud. I don't know why it comes to me, but it does. Grief's talons clutched tightly to the perch of the heart. I am not even certain I know what it means for grief to be the thing with feathers. I know only that the crow haunts Porter's mourning as he moves between allusions to the literary imaginations of Edgar Allan Poe, Ted Hughes, Sylvia Plath, and Emily Dickinson. I am not sure I have ever fully understood what it means, even, for hope to be the thing with feathers, as Emily Dickinson writes.[4] Hope, the feathered thing that takes hold, that shall not be abashed and asks so little of us. Hope against hope upon hope. Without some sense of hope, how else do we continue in the realm of the living? Grief, both ruffled and downy, the raven of nightmares and the crow of romantic lore. Yet we haven't killed the black birds like we have the wolves. Their talons no match for fangs. Grief, the thing with feathers. The thing that, when grasped at, hardly perches in the soul, but slips away and takes flight. Hope so allegedly steady, grief so unstable in its waves. With each utterance, with each step through the fallen leaves, I feel as though I am stumbling upon my grief. I am both losing myself in the grief that clutches and steeling myself against the waves of grief I know are yet to come. Chronic illness; chronic pain; chronic grief.

---

4   Emily Dickinson, "'Hope' Is the Thing with Feathers," *Poetry Foundation,* https://www.poetryfoundation.org/poems/42889/hope-is-the-thing-with-feathers-314.

* * *

I remember the wet chill of a Pacific Northwest December, the way I curled my body into a chair in front of *L*'s living room window. I hadn't eaten in days, my body wracked with fever, as a deep slow ache crept through my torso and limbs. I remember wrapping my arms around myself as I watched the world outside go on: people passing and buses and cars shuttling through the streets. I felt certain that I could not and would not go on. Melodramatic as it may seem, in this memory, I must let myself indulge the melodrama. I think again of Audre Lorde, who wrote in her journals of her own melodrama in the face of her own mortality, "every once in a while I would think, 'what do I eat? how do I act to announce or preserve my new status as temporary upon this earth?' and then I'd remember that we have always been temporary, and that I had just never really underlined it before, or acted out of it so completely before. And I would feel a little foolish and needlessly melodramatic, but only a little."[5] But only a little.

I wonder to what extent we all become a bit melodramatic in the face of our temporality, as illness brings us closer to a sense of impending death, when the grunt and grit of living doubles down on us. Barthes, after losing his mother, writes in *Mourning Diary* of the everyday encounters of our having-to-die, "now, everywhere, in the street, the café, I see each individual under the aspect of ineluctably *having-to-die,* which is exactly what it means to be *mortal.* — And no less obviously, I see them as *not knowing this to be so*."[6] I am not necessarily dying. But there is nothing like illness to push us that much closer to our status as temporary, our having-to-die and our own abjection. I feel a bit foolish and needlessly melodramatic lamenting my fate in a window on an urban thruway. But only a little. As I curl into myself, knees to my chest, chin on knee, I remember *L* walking

---

5   Lorde, *The Cancer Journals,* 52.
6   Roland Barthes, *Mourning Diary,* ed. Nathalie Léger, trans. Richard Howard (New York: Hill and Wang, 2010), 52.

into the room and sitting down on a chair about an arm's reach away. I remember telling her that everyone always wants to tell you that things are going to be okay, that everything's gonna be all right, but it feels like it will never be okay again; it will never be alright. And with those words, I burst into tears, shocking myself with the sobs that rose from my gut. I hadn't cried like that in years.

I remember precisely the last time I had cried such full-bodied, gasping sobs. But they had been pulled out of me with the force of a flogger and a determined dominatrix, just a couple years earlier in the dungeon. About six months before my time in the dungeon, there was one other instance in which I released my grief in heaving sobs. While I was still dating *R,* there was a week in which my father started calling me incessantly, out of the blue. I hadn't spoken to him in years. I asked my sister if she knew what he might want. "I don't know," she said, "maybe he finally wants to apologize." I eventually called him back. He asked me how I'd been and talked about the weather. He called me again a week later. He told me things actually weren't so great, and that he needed money. I told him surely someone could help him out. He insisted he had asked everyone he could think of, but nobody had money to give him. With my father, most people he might ask for money know by now they will never get it repaid. I waited for him to ask me. I wanted him to ask me, so I could say *no.* I wanted to say *no* to him, a direct *no* to him for perhaps the first time in my life. He didn't ask. I didn't offer. We hung up the phone, and I did not take any more of his calls again.

That evening, I lay in bed, feeling angry at myself for getting my hopes up, for thinking my father actually wanted to reconnect and apologize. Would I never learn? I texted *R* and asked her if she could come over. She did. She crawled into bed with me and wrapped her arms around me. As I fell into her, I burst into sobs and let out some of that anger at myself along with the grief of an unrequited fatherly love. She held me while I heaved and sobbed; no questions, just pure comfort. That moment is still one of the fondest memories I have of my time with *R*, the one time she made space and held my pain, an antidotal salve to the pain caused by my father's neglect. So attentive she was, so unlike him, just for that night.

That was the last time I really let the grief pour out of me in front of a lover, much less in front of myself, until that night in Vancouver in the midst of a feverish and painful illness. "It feels like it's never going to be okay again," I said, just before I burst into tears. It was days into the onset of illness, and it was the first time I cried at all since I became ill. I remember *L* reaching out a hand tentatively to touch my shoulder. I don't remember if she said anything. I remember wishing she had scooped me up into her arms and held me, cradled my body into hers, and told me that, no matter what, she was there for me. I still wish she had done that. I still resent that she didn't.

We will replay this scene months later in my Ohio apartment. Sitting down to brunch just days before the surgery I must have to cut my hole back open, I am suddenly panic-stricken. I hadn't been feeling well that morning, and, just before I sat down at the table, I noticed some swelling in my lymph nodes. I began to panic about what was happening in my body, afraid I wouldn't be able to have this surgery if I were ill or if my immune system was compromised again. I was already terrified of this surgery, this surgery that I had so carefully scheduled at the start of my spring break. I would have just enough time to recover before I had to be back in the classroom. I sat there staring at my plate, holding back tears. *L* had already cleared nearly half her plate when she noticed I wasn't eating. She paused and asked me what was wrong. I told her between choked-back tears about my fears, and, before long, my head was in my hands as I did my best to hold back the sobs that wanted to surge forth from my body. She stood and walked over to me, placing an arm around my shoulders and giving me a few pats. I think she told me to schedule an appointment with my doctor immediately. Then she went back to her seat and resumed eating. I stood, walked away, and closed myself in the bathroom until I felt composed enough to return to the table. I remember staring at my swollen face in the mirror, longing yet again for a tangible memory, repeating the wish, this time without difference, that she had scooped me up into her arms and held me, cradled my body into hers, and told me that, no matter what, she was there for me. I still wish she had done that. I still resent that she didn't.

But sometimes I wonder if I resent a false memory. Part of me believes I must have forgotten the ways in which L surely reached out to me and held me, how she must have offered what comfort and solace she knew how. In more recent months since L and I split up, I found myself shifting my focus to all the ways in which I loved her, the memories I cherish, and the ways in which she brought me joy and happiness. I remember us awe-struck on mountaintops and captivated as we watched the waves roll in from the beach. I remember zipping through crowded cities together, stopping for cocktails in any number of hip bars, and leaving tangled in each other's arms. I remember savoring long nights and slow mornings in bed. I remember the ebullient moments of laughter, the ways she would surprise me with her unexpected humor.

I find myself rehearsing and clinging to these stories because I recognize how readily we can latch onto the painful memories. All the times of hurt and let-down seem so much easier to recall, especially when we are continuing to feel hurt and let down. I think of the way Sara Ahmed writes in *Living a Feminist Life* about memory work: "we work to remember what sometimes we wish would or could just recede."[7] Throughout this book, I have worked so hard to call up and live in the memories I had long wished would recede into an oblivion of the forgotten. But those memories will not recede. They always leave their mark. I want to work, too, to remember that which so easily wants to recede, those moments that warm my heart and fill me with love and gratitude despite, or alongside, the pain and heartache. They do, in fact, leave a different kind of mark, if we let them. We must, also, let the love spill.

---

7   Sara Ahmed, *Living a Feminist Life* (Durham: Duke University Press, 2017), 22.

* * *

What a shock to my system, then, when, after our breakup, *L* tells me the reason she is cutting off communication with me is because I treated her horribly for the last half of our relationship and that it would be damaging for her mental health to maintain contact. She has also accused me of having "abusive tendencies." I take such accusations seriously, which give me pause and require me to take stock of the ways in which I myself have done harm and can do harm. I remember one particularly bad week in Ohio when *L* came to visit, just before my surgery. I remember lashing out in ways I am embarrassed to admit, fearing that my actions are too closely aligned with things my father would do. I remember slamming the toilet lid down every time *L* left it up. I remember growing angry at her for small things, like putting the dishes away in the wrong place or sleeping on my side of the bed. I was no doubt cruel to her in these moments of frustration. I am embarrassed and remorseful.

But I also remember feeling like a wounded animal backed into a corner while someone incessantly poked directly at the scrapes and gouges. *L*'s repetitious diminishment of my pain and suffering as "not a big deal" and "not the worst thing that could happen" is that jab into the festering wound. With each prod, the animal shrinks smaller and smaller away from the threat until it cannot withdraw any further, pressed tightly against the wall. The next jab evokes so much pain and, with nowhere to retreat, the animal lunges forward, teeth bared. What appears as an attack is actually a defense.

This analogy is not designed to excuse my behavior but rather to recognize the ways in which we crumble when our own capacity for pain is tested and put to the limit. I also trust myself to recognize how easily the isolated moments — a day here, a week or so of unbridled arguing there — in which I had caused her pain or mistreated her became months of horrible treatment in her memory. But she is allowed her story. My therapist once said to me, "the only people who know what happened in a relationship are the people inside the relationship." What does

L know? She knows what happened. What do I know? I know what happened. Even if those stories are not corroborative, they happened for each of us. And I think, too, how easily I villainize *L* in my own memories. How easily I villainize *R*. How easily I villainize my mother and father. What a sadness; what a violence too. How easily we forget and let go of the good times, the love, and the ways we were there for one another.

* * *

On a cool December morning, I return home from the doctor's office, the last post-surgical visit I will have for some time. It is still early, and I have a plan for all the writing and grading I will do that day. Instead, I find myself crawling back into bed, feeling depressed and despondent. I eventually move from the bed to the couch, where I begin scrolling through old photos on my phone. The time-stamped images help me piece together a timeline. I realize it was exactly one year ago to the day that I woke up in the burn of fever, completely drenched in my own sweat with the length and depth of my body aching. I wonder if I might chalk up my lethargy and despondency today to somatic memory, the body storing its own anniversary response, keeping the score, so to speak.[8]

I decide to let myself take a sick day. I drink bubbly water and binge-watch online television. The next day, I speak with a dear love on video chat and she asks how my doctor visit went. I tell her about how my doctor, who is usually the one to light up hope in moments I find myself falling into hopeless despair, confirmed what I thought I had already accepted. She told me that at this stage in the rehabilitative process, we may have reached the point where it's as good as it's going to get. She was so sorry to tell me that it's likely I will have to live the rest of my life with this chronic pain that doesn't seem to be resolving with

---

8   "Keeping the score" is a reference to Bessel A. van der Kolk, *The Body Keeps the Score: Brain, Mind, and Body in the Healing of Trauma* (New York: Penguin Books, 2014).

treatment. I told her that yes, I kind of already assumed that. "Anyway," I say. "No, not anyway," she says, "that's huge. That's a big and difficult thing to hear. Of course you went home feeling the way you did." I do everything I can to fight bursting into tears in that moment. She is right. I hadn't let myself account for the impact of this news and the impeccable timing of its arrival. But to my shock, through the sadness, I feel, above all, a sudden surge of rage.

A year ago nearly to the day, I lay feverish and almost certain of death's approach, while *L* told me she couldn't understand why I was making such a big deal of it all. A year later, I am *still* in a doctor's office. I am *still* in pain. It *still* feels like a big deal to me. I tell my confidante that I feel suddenly angry about how all of this — the illness, the pain, the wanting from *L* — follows me and haunts me, yet it was so easy for *L* to… to… I cannot find the right words. "Peace out?," my friend finishes my thought. Yes! How easily *L* turned her back and never looked back, never wanted to know if or how I was healing; how in her last message to me, the one in which she asked me to refrain from contacting her ever again, she signed off by wishing me a productive and relaxing summer, as if she had willfully forgotten that my summer would be pockmarked by frequent doctor visits and pain treatment.

I am reminded of a letter I recently wrote to another friend, who sat with me in the corner of a bar in San Francisco, cradling all the suffering I poured into her lap. I continued to pour it out later as I wrote,

the other night, I was reading Audre Lorde's T*he Cancer Journals,* which I oddly enough approached with renewed interest after moderating the roundtable at [redacted]. The conversations we had made me want to return to Lorde's work, especially in thinking about pain and illness. I was struck by these words she wrote after her unilateral mastectomy, reflecting on a moment in which a nurse withdraws from her upon noticing she has refused to wear a prosthesis to fill the space of her missing breast: "the status of untouchable is a very unreal and lonely one, although it does keep everyone at arm's length, and protects as it insulates. But you can die of that specialness, of the cold, the isolation. It does not serve living. I began quickly to yearn for the warmth of the fray, to be good as the old even while the slightest touch meanwhile threatened to be unbearable."[9] She is writing from a different place, but I am so stricken by these words, feeling to be now damaged, untouchable and unlovable, giving myself over to a solitude that can be as life-giving at times as it is a cold and isolating movement toward death. It does not serve living. I too want to be as good as the old me, eager to jump into the fray of living. But I feel as though such vitalization and hope has been taken from me by someone who has so easily walked away from the damage she has caused.

Rereading the words I wrote, I imagine L standing in a doorway. "Peace out," she says, as she turns and walks away into the fray of her new life.

Anamnesis, a desire:

Rewind. Fluorescent lights. The starched sheets of a hospital bed. Rewind. Fluorescent lights. A hallway. Rewind. Dim house lights. A hallway. My father's hand raised. A couple stomps in my direction. A dive under worn bedsheets. Silence. Fast forward. Fluorescent lights. A hallway. R's finger pointed at me. A couple stomps in my direction. The pull of a doorway. Sunlight. The slam of a door. Fast forward. Fluorescent lights. The starched sheets of a hospital bed. A pool of blood at my elbow. IV lines in the tops of my hands. L's hand on my shoulder. A kiss over the bedrails. Sleep. Rewind. The starched sheets of a hospital bed. A pool of blood at my elbow. IV lines

---

9   Lorde, *The Cancer Journals*, 49.

in the tops of my hands. *L*'s hand on my shoulder. A kiss over the bedrails. Sleep. Rewind. A pool of blood at my elbow. IV lines in the tops of my hands. *L*'s hand on my shoulder. A kiss over the bedrails. Sleep. Rewind. IV lines in the tops of my hands. *L*'s hand on my shoulder. A kiss over the bedrails. Sleep. Rewind. *L*'s hand on my shoulder. A kiss over the bedrails. Sleep. Rewind. A kiss over the bedrails. Pause. A kiss over the bedrails. A kiss. The kiss. Let me hold onto this kiss over the hospital bed. Let me hold onto those moments before she walks through that doorway. Let me hold onto this.

* * *

The first lines of Phoebe Bridger's song, "Motion Sickness," replay over and over in my head, as I reflect on *L*'s walkout: "I hate you for what you did. And I miss you like a little kid."[10] For so long, after a shared life with *L* ended, I missed her and missed her and missed her despite also feeling so angry and betrayed. So much energy put into missing and worrying about someone who has so denied and been in denial to my pain and suffering that she wished me a productive and relaxing summer. So much missing.

I think of myself as a little kid missing and missing and missing the love of my parents even as they beat the want for it out of me or deeper into me, sometimes a little of both. I think of all the ways I missed my father, the scruff of his beard, the fishing trips, the moments when it felt like he really loved me. I think of how I felt like a little kid every time *R* berated me or called me a "petulant child," verbally pushing me backward into childhood. Or, maybe she was simply calling out the childlike ways

---

10   Phoebe Bridgers, "Motion Sickness," on *Stranger in the Alps* (Dead Oceans, 2017).

I responded to such abuse, undoubtedly the only ways I knew how, patterned responses developed in a childhood in which I had learned how to survive similar abuses.

I think of how I felt like a little kid pressed against the door as *R* came at me down the hallway the last time I saw her. I think about how I missed *R* for months and months after I walked through that doorway, how much I wanted her to reach out with an apology or an acceptance of responsibility for the pain she'd wrought. I hated her for what she did, but I missed her like that little kid I became with her.

And now *L*. It's been so much missing, never hating. But after my most recent doctor's visit, a year to the day of what felt like my undoing and after several sleepless nights of anguish and despair, I find myself on the morning of New Year's Eve fully consumed with a burning rage. The missing is gone. All the effort put into remembering the good times together has dissolved into a burning anger teetering on the edges of hatred. After so much time spent wanting rage and only finding sadness, I do not know what to do with the rage that finally broils inside me, almost on cue as the year turns.

From Yanyi's *The Year of Blue Water,* "And on cue the cedars become green and then stone, this person unmaking love from you and placing the pieces elsewhere, again, on earth."[11] Unmaking love *from* you, not *to* you. Because the unmaking is a taking. Taking so much love from you until all that is left turns to stone. All that is left is rage. All that is left is hatred. It breaks us into pieces. We are scattered. We cannot be pieced back together in the wake of it.

* * *

The wolves are relentless in their haunted hunt, or I am relentless in mine. Because in my grief, I want also to access my anger, to be wild with anger, to let anger rewild me. I want to let myself rage at all that is unjust and unfair, at all the pain that

---

11 Yanyi, *The Year of Blue Water* (New Haven: Yale University Press, 2019), 1.

perpetuates not only in my own body but in the world, in all its violences and ongoing harms. I want to write the rage, but, still, sadness comes. All that comes is sadness. I am crying again. Don't believe what they tell you about testosterone working to dam the tears. I am crying because I am also afraid. I am afraid of letting the anger out of my body, afraid of sounding like my father, afraid of becoming a man, afraid of becoming a wolf.

I still startle awake at night, all the rage and grief caught in my throat, my body covered in the sweat of memory. I continue to dream in monsters and in the nightmares of wolves. I have become my own ghosts, howling through this cavernous landscape of bone and blood and tissue. I was and am afraid of my father. I have never actually attributed my father's rage and aggression to the testosterone his body produces, yet I somehow fear that the testosterone I inject into my body will bring me even closer to his likeness. In fact, I have speculated that my body may have erected its own blockage around this fear, refusing to take up the testosterone molecule toward the atrophy of my vocal chords. My voice has changed very little since starting testosterone, and I am convinced it is because I am too afraid that if I sound like my father, I will become him. But in this fear, I must remember that I am not father. My voice is my own, and my howls carry a different register.

I recall Marquis Bey's invective to unbecome the men we don't want to be and to become the men we ought to and need to be.[12] Testosterone will not turn me into my father. Testosterone will not turn me into a wolf. Nevertheless, I remain afraid that it will.

12 Marquis Bey, *Them Goon Rules: Fugitive Essays on Radical Black Feminism* (Tucson: The University of Arizona Press, 2019), 78.

A body, a transit:

Writing these last pages, I have noticed a shift in which strangers have begun to read me more and more often as male, even still with little change in my voice. There are palpable moments at the airport. For years, I experienced anxiety as I approached TSA screening, where the security personnel would either ask me directly which gender they should select on the scanning system or ask me how I am doing today with the idea that my voiced response provides an audible cue for gender when it is not visually determinable. But on two recent trips, I stepped into the body scanner and the agent simply pushed the button. Glancing over my shoulder as I stepped out of the scanner, I noticed the agent had selected "male" for my scan. On one occasion, a zipper on the side of my sweatshirt set off an alert, and without pause or question, a male TSA officer moved in for the pat down. All clear, he wished me a nice day. Later, I tell *M* about this encounter, and I wonder aloud, when did I become a man? Maybe the question is not how did I go from being like a man to being a man; rather, I might ask, when, where, and to whom am I like a man or simply a man? And does testosterone have anything to do with it? *M* says it's not really just a question of when, but where. He describes our legibility as men as points that move through time and space, contextually dependent as to where, when, and how people will see what they see. A man is something I am becoming for others even as I remain unsure what I am becoming or unbecoming for myself.

I have long been skeptical and remain resistant to the mythologies of testosterone as a powerful chemical, or an elixir even, that makes people do and want things in ways that put so much agency on the hormone. As I have highlighted, in *Testosterone*

Rex, Cordelia Fine works through study after study in order to dispel these myths of the so-called "Testosterone Rex," the testosterone-fueled monster that causes aggression and violence. In a corollary, Rebecca Jordan-Young and Katrina Karkazis uncover the socio-cultural contexts and methodological practices that allow such myths to persist. These stories of the testosterone-charged monster are inevitably caught up in ideologies of white supremacy and an imagined ideal order to hormonal balance and its attendant conceptualization of "right" or "proper" masculinity.

Still, yes, I do think testosterone does things; this whole book has been a meditation on what testosterone can and cannot do. But this book is also about what the body does with testosterone and how we are the artisans of who we become. Further, I am wary and weary of the idea that testosterone can make us do particular things. Testosterone will not make me angry; it will not suddenly make me sexist. I have heard trans men make this claim, even seen it in writing, about how testosterone shifts their views of women so much that they suddenly understand where sexism lives in a body fueled by testosterone. Testosterone will not make me more aggressive; it will not make me become my father. It may reshape how I experience my anger, just as so many other things shape and reshape our affective lives right alongside our hormonal shifts. Jordan-Young and Karkazis write, "T is at once a specific molecule and a mercurial cultural figure."[13] How do we distinguish what the molecule does and what we want it to do? How much of our own wanting makes testosterone into that mercurial cultural figure and not the other way around?

I am angry. I am wild with anger. But it is not testosterone that makes me angry or increases my anger. It is my own wounding, my attachment to closure, and my inability to let go of that which will likely always remain unresolved. In *Sovereignties in Question,* Derrida writes, "the wound consists precisely

---

13   Rebecca M. Jordan-Young and Katrina Karkazis, *Testosterone: An Unauthorized Biography* (Cambridge: Harvard University Press, 2019), 11.

in claiming to discover and to master meaning, in claiming to suture or to saturate, to fill this emptiness, to close the mouth."[14] But I have written how the wound refuses the mastery of meaning, refuses closure, and pops open the sutures. I have become preoccupied with the question of how to live on when one is still gaping, leaking, and bleeding. I think about this as I watch Ricky Gervais's Netflix series, *After Life,* which follows a man, Tony, as he figures out how to live on after his wife's life has ended. She died of cancer, no less. Tony is miserable and suicidal, and, rather than kill himself, he makes everyone around him miserable with his despair-driven cruelty. I cannot say I relate to Tony's turn to reckless cruelty toward others. But I do empathize with the feelings of hopelessness and unmattering that drive Tony's actions, after having journeyed so recently through intense episodes of suicidality in relation to living on after illness and living in illness, after feeling like life had been sapped out of me.

Anamnesis, a decision:

At the beginning of our relationship, L and I went on a camping and canoe trip in northern British Columbia. Heading out of Vancouver in the middle of a weekday afternoon, we were surprised to suddenly be stopped in gridlock traffic on the Lions Gate Bridge. As we began to cross the bridge, traffic was funneled into one lane. I spotted several police cruisers parked in the right lanes ahead, and I noticed several uniformed officers forming a small semi-circle on the sidewalk. As L drove, I watched out my window as we passed the crowd of officers. Just beyond them, I saw a person on the other side of the railing, perched on the edge of the bridge, hugging a pole. If they

14 Jacques Derrida, *Sovereignties in Question: The Poetics of Paul Celan,* eds. Thomas Dutoit and Outi Pasanen (New York: Fordham University Press, 2005), 167.

let go and leaned back, they would plummet into the Burrard Inlet below. As we rolled past in our traffic-slowed crawl, I caught the person's face, gaze turned downward, a quietude in their being. I remember an officer with a pleading look, another with arms outstretched as if to hold everyone back from any sudden moves. I remember a solemnity and deep sadness hanging thick in the air. The image and its attendant affective and somatic memories have haunted me ever since. For days, upon our return from our trip, I scoured the internet for any information as to what became of that person I felt so fleetingly present with. I never turned up any news. My hope is that my fruitless searches were an indication that the person clinging to that edge made the climb back over the rail into the fray of the living.

I recall this story because I have thought of that moment on the bridge again and again since it happened. When I was in the deepest aches and throes of fever and sickness, I felt only that I wanted to die. I became reckless with my life, stepping into the street without double-checking for oncoming traffic, abusing alcohol with the medications I was on, and fantasizing endlessly about how I would end my own life. Every time I closed my eyes, I saw the person on the bridge, their arms around the pole, and their face quiet and forlorn. Every time I closed my eyes, I saw the person on the bridge, but with every repetition, my mind created a new story. In some versions, the person looks up and directly into my eyes, inviting; sometimes a slight smile cracks across their lips; sometimes a tear glints in their eye; sometimes a wink, a wave, a kiss blown on the wind. Every time an invitation, every time another uncanny return, every time a want, every time a need, every time another fall, every time a face, every time a bridge, every time another time, every time the last time.

A couple days after my fever broke and I regained enough of an appetite to try to eat something, I told L I was going to walk to the store on the corner to purchase some juice and some yogurt. She asked me if I would be okay going alone, and I said yes. When I stepped outside, I was shocked by the crispness of the air on a sunny afternoon following a cold morning rain shower. The mountains were in full view in all their spectacularity, never ceasing to catch my breath with their beauty even in moments when nothing seems worth pausing to live with or for. In this dazed reverie, I walked past the grocery store and kept walking and walking until I found a park bench. I sat there and watched a group of young people play soccer while the sun sank lower in the sky, and the mountains took on a deep orange glow. In this moment, watching the world light up around me, I told myself, "you have to decide to live."

As the sky grew darker, I realized I should be getting back. I didn't bring my phone, so I had no idea what time it was. When I returned to L's place, no one was home, and I was locked out. I sat down on the porch and lay back in exhaustion while I waited, whispering to myself like a mantra, "you have to decide to live." About five minutes later, L returned home, frantic and relieved to find me on the porch. She said she had been driving around town looking for me. She drove to all the nearest bridges, fearing I had decided to jump. She almost went to Lions Gate before she turned back, thinking there was no way I could have made it that far on foot. I told her I was so sorry, that I didn't mean to make her worry, that I lost track of time, and that to the contrary, I had told myself that it was time to decide to live.

But in the ensuing months, whenever I dip back down into the not-wanting-to-live, I think of L heading to the Lions Gate Bridge. I think of myself hugging the pole. I think of closing my eyes and letting go. I imagine the roar of water in my ears, the cold shock of the sea, the quietness of death. I imagine, in a parallel universe, I did jump, and I am now living a life I am not supposed to have lived. I cannot help but think that I should have jumped. I should have jumped. I could have jumped. But I decided to live.

By the end of the first season of *After Life,* Tony has a bit of an epiphany. He tells his acquaintance in the cemetery, a woman whose husband is buried next to Tony's wife, "even though I'm in pain, it's worth sticking around to maybe make my little corner of the world a slightly better place."[15]Although Tony states that his own happiness is a long shot, he realizes he can bring moments of happiness to others. He soon undertakes small acts of kindness: he leaves a bottle of scotch for his postman; he leaves a bicycle for a child on the playground he had earlier threatened; he places a picture of his co-worker's favorite comedian in her snow globe. In these small actions, he finds a reason to keep living — to bring others joy even though his own joy seems so far off and impossible. As silly as it may seem, this television show flickers a small light of hope, in recognizing that even if my own happiness feels so far off it seems impossible, that underneath the burning rage and anger, I still have so much love to give. And for that, I must decide to live. I still want to find the love story here.

* * *

Through love, Diane Enns writes, "we let ourselves into another life and our own alters irrevocably. In this way, our lives are inhabited by others, and even when we lose them, they remain lodged within us."[16] Even when we lose those we have loved, they remain with us — their hair, their memory, their ghosts — so many ways they lodge within us, both taking and giving. Of the things that may haunt us, Avery Gordon names "the unexpected arrival of ghosts or wolves or eerie photographs," all of which

---

15 Ricky Gervais, dir., *After Life,* Episode 6 (Netflix, 2019).

16 Dianne Enns, *Love in the Dark: Philosophy by Another Name* (New York: Columbia University Press, 2016), 42.

have haunted these pages.[17] Fort. Da. Gone. There. Gone. Here. Eternal return. How uncanny. How at home. Lodged. The question is in what we do with those lodgings. How do we live on, live in them, and live with them?

I have written here an inquiry into how ghosts — especially the ghosts of trauma — haunt and impress upon the living body, and how our narratives — our tellings and retellings — can heal or suffer or reshape the body in pain, the body abused and traumatized, the body cut and sutured, the body in transition. I have pondered how the rigid scar tissue arcing across my chest stitches me into a fabric of biomedical technologies, bodies modified and pieced together, each ridge of flesh telling a different story of holding trauma and conjuring ghosts. I have written of how this wolf hunt is also something of a ghost haunt, linked to my usage of testosterone. I have written of how each plunge of the needle into my thigh muscle calls up histories of colonial violence through hormone extraction, in addition to my own buried memories of abuse suffered at the hands of those I loved and wanted love from.

Yet testosterone has helped me to call up the memories, chase down the monsters, and summon the ghosts; to write a counter-memory for today; and to make contact that touches the past in order to reshape more livable todays and tomorrows. Testosterone has become my vehicle of inheritance. Carol Rambo writes, "when I allow the remembering and the crying, a piece of myself comes back to me and I am more than I was as a result."[18] I think of what this idea of remembering as a recovery of the pieces of oneself means for that notion of the impossibility of wholeness, that we are always undoing and undone, always in parts and pieces. Always piecing together all that we inherit. What does it

---

17 Avery Gordon, *Ghostly Matters: Haunting and the Sociological Imagination* (Minneapolis: University of Minnesota Press, 2008), 53; "Fort. Da." is of course a reference to Sigmund Freud, *Beyond the Pleasure Principle,* trans. James Strachey (New York: W.W. Norton, 1961), 13–17.

18 Carol Rambo, "Twitch: A Performance of Chronic Liminality," in *Handbook of Autoethnography,* eds. Stacy Holman Jones, Tony E. Adams, and Carolyn Ellis (Walnut Creek: Left Coast Press, 2013), 634.

mean to become more? To become more than? To become more than we were?

How does memory continue to mark us and remake us beyond the event itself, each recollection a new event, a repetition with a difference? In *Two Kinds of Decay,* Sarah Manguso ends the book with this sentiment, "everything that happens is the last time it happens. We see things only as their own fatal brightness, and there is nothing after that brightness. You can't learn from remembering. You can't learn from guessing. You can learn only from moving forward at the rate you are moved, as brightness, into brightness."[19] But I wonder what it means to move into brightness as brightness when brightness is also fatal, a reminder perhaps that we are hurtling always towards death.

I think of how Tanya Davis sings of wanting more radiance, a word with a nearness to brightness but with more planes of register.[20] Radiance is evocative of both light and heat, warmth and cheer. I imagine radiance as less fatal and more vivacious. I want to move forward into a radiant remainder of life rather than into the fatality of brightness. But I also need to revisit and remember those brightnesses that convinced me there would be nothing after in order to remember there has indeed been so much after. I think of how Thomas Page McBee and Amy Berkowitz need to remember in order to learn and need to look backward in order to move forward. I think of how Christina Crosby refuses to forget the past. Describing forgetting as both impossible and "imperiously necessary," she writes, "I can't forget the past. I won't. I need it, I want and I need to remember the body that I once was."[21] We do learn from remembering. Maybe we need to call up those past moments of brightness and darkness both to brighten us, to propel us into the radiance that awaits, and to let ourselves fully mourn the bodies we once were and the pieces we gave away, gave up, or had taken from us.

---

19 Sarah Manguso, *The Two Kinds of Decay* (New York: Farrar, Straus, and Giroux, 2008), 184.

20 Davis, "Eulogy for You and Me."

21 Christina Crosby, *A Body, Undone: Living On after Great Pain* (New York: New York University Press, 2017), 201.

And let us not forget Derrida (again): repetition and first time, repetition and last time, the first time is the last time. The happening is singular. When it happens, it is the last time it happens, its own fatal brightness and nothing more. Until it happens again. But that is a new happening, each repetition its own singularity, its own first and last. We remember and we forget. We do and we redo. Everything happens for the last time, but nothing is once and for all. All we can do is let it happen, or, let ourselves happen. Clarice Lispector writes, simply, in the face of a world with no order, "I let myself happen."[22] Our happening is our being, our constant becoming (undone). It is no way to live, but it is how we live. It is how we happen.

Just as Manguso ends her book with a propulsion toward brightness, Crosby ends hers with a propulsion toward life: "all of us who live on are not what we were, but are becoming, always becoming."[23] I recall a session with my therapist in which I reach the assertion, "I can be a better man (than my father)" through the chain of thoughts, "I can become a man if I want to… I can be a man if I want to be… I don't have to become a man… I don't have to be a man… If I do want to be a man, I can become the man I want to be… I can be a better man (than my father)." "Yes," she replies, "you can… and you are." My eyes pool. I nearly cry.

Tears of joy and tears of grief. The recognition of what one is or is becoming is both painful and pleasant. We are always living in and between. In her call to live on, Crosby also writes of choosing to live fully and passionately. "Every time I make that choice," she writes, "I move further from the past, and am increasingly detached from what once was."[24] I am afraid to detach myself from the pasts I have recounted here, but I am also determined to let go of that which I have forgiven as well

---

22 Jacques Derrida, *Specters of Marx: The State of the Debt, The Work of Mourning, and The New International,* trans. Peggy Kamuf (New York: Routledge, 1994), 10; Clarice Lispector, *Água Viva,* ed. Benjamin Moser, trans. Stefan Tobler (New York: New Directions Books, 2012), 17.

23 Crosby, *A Body, Undone,* 202.

24 Ibid.

as that which I cannot forgive. But that does not mean forgetting. Rather, letting go is a way of living on, in, through, and with. Such a patchwork of living. Becoming in the gaps, in the cuts, in the wounds, in the gapes, and even within the stitches, bandages, and sutures. Gender without telos. Love without telos. Pain without end. Love without end. Being as becoming. Happening. Doing and undoing. Becoming, becoming. Always becoming. What happened surely did change me. It marked me. It created wounds that are still healing, that are always ripe for reopening where the sutures cannot hold. The hereafter cannot be anything but raw and sad and yes, even passionate, radiant, and oh so sweet.

Bibliography

Abdurraqib, Hanif. *They Can't Kill Us Until They Kill Us.*
Columbus: Two Dollar Radio, 2017.

Ahmed, Sara. *Living a Feminist Life.* Durham: Duke University
Press, 2017.

———. *Queer Phenomenology: Orientations, Objects, Others.*
Durham: Duke University Press, 2006.

———. *The Cultural Politics of Emotion.* New York: Routledge,
2004.

Akbar, Kaveh. *Calling a Wolf a Wolf.* Farmington: Alice James
Books, 2017.

Allison, Dorothy. *Bastard Out of Carolina.* New York: Penguin
Books, 1992.

———. "Notes to a Young Feminist." *In These Times,* April 27,
2004. https://inthesetimes.com/article/notes-to-a-young-
feminist.

Alsous, Zaina. *A Theory of Birds.* Fayetteville: University of
Arkansas Press, 2019.

Anzengruber, Florian, Katrin Ruhwinkel, Adhideb Ghosh,
Richard Klaghofer, Undine E. Lang, and Alexander
A. Navarini. "Wide Range of Age of Onset and Low
Referral Rates to Psychiatry in a Large Cohort of
Acne Excoriée at a Swiss Tertiary Hospital." *Journal of
Dermatological Treatment* 29, no. 3 (2017): 277–80. DOI:
10.1080/09546634.2017.1364693.

Apps, Aaron. *Intersex: A Memoir*. Grafton: Tarpaulin Sky Press, 2015.

Axel, Bob. "Rockville Centre Parking." PAIN EXHIBIT: A *Non-Profit Art Exhibit*. http://painexhibit.org/en/galleries/isolation-and-imprisonment/ag04_axel/.

Bakhtin, Mikhail. *Rabelais and His World*. Translated by Helene Iswolsky. Cambridge: MIT Press, 1968.

Barad, Karen. "Quantum Entanglements and Hauntological Relations of Inheritance: Dis/continuities, SpaceTime Enfoldings, and Justice-to-Come." *Derrida Today* 3, no. 2 (2010): 240–68. DOI: 10.3366/drt.2010.0206.

——. "TransMaterialities: Trans*/Matter/Realities and Queer Political Imaginings." GLQ: *A Journal of Lesbian and Gay Studies* 21, nos. 2–3 (2015): 387–422. https://muse.jhu.edu/article/581607.

Barthes, Roland. *Camera Lucida: Reflections on Photography*. Translated by Richard Howard. New York: Hill and Wang, 1981.

——. *Mourning Diary*. Edited by Nathalie Léger. Translated by Richard Howard. New York: Hill and Wang, 2010.

Beauchamp, Toby. *Going Stealth: Transgender Politics and U.S. Surveillance Practices*. Durham: Duke University Press, 2019.

Beckett, Samuel. *Not I*. London: Faber, 1973.

Bellamy, Dodie. *When the Sick Rule the World*. South Pasadena: Semiotext(e), 2015.

Berkowitz, Amy. *Tender Points*. Oakland: Timeless, Infinite Light, 2015.

Berlant, Lauren. "Intimacy: A Special Issue." *Critical Inquiry* 24, no. 2 (1998): 281–88. http://www.jstor.org/stable/1344169.

"Between the Worlds." *Dori Midnight*. https://dorimidnight.com/apothecary/between-the-worlds/.

Bey, Marquis. *Them Goon Rules: Fugitive Essays on Radical Black Feminism*. Tucson: The University of Arizona Press, 2019.

———. "The Trans*-Ness of Blackness, the Blackness of Trans*Ness." *Transgender Studies Quarterly* 4, no. 2 (2017): 275–95. DOI: 10.1215/23289252-3815069.

Biss, Eula. *On Immunity: An Inoculation.* Minneapolis: Graywolf Press, 2015.

———. "The Pain Scale." *Creative Nonfiction* 1, no. 32 (2007): 65–84. https://www.jstor.org/stable/44363570.

Blackman, Lisa. "Affective Politics, Debility, and Hearing Voices: Towards a Feminist Politics of Ordinary Suffering." *Feminist Review* 111, no. 1 (2015): 25–41. DOI: 10.1057/fr.2015.24.

Bottoms, Stephen. "Diane Torr Obituary." *The Guardian,* June 29, 2017. https://www.theguardian.com/artanddesign/2017/jun/29/diane-torr-obituary.

Brison, Susan J. *Aftermath: Violence and the Remaking of a Self.* Princeton: Princeton University Press, 2003.

Brocq, M.L. "L'acné excoriée des jeunes filles." *Revue generale de clinique et de therapique* 12 (1898): 139–97.

Burroughs, Augusten. *A Wolf at the Table: A Memoir of My Father.* New York: Picador, 2008.

Butler, Judith. *Bodies That Matter: On the Discursive Limits of Sex.* New York: Routledge, 1993.

———. *Undoing Gender.* New York: Routledge, 2004.

Calou, Yana. "The Picking Diaries." *Hematopoiesis* 3 (2018).

Campt, Tina M. *Listening to Images.* Durham: Duke University Press, 2017.

Cannon, Jeffrey S., and Larry E. Overman. "Is There No End to the Total Synthesis of Strychnine? Lessons Learned in Strategy and Tactics in Total Synthesis." *Angewandte Chemie International Edition* 51, no. 18 (2012): 4288–311. DOI: 10.1002/anie.201107385.

Caruth, Cathy. *Unclaimed Experience: Trauma, Narrative, and History.* Baltimore: Johns Hopkins University Press, 1996.

———. "Violence and Time: Traumatic Survivals." *Assemblage* 20 (1993): 24–25. DOI: 10.2307/3181682.

Celan, Paul. *Selected Poems and Prose of Paul Celan.* Translated by John Felstiner. New York: W.W. Norton, 2001.

Cerankowski, KJ. "Illegible: Asexualities in Media, Literature, and Performance." PhD Thesis, Stanford University, 2014. https://purl.stanford.edu/nh910mw8702.

Chen, Mel Y. *Animacies: Biopolitics, Racial Mattering, and Queer Affect.* Durham: Duke University Press, 2012.

Ciston, Sarah. "TRAVELNET / 37° 45'7.87"N, 122° 25'12.50"W." *Poecology* 2 (2012). http://poecology.org/issue-2/sarah-ciston/.

Clare, Eli. *Brilliant Imperfection: Grappling with Cure.* Durham: Duke University Press, 2017.

———. *Exile and Pride: Disability, Queerness, and Liberation.* Cambridge: South End Press, 1999.

Coan, Jaime Shearn. *Troubling the Line: Trans and Genderqueer Poetry and Poetics.* Edited by TC Tolbert and Trace Peterson. Brooklyn: Nightboat Books, 2013.

Coates, Ta-Nehisi. "In Defense of a Loaded Word." *The New York Times,* November 23, 2013. https://www.nytimes.com/2013/11/24/opinion/sunday/coates-in-defense-of-a-loaded-word.html.

Coleman, Jon T. *Vicious: Wolves and Men in America.* New Haven: Yale University Press, 2004.

Cooper, T. *Real Man Adventures.* San Francisco: McSweeney's Books, 2012.

Cremins, Brian. "Bodies, Transfigurations, and Bloodlust in Edie Fake's Graphic Novel 'Gaylord Phoenix.'" *Journal of Medical Humanities* 34 (2013): 301–13. DOI: 10.1007/s10912-013-9214-z.

Crosby, Christina. *A Body, Undone: Living On after Great Pain.* New York: New York University Press, 2017.

Cukor, George, dir. *Gaslight.* 1944; Metro-Goldwyn-Mayer, 2004.

Cvetkovich, Ann. *An Archive of Feelings: Trauma, Sexuality, and Lesbian Public Cultures.* Durham: Duke University Press, 2003.

Delany, Samuel R. *Times Square Red, Times Square Blue.* New York: New York University Press, 1999.

Deleuze, Gilles, and Félix Guattari. *A Thousand Plateaus: Capitalism and Schizophrenia*. Translated by Brian Massumi. Minneapolis: University of Minnesota Press, 1987.

Derrida, Jacques. *Sovereignties in Question: The Poetics of Paul Celan*. Edited by Thomas Dutoit and Outi Pasanen. New York: Fordham University Press, 2005.

———. *Specters of Marx: The State of the Debt, The Work of Mourning, and The New International*. Translated by Peggy Kamuf. New York: Routledge, 1994.

Diagnostic and Statistical Manual of Mental Disorders, Fifth Edition (DSM-5). Arlington: American Psychiatric Association, 2013.

Dickinson, Emily. "'Hope' Is the Thing with Feathers." *Poetry Foundation*. https://www.poetryfoundation.org/poems/42889/hope-is-the-thing-with-feathers-314.

Didion, Joan. *The White Album*. New York: Farrar, Straus and Giroux, 1979.

Dombek, Kristin. *The Selfishness of Others: An Essay on the Fear of Narcissism*. New York: Farrar, Straus and Giroux, 2016.

Driskill, Qwo-Li. *Walking with Ghosts*. Cambridge: Salt Publishing, 2005.

Easton, Dossie, and Janet W. Hardy. *The New Bottoming Book*. Emeryville: Greenery Press, 2001.

Ellis, Melody. "Writing Ugly." In *On the Politics of Ugliness*, edited by Sara Rodrigues and Ela Przybylo, 291–307. London: Palgrave Macmillan, 2018.

Enns, Diane. *Love in the Dark: Philosophy by Another Name*. New York: Columbia University Press, 2016.

Evans, Marc, dir. *Snow Cake*. Alliance Atlantis, 2006.

Fake, Edie. *Gaylord Phoenix*. Jackson Heights: Secret Acres, 2010.

———. *Gaylord Phoenix #7*. Chicago: Perfectly Acceptable Press, 2017.

———. *Gaylord Phoenix #8*. Brooklyn: Pegacorn Press, 2017.

"Film & Music." *Cris Mazza*. http://cris-mazza.com/projects/.

Fine, Cordelia. *Testosterone Rex: Myths of Sex, Science, and Society.* New York: W.W. Norton, 2017.

Fjelstad, Margalis. *Stop Caretaking the Borderline of Narcissist: How to End the Drama and Get On with Life.* Lanham: Rowman & Littlefield Publishers, 2013.

Foucault, Michel. *Language, Counter-Memory, Practice: Selected Essays and Interviews.* Edited by Donald F. Bouchard. Translated by Donald F. Bouchard and Sherry Simon. Ithaca: Cornell University Press, 1977.

Freccero, Carla. "Wolf, or Homo Homini Lupus." In *Arts of Living on a Damaged Planet: Ghosts and Monsters of the Anthropocene,* edited by Anna Lowenhaupt Tsing, Heather Swanson, Elaine Gan, and Nils Bubandt, M91–M105. Minneapolis: University of Minnesota Press, 2017.

Freud, Sigmund. "'A Child is Being Beaten': A Contribution to the Study of the Origin of Sexual Perversions." In T*he Standard Edition of the Complete Psychological Works of Sigmund Freud, Vol. 17: An Infantile Neurosis and Other Works (1917–1919),* edited and translated by James Strachey with Anna Freud, 175–204. London: Hogarth Press, 1955.

———. *Beyond the Pleasure Principle.* Translated by James Strachey. New York: W.W. Norton, 1961.

———. *Civilization and Its Discontents.* Translated by James Strachey. New York: W.W. Norton, 1961.

———. "On Narcissism." In *The Standard Edition of the Complete Psychological Works of Sigmund Freud,* Vol. 14: O*n the History of the Psycho-Analytic Movement, Papers on Meta-psychology and Other Works (1914–1916),* edited and translated by James Strachey with Anna Freud, 67–102. London: Hogarth Press, 1964.

——— "Remembering, Repeating, and Working-Through." In *The Standard Edition of the Complete Psychological Works of Sigmund Freud,* Vol. 12: *Case History of Schreber, Papers on Technique and Other Works (1911–1913),* edited and translated by James Strachey with Anna Freud, 147–56. London: Hogarth Press, 1958.

————. *The Interpretation of Dreams*. Translated by A.A. Brill. 3rd edn. New York: The Macmillan Company, 1913.

————. *Three Contributions to the Theory of Sex*. Translated by A.A. Brill. New York: Nervous and Mental Disease Publishing Company, 1918.

————. *Three Essays on the Theory of Sexuality*. Edited and translated by James Strachey. New York: Basic Books, 1962.

————. "The 'Uncanny.'" In *The Standard Edition of the Complete Psychological Works of Sigmund Freud*, Vol. 17: *An Infantile Neurosis and Other Works (1917–1919)*, edited and translated by James Strachey with Anna Freud, 217–56. London: Hogarth Press, 1955.

Frosh, Stephen. *Hauntings: Psychoanalysis and Ghostly Transmissions*. London: Palgrave Macmillan, 2013.

Gay, Ross. *The Book of Delights*. Chapel Hill: Algonquin Books, 2019.

Gay, Roxane. *Hunger: A Memoir of (My) Body*. New York: HarperCollins, 2017.

Gervais, Ricky, dir. *After Life*. Netflix, 2019.

Gilbert, Scott F. "Holobiont by Birth: Multilineage Individuals as the Concretion of Cooperative Processes." In *Arts of Living on a Damaged Planet: Ghosts and Monsters of the Anthropocene*, edited by Anna Lowenhaupt Tsing, Heather Swanson, Elaine Gan, and Nils Bubandt, M73–M89. Minneapolis: University of Minnesota Press, 2017.

Gill-Peterson, Jules. "The Technical Capacities of the Body: Assembling Race, Technology, and Transgender." *Transgender Studies Quarterly* 1, no. 3 (2014): 402–18. DOI: 10.1215/23289252-2685660.

Gilmore, Leigh. "Agency without Mastery: Chronic Pain and Posthuman Life Writing." *Biography* 35, no. 1 (Winter 2012): 83–98. DOI: 10.1353/bio.2012.0011.

Girmay, Aracelis. *Kingdom Animalia*. Rochester: BOA Editions, 2011.

Gordon, Avery. *Ghostly Matters: Haunting and the Sociological Imagination*. Minneapolis: University of Minnesota Press, 2008.

Grover, Martha. *The End of My Career*. Portland: Perfect Day Publishing, 2016.

Gumbs, Alexis Pauline. *M Archive: After the End of the World*. Durham: Duke University Press, 2018.

Hanh, Thich Nhat. *How to Love*. Berkeley: Parallax Press, 2014.

Haraway, Donna. "Symbiogenesis, Sympoiesis, and Art Science Activisms for Staying with the Trouble." In *Arts of Living on a Damaged Planet: Ghosts and Monsters of the Anthropocene,* edited by Anna Lowenhaupt Tsing, Heather Swanson, Elaine Gan, and Nils Bubandt, M25–M50. Minneapolis: University of Minnesota Press, 2017.

Harris, Nadine Burke. *The Deepest Well: Healing the Long-Term Effects of Childhood Adversity*. Boston: Houghton Mifflin Harcourt, 2018.

Hartman, Saidiya. *Lose Your Mother: A Journey Along the Atlantic Slave Route*. New York: Farrar, Straus, and Giroux, 2008.

Hayward, Eva. "More Lessons from a Starfish: Prefixial Flesh and Transspeciated Selves." *Women's Studies Quarterly* 36, nos. 3–4 (Fall/Winter 2008): 64–85. DOI: 10.1353/wsq.0.0099.

Heath, Stephen. *The Sexual Fix*. London: Macmillan, 1982.

Hedva, Johanna. "Sick Woman Theory." *Mask Magazine,* January 2016. https://johannahedva.com/SickWomanTheory_Hedva_2020.pdf.

Hegel, Georg W.F. *The Phenomenology of Spirit*. Translated by Terry Pinkard. Cambridge: Cambridge University Press, 2017.

Herman, Judith Lewis. *Trauma and Recovery: The Aftermath of Violence from Domestic Abuse to Political Terror*. New York: Basic Books, 1997.

Herring, Scott. "Material Deviance: Theorizing Queer Objecthood." *Postmodern Culture* 21, no. 2 (January 2011). DOI: 10.1353/pmc.2011.0009. http://www.pomoculture.org/2013/09/03/material-deviance-theorizing-queer-objecthood/.

Hersch, Matthew H. "'Calm, But Still Alert': Marketing Stelazine to Disturbed America, 1958–1980." *Pharmacy in History* 50, no. 4 (2008): 140–48. http://www.jstor.org/stable/41112401.

Hotchkiss, Sandy. *Why Is It Always About You? The Seven Deadly Sins of Narcissism*. New York: Free Press, 2003.

Jagose, Annamarie. *Orgasmology*. Durham: Duke University Press, 2013.

Jamison, Leslie. *The Empathy Exams: Essays*. Minneapolis: Graywolf Press, 2014.

———. *The Recovering: Intoxication and Its Aftermath*. New York: Little, Brown and Company, 2018.

Jones, Ernest. "The Early Development of Female Sexuality." In *Psychoanalysis and Female Sexuality*, edited by Hendrik M. Ruitenbeek, 21–35. New Haven: College & University Press, 1966.

Jones, Saeed. *How We Fight for Our Lives: A Memoir*. New York: Simon & Schuster, 2019.

Jordan-Young, Rebecca M., and Katrina Karkazis. *Testosterone: An Unauthorized Biography*. Cambridge: Harvard University Press, 2019.

Kafka, Franz. *Letters to Friends, Family, and Editors*. Translated by Richard Winston and Clara Winston. New York: Schocken Books, 1977.

Khumalo, Nonhlanhla P., Gasnat Shaboodien, Sian M.J. Hemmings, Johanna C. Moolman-Smook, and Dan J. Stein. "Pathologic Grooming (Acne Excoriée, Trichotillomania, and Nail Biting) in Four Generations of a Single Family." *JAAD Case Reports* 2, no. 1 (2016): 51–53. DOI: 10.1016/j.jdcr.2015.11.002.

Kligerman, Eric. *Sites of the Uncanny: Paul Celan, Specularity and the Visual Arts*. New York: Walter de Gruyter, 2007.

Kolbeins, Graham. "Rad Queers: Edie Fake." *The Comics Journal*, February 5, 2014. http://www.tcj.com/rad-queers-edie-fake/.

Kristeva, Julia. *Powers of Horror: An Essay on Abjection*. Translated by Leon S. Roudiez. New York: Columbia University Press, 1982.

Lanzoni, Susan. "A Short History of Empathy." *The Atlantic,* October 15, 2015. https://www.theatlantic.com/health/archive/2015/10/a-short-history-of-empathy/409912/.

Laub, Dori. "Bearing Witness, or the Vicissitudes of Listening." In *Testimony: Crises of Witnessing in Literature, Psychoanalysis, and History,* edited by Shoshana Felman and Dori Laub, 57–74. New York: Routledge, 1992.

Le Guin, Ursula K. "Deep in Admiration." In *Arts of Living on a Damaged Planet: Ghosts and Monsters of the Anthropocene,* edited by Anna Lowenhaupt Tsing, Heather Swanson, Elaine Gan, and Nils Bubandt, M15–M21. Minneapolis: University of Minnesota Press, 2017.

Levine, Peter A. *In an Unspoken Voice: How the Body Releases Trauma and Restores Goodness.* Berkeley: North Atlantic Books, 2010.

Lewis, C.S. *The Problem of Pain.* New York: The Macmillan Company, 1948.

Leys, Ruth. *Trauma: A Genealogy.* Chicago: The University of Chicago Press, 2000.

Lispector, Clarice. *Água Viva.* Edited by Benjamin Moser. Translated by Stefan Tobler. New York: New Directions Books, 2012.

———. *The Passion According to G.H.* Edited by Benjamin Moser. Translated by Idra Novey. New York: New Directions Books, 2012.

Liu, Kenji C. *Monsters I Have Been.* Farmington: Alice James Books, 2019.

Lopez, Barry Holstun. *Of Wolves and Men.* New York: Charles Scribner's Sons, 1978.

Lorde, Audre. *The Cancer Journals.* San Francisco: Aunt Lute Books, 1980.

Love, Heather. *Feeling Backward: Loss and the Politics of Queer History.* Cambridge: Harvard University Press, 2007.

Machado, Carmen Maria. *In the Dream House.* Minneapolis: Graywolf Press, 2019.

Malatino, Hil. "Biohacking Gender." *Angelaki: Journal of the Theoretical Humanities* 22, no. 2 (2017): 179–90. DOI: 10.1080/0969725X.2017.1322836.

———. *Queer Embodiment: Monstrosity, Medical Violence, and Intersex Experience*. Lincoln: University of Nebraska Press, 2019.

———. "Tough Breaks: Trans Rage and the Cultivation of Resilience." *Hypatia: A Journal of Feminist Philosophy* 34, no. 1 (Winter 2019): 121–40. DOI: 10.1111/hypa.12446.

Manguso, Sarah. *300 Arguments*. Minneapolis: Graywolf Press, 2017.

———. *Ongoingness: The End of a Diary*. Minneapolis: Graywolf Press, 2015.

———. *The Two Kinds of Decay*. New York: Farrar, Straus, and Giroux, 2008.

Manning, Erin. "What If It Didn't All Begin and End with Containment? Toward a Leaky Sense of Self." *Body & Society* 15, no. 3 (2009): 33–45. DOI: 10.1177/1357034X09337785.

Maté, Gabor. *In the Realm of Hungry Ghosts: Close Encounters with Addiction*. Berkeley: North Atlantic Books, 2010.

Mazza, Cris. *Something Wrong With Her: A Real-Time Memoir*. Los Angeles: Jaded Ibis Press, 2013.

McBee, Thomas Page. *Man Alive: A True Story of Violence, Forgiveness, and Becoming a Man*. San Francisco: City Light Books, 2014.

Mech, L. David. *The Wolf: The Ecology and Behavior of an Endangered Species*. Garden City: The Natural History Press, 1970.

Milks, Megan. "Doing it Wrong." *The New Inquiry*, November 12, 2013. https://thenewinquiry.com/doing-it-wrong/.

———. "Edie Fake's Radical Bloodlust." *Mildred Pierce Zine*, no. 4 (2011): 6–10.

Moore, Lisa Jean. "Incongruent Bodies: Teaching While Leaking." *Feminist Teacher* 17, no. 2 (2007): 95–106. http://www.jstor.org/stable/40546013.

Moschovakis, Anna. *You and Three Others Are Approaching a Lake*. Minneapolis: Coffee House Press, 2011.

Muñoz, José Esteban. *Cruising Utopia: The Then and There of Queer Futurity*. New York: New York University Press, 2009.

———. *Disidentifications: Queers of Color and the Performance of Politics*. Minneapolis: University of Minnesota Press, 1999.

Murphy, Timothy. "Brief History of a Recurring Nightmare." *The Gay & Lesbian Review,* January 1, 2008. https://glreview. org/article/article-42/.

Nelson, Maggie. *The Argonauts*. Minneapolis: Graywolf Press, 2015.

Notley, Alice. *Benediction*. Tucson: Letter Machine Editions, 2015.

Pellow, David Naguib. *Resisting Global Toxics: Transnational Movements for Environmental Justice*. Cambridge: MIT Press, 2007.

Patsavas, Alyson. "Recovering a Cripistemology of Pain: Leaky Bodies, Connective Tissue, and Feeling Discourse." *Journal of Literary & Cultural Disability Studies* 8, no. 2 (2014): 203–18. DOI: 10.3828/jlcds.2014.16.

Porter, Max. *Grief Is the Thing with Feathers*. Minneapolis: Graywolf Press, 2015.

Preciado, Paul B. *Testo Junkie: Sex, Drugs, and Biopolitics in the Pharmacopornographic Era*. Translated by Bruce Benderson. New York: The Feminist Press, 2013.

Puar, Jasbir K. *The Right to Maim: Debility, Capacity, Disability*. Durham: Duke University Press, 2017.

Pulkoski-Gross, Ashleigh, Jian Li, Carolina Zheng, Yiyi Li, Nengtai Ouyang, Basil Rigas, Stanley Zucker, and Jian Cao. "Repurposing the Antipsychotic Trifluoperazine as an Antimetastasis Agent." *Molecular Pharmacology* 87, no. 3 (March 2015): 501–12. DOI: 10.1124/mol.114.096941.

Rambo, Carol. "Twitch: A Performance of Chronic Liminality." In *Handbook of Autoethnography,* edited by Stacy Holman Jones, Tony E. Adams, and Carolyn Ellis, 627–38. Walnut Creek: Left Coast Press, 2013.

Random House. "Ta-Nehisi Coates on Words that Don't Belong to Everyone | 'We Were Eight Years in Power' Book

Tour." *YouTube,* November 7, 2017. https://www.youtube.
com/watch?v=QO15S3WC9pg.

Rankine, Claudia. *Citizen: An American Lyric.* Minneapolis:
Graywolf Press, 2014.

Roberts, David C. "The Secret Life of Pain." *The New York
Times,* August 1, 2017. https://www.nytimes.com/2017/08/01/
well/live/the-secret-life-of-pain.html.

Salamon, Gayle. *Assuming a Body: Transgender and the
Rhetorics of Materiality.* New York: Columbia University
Press, 2010.

Savich, Zach. *Diving Makes the Water Deep.* Chicago: Rescue
Press, 2016.

sax, sam. *Madness.* New York: Penguin Books, 2017.

Scarry, Elaine. *The Body in Pain: The Making and Unmaking of
the World.* Oxford: Oxford University Press, 1985.

Shah, Nayan. *Stranger Intimacy: Contesting Race, Sexuality, and
the Law in the North American West.* Berkeley: University of
California Press, 2012.

Sharpe, Rachel Frances, and Sophie Sexon. "Mother's Milk and
Menstrual Blood in 'Puncture': The Monstrous Feminine in
Contemporary Horror Films and Late Medieval Imagery."
Studies in the Maternal 10, no. 1 (2018): 10. https://www.
mamsie.bbk.ac.uk/articles/10.16995/sim.256/.

Shildrick, Margrit. *Leaky Bodies and Boundaries: Feminism,
Postmodernism, and (Bio)ethics.* New York: Routledge, 1997.

Shipley, Ely. *Boy with Flowers.* New York: Barrow Street Press,
2008.

Singh, Julietta. *No Archive Will Restore You.* Earth: punctum
books, 2018.

Slattery, Dennis Patrick. *The Wounded Body: Remembering the
Markings of the Flesh.* Albany: State University of New York
Press, 2000.

Snaza, Nathan. *Animate Literacies: Literature, Affect, and the
Politics of Humanism.* Durham: Duke University Press, 2019.

Sneddon, Joan, and Ian Sneddon. "Acne Excoriée: A Protective
Device." *Clinical and Experimental Dermatology* 8, no. 1
(1983): 65–68. DOI: 10.1111/j.1365-2230.1983.tb01746.x.

Sontag, Susan. *Regarding the Pain of Others.* New York: Farrar, Straus, and Giroux, 2003.

Stawarska, Beata. "From the Body Proper to Flesh: Merleau-Ponty on Intersubjectivity." In *Feminist Interpretations of Maurice Merleau-Ponty,* edited by Dorothea Olkowski and Gail Weiss, 91–106. University Park: Penn State University Press, 2006.

Stolorow, Robert. *Trauma and Human Existence: Autobiographical, Psychoanalytic, and Philosophical Reflections.* New York: Routledge, 2011.

Stone, Bianca. *Someone Else's Wedding Vows.* Portland: Tin House Books, 2014.

Stone, Oliver, dir. *The Hand.* 1981; Warner Bros. Pictures, 2007.

Stryker, Susan. "My Words to Victor Frankenstein above the Village of Chamounix: Performing Transgender Rage." In *The Transgender Studies Reader,* edited by Susan Stryker and Stephen Whittle, 244–56. New York: Routledge, 2006.

Stryker, Susan, and Nikki Sullivan. "King's Member, Queen's Body: Transsexual Surgery, Self-Demand Amputation and the Somatechnics of Sovereign Power." In *Somatechnics: Queering the Technologisation of Bodies,* edited by Nikki Sullivan and Samantha Murray, 55–67. London: Routledge, 2016.

Sullivan, Nikki. "Transmogrification: (Un)Becoming Other(s)." In *The Transgender Studies Reader,* edited by Susan Stryker and Stephen Whittle, 552–64. New York: Routledge. 2006.

Sundén, Jenny. "On Trans-, Glitch, and Gender as Machinery of Failure." *First Monday* 20, no. 4 (2015). DOI: 10.5210/fm.v20i4.5895.

Teare, Brian. *The Empty Form Goes All the Way to Heaven.* Boise: Ahsahta Press, 2015.

Teed, Corinne. "Dear Gray Wolf." *Leaf Litter* #5: The Wolf Issue. Portland: Signal Fire, 2015.

Thomas, Shannon. *Healing from Hidden Abuse: A Journey Through the Stages of Recovery from Psychological Abuse.* Arlington: MAST Publishing House, 2016.

Tippett, Krista, and Alain de Botton. "The True Hard Work of Love and Relationships." *On Being,* February 9, 2017. https://onbeing.org/programs/alain-de-botton-the-true-hard-work-of-love-and-relationships.

Tsing, Anna Lowenhaupt. *The Mushroom at the End of the World: On the Possibility of Life in Capitalist Ruins.* Princeton: Princeton University Press, 2015.

Tuck, Eve, and C. Ree. "A Glossary of Haunting." In *Handbook of Autoethnography,* edited by Tony E. Adams, Stacy Holman Jones, and Carolyn Ellis, 639–58. Walnut Creek: Left Coast Press, 2013.

Valerio, Max Wolf. *Testosterone Files: My Hormonal and Social Transformation from Female to Male.* Emeryville: Seal Press, 2006.

van der Kolk, Bessel A. "Developmental Trauma Disorder: Toward a Rational Diagnosis for Children with Complex Trauma Histories." *Psychiatric Annals* 35, no. 5 (2005): 401–8. DOI: 10.3928/00485713-20050501-06.

———. *The Body Keeps the Score: Brain, Mind, and Body in the Healing of Trauma.* New York: Penguin Books, 2014.

Vanasco, Jeannie. *Things We Didn't Talk About When I Was a Girl: A Memoir.* Portland: Tin House Books, 2019.

Vertosick, Frank T., Jr. *Why We Hurt: The Natural History of Pain.* New York: Harcourt, 2000.

Vitale, Frank, dir. *Anorgasmia: Faking It in a Sexualized World.* Produced, written, and performed by Cris Mazza. 2015.

Vitello, Paul. "The Trouble When Jane Becomes Jack." *The New York Times,* August 20, 2006. https://www.nytimes.com/2006/08/20/fashion/20gender.html.

Vuong, Ocean. *Night Sky with Exit Wounds.* Port Townsend: Copper Canyon Press, 2016.

Wall, Patrick. *Pain: The Science of Suffering.* New York: Columbia University Press, 2000.

Weaver, Harlan. "Monster Trans: Diffracting Affect, Reading Rage." *Somatechnics* 3, no. 2 (September 2013): 287–306. DOI: 10.3366/soma.2013.0099.

Weber, Bob. "Alberta's Use of Poison as Wolf Control Criticized, Feds Asked to Review." *Global News,* December 18, 2020. https://globalnews.ca/news/7530444/alberta-wolf-control-strychnine-poison/.

Wolynn, Mark. *It Didn't Start with You: How Inherited Family Trauma Shapes Who We Are and How to End the Cycle.* New York: Penguin Books, 2016.

Wrong, Norman M. "Excoriated Acne of Young Females." *Archives of Dermatology and Syphilology* 70, no. 5 (1954): 576–82. DOI: 10.1001/archderm.1954.01540230026003.

Yan, Bernice Y., and Joseph L. Jorizzo. "Management of Morgellons Disease with Low-Dose Trifluoperazine." *JAMA Dermatology* 154, no. 2 (2018): 216–18. DOI: 10.1001/jamadermatol.2017.5175.

Yanagihara, Hanya. *A Little Life.* New York: Doubleday, 2015.

———. "Don't We Read Fiction Exactly to Be Upset?" *The Guardian,* March 4, 2016. https://www.theguardian.com/books/2016/mar/04/hanya-yanagihara-a-little-life-what-is-brave.

Yanyi. *The Year of Blue Water.* New Haven: Yale University Press, 2019.

Discography

Animal Prufrock. "Emotional Boner." On *Congratulations; Thank You + I'm Sorry.* Righteous Babe Records, 2010.

Bridgers, Phoebe. "Motion Sickness." On *Stranger in the Alps.* Dead Oceans, 2017.

Davis, Tanya. "Eulogy for You and Me." On *Clocks and Hearts Keep Going.* Sandbar Music, 2010.

DiFranco, Ani. "Out of Habit." On *Ani DiFranco.* Righteous Babe Records, 2019. Remastered.

Iron & Wine. "Bitter Truth." On *Beast Epic.* Black Cricket Recording Company/Sub Pop, 2017.

Pansy Division. "Luv Luv Luv." On *Absurd Pop Song Romance.* Lookout! Records, 1998.

The Weeknd. "Tell Your Friends." On *Beauty Behind the Madness.* Republic Records, 2015.

———. "Wicked Games." On *House of Balloons.* XO, 2011.

Made in the USA
Monee, IL
05 March 2022